DYNAMICS OF CHANGE IN THE MODERN HINDU FAMILY

DR. RAGHUVIR SINHA (*b.* 1933) took a Master's Degree in the Faculty of Science at University of Saugar in 1956 followed by several doctoral and post-doctoral degrees during his academic career spread to some thirty years. These include a Ph.D. in Sociology (Bhopal University), Ph.D. in Anthropology (Ravi Shankar University, Raipur), a Doctoral Degree from Stanton University, New York, and a Cultural Doctorate in Business Management from World University, Los Angeles. His recent interests in medical science have earned him a Doctorate in Alternative Systems of Medicines under the Council of Alternative Systems of Medicines, Calcutta. He has also received several academic awards for his rich and incessant contribution to knowledge like the honour of Fellowship of United Writers Association, India (FUWAI). He is a life member of several scientific and academic and cultural organizations.

Dr. Sinha has worked in various cultural areas of India like NEFA, Bihar, Delhi, Madhya Pradesh under different responsible positions. At present he is associated with Management Promotion Institute, New Delhi as faculty Advisor and Kothari Institute, Indore as Advisor & Specialist. He is also teaching as Professor College of Medical Sciences, Indore. His special areas of interest are Family, Change, Social Change, Sociology of Literature, Human Genetics, and now also Alternative Systems of Medicines. As a social scientist of repute, Dr. Sinha is included in several *Who is Who of India and Asia*. He has published some eight important works in Anthropology and Sociology.

DYNAMICS OF CHANGE IN THE MODERN HINDU FAMILY

RAGHUVIR SINHA

Professor

College of Medical Science, Indore

and

Ex-officio Advisor

Kothari Institute, Indore

CONCEPT PUBLISHING COMPANY, NEW DELHI-110059

ISBN 81-7022-448-9

First Published 1993

Published and Printed by
Ashok Kumar Mittal
Concept Publishing Company
A/15-16, Commercial Block, Mohan Garden
NEW DELHI 110059 (India)

Lasertypeset by
Microtech Advance Printing Systems (Pvt.) Ltd.
H-13, Bali Nagar,
NEW DELHI 110015

TO

MY SISTER

SHAKUNTALA

ACKNOWLEDGMENTS

I owe a high sense of gratitude to several scholars who have inspired or helped me in this intensive research on the urban Hindu family in the context of change. I specially owe my basic inspiration to Professor M.N. Srinivas whose studies gave me an impulse to study my own society.

I can hardly express my true and sincere gratitude to my own family, joint as it is in itself, where I had first thought of my research and where I had given it a form. My own family has been the base of all my thinking on the Hindu family. My father, mother, sisters, brothers and my wife and children have all played their big and small roles in providing me an atmosphere as well as strength to accomplish my painstaking research work. Here a serious research of this kind can be pursued with patience for such a long period. And to this large family of mine I owe a deep sense of obligation.

My absorption in this research meant strains on the family but I was never allowed to feel and adjustments and re-adjustments to my own family were made without demur or grudge. The Indian cultural tradition does not permit any formal expression of acknowledgment to these great role players of the Hindu family, and in all my sincerity I can only feel the humble acknowledgment within me.

RAGHUVIR SINHA

CONTENTS

LIST OF TABLES

LIST OF FIGURES

1

INTRODUCTION

There has been a change in the family process in Indian society during the past few decades and more especially after Independence. This change works subtly within the institutional set up of the family and brings about structural and functional changes in its organization. This will continue until Indian society assumes total change or modernization. Family change in this respect also becomes an important index of social change in society. Organization or disorganization of society can thus be best understood in terms of organization or disorganization of family. A study of family changes thus becomes an integral part of social change in Indian society.

Having made an intensive theoretical research on the universal Hindu family in India over the past twenty-five years, author has found that there has been a lot of research done on the family during past four or five decades. Through these researches various aspects of the family were studied but most of them had focused only on structural changes. The research also provided author with a greater knowledge about the scope of work in those areas which have not been studied at all, or have been studied inadequately. The role dynamics in the family gained author's attention and therefore, author, decided to study the areas of roles and status, role expectations, role obligations of the family and the actual role discharge in the urban Hindu family, so as to assess how far these have been actually effected by urbanization and other modern conditions, it is through these that author wanted to study the process and trends of family change in Indian society. In this study author had also wanted to test another part of his theoretical assumption that change in society comes mainly through the family.

The hypothesis author had formulated for testing through the study of family change based on empirical research was, that the urban Hindu family has recently shown (some) definite trends of functional changes in the organization of the family, apart from the structural changes, which have been in process for a longer time. With the structural changes in the different roles of the urban Hindu family there has been marked a related functional change in the different role sets, and their associated role expectations and role obligations.

Author has studied Family Change in a limited area of urban setting in Madhya Pradesh and have strengthened his arguments on the basis of research done by other scholars and social scientists in different parts of India. The empirical study has been made in growing cosmopolitan town of Bhopal, the capital of Madhya Pradesh. It is situated in the heart of India and people of different cultures, though belonging to a common Hindu religion which binds them together, are living here in a heterogeneous environment sharing the problems and strains of a common urban society. Bhopal, the universe of this empirical research has been the capital of Madhya Pradesh since the Reorganization of States in 1956, and has passed through a rapid process of urbanization for more than twenty-five years. Before Independence it was the capital seat of a small Muslim State ruled by the Nawab. It grew from a small town to a capital city of the largest State of the nation, and it was subsequently made the seat of a heavy electrical plant of the Government of India Bharat Heavy Electricals Ltd. A few other allied industries installed; such as Card Board, Steel and Carbide plants, the industrial sectors such as Union Carbide now closed since 1984 after explosion of gas have made the city a subject of industrialization.[1]

But since, industrialization warrants an independent study and since these industries are situated outside the municipal limits, thus have been studied here. The rapid growth of population in the city of Bhopal has been marked during past two decades. It had increased about three-fold by 1971 from what it was in 1951. Table 1.1 indicates the growth of the population in past twenty years.

TABLE 1.1: Growth of Urban Population in the City of Bhopal

Population Figures as per 1951 census	Population figures as per the 1961 census	Population Figure as per 1971 census
102,333	185,374	304,550

Certain parts of the city such as in the old *Mohallas* and on the fringes of the city have retained kasbaic traits.[2]

Bhopal city also provides a cross-cultural complex, as persons belonging to different cultural ethnics has come to reside in the city for employment or business purpose or for permanent settlement in the town in large numbers during the past twenty-five years.

The city of Bhopal thus provides rich socio-cultural avenues for studying changes in the family organization under different cultural environment although under the common urban habitat. The family could de studied under the different stages of urbanization as well as under its direct impact and influence.

A large number of families in the sample studied, immigrant families, that is, those who have come to live in Bhopal for employment, professional or business purposes, from outside the State, after Independence, but who maintain a kind of functional tie with their large families in the home towns of their provinces and who also maintain a kind of cultural continuity with their original culture. About twenty-five per cent of the households belong to the local resident group comprising of those who have been born and brought up in Bhopal town, in the erstwhile Bhopal State, or in its neighbouring sub-urban villages within the Municipal limits and have, since then, settled permanently in Bhopal for the past three or four generations.

For the purpose of determining immigration, the State has been made the determining unit, and the post-independent, era has been made a period of reference. In other words, those families which have come to Madhya Pradesh for occupational purposes from outside the State after Independence (1947), and which are either temporarily or permanently in the town after retirement have been classified as immigrant families.

The city of Bhopal was thus first chosen as the universe of study. From within this universe and from within the canvas of Hindu society living in an urban setting, a single economic class – the Middle Class was selected as a unit of inquiry. The three sub-components of the middle class, the upper-middle class, the middle-middle class and the lower-middle class were classified distinctly and a proportionate selection of households from each of these sub-component classes was ensured for the samp'^ selection was proportionately made from two distinct parts of the ^ı.y, the old Bhopal and the new Bhopal. Author had been almost convinced that it is this middle class that reflects maximum change in society.

From within the urban Hindu society, the four main castes of Hindus – Brahmin, Kshatriya, Vaishya and Kayastha – were chosen for study. While selecting a sample from these castes due care was taken to see that the five cultural regions normally recognised in India (*cf.* Karve, 1955), were properly represented.

The caste-wise selection of sample from the universe of study, Bhopal, is shown in Table 1.2.

TABLE 1.2: Caste-wise Selection of Sample from Universe

Sl.No.	Name of caste	No. of families in the universe defined		No. of families taken as ten per cent sample from the universe	
1.	Brahmin	1180		118	
2.	Kshatriya	220		20	
3.	Vaishya including Agarwala Nagar, Gupta etc.	420		42	
4.	Kayastha	422		42	
Total: 4 Castes		2222	families in the universe	222	families taken in representative sample

While presenting this work to his readers, author recalls three significant studies previously done on the family in India and which have been a basic source of inspiration to him in this study of family change. These are: A.M. Shah's, *The Household Dimension of the Family in India* (1973), Aileen D. Ross' *The Hindu Family in its Urban Setting* (1961), and K.M. Kapadia's *Marriage and Family in India* (1955). Besides these there have been a number or smaller studies made in different cultural zones of India which have impressed as very much. Aurhor has made a reference to all these studies in his discussion on family change. This work is based on his doctoral research on the Urban Hindu Family. Author has thus studied family change in India both in its universal sense and on a wider plane, as well as in a limited area of selected universe in an urban setting through empirical research. Author may mention here that this study of family change with a special discussion of role dynamics in the Hindu family is probably the first of its kind in India. Author does hope that this discussion stimulates other scholars to discover new avenues of research and greater dimensions in the area of family change in Indian society.

NOTES

1. Based on *Census of India*, Part II-1971, Series 10, General Population Tables (Director of Census Operation, Madhya Pradesh, 1974).
2. Culturally rural based traits.

2

THE JOINT FAMILY CONCEPT IN INDIAN SOCIETY

The Hindu Family has been a subject of significant importance and study during the past three or four decades. It has also perhaps, equally been a subject of controversy through the years.

The Hindu Family has been studied by sociologists, social anthropologists and Indologists. Besides, it has also been studied by lawyers and constitution writers. It is perhaps because of these various studies and approaches that the concept of the Hindu Joint Family has been variously and loosely used.

Whereas the joint family system as prevalent in India is totally unfamiliar to Western society, the extended family of the Western industrial economy is practically absent in India. But for want of conceptual clarity, the two terms, "joint family" and "extended family" have sometimes been used inter-changeably.

Parsons (1934, 1949 and 1961), Weber (1950), Ogburn and Nimkoff (1950), Linton (1952), Burgess and Locke (1953) have more or less incited this argument. It is because of such controversial hypotheses that there has been a crop of extensive studies of family organization all over the world during the past few decades. Levy (1949), Young and Wilmokt (1951), Nimkoff and Middleton (1960), William J. Goode (1964), Johnson (1964) have done significant research work in different societies of the world, especially in countries like Japan, China and England. In India, Srinivas (1942), Kapadia (1955), Desai (1955), Agarwala (1955), M.S.A. Rao (1957), Bailey (1960), Ross (1961), Sahani (1961), Oreinstein (1961), Madan (1962), Sarma (1964), Oreinstein and Micklin (1966) and Saha (1964), (1973) have analytically studied the Indian family. Studies of Mandelbaum (1949, 1972), Ghurye (1952), Dube (1955), and Hitchcock (1965) have also indirectly dealt with traditional family organization which is of course, the joint family. In the discussion in the present chapter, author will attempt to point out the differences between concepts of the joint family and the traditional family organizations as well as elucidate the two concepts in their individual contexts as studied by earlier researches, author shall then try to determine the definition of the joint family in the light of its different interpretations. This discussion will enable us to examine the joint family structure and its function as compared to the nuclear family structure in the context of Hindu society.

Studies of the joint family have been emphasized more especially during the past few decades because of the growing theses in Sociology of the Family in India, because these have often indicated that the joint family of the traditional type is breaking up into smaller nuclear families as a result of industrial and urban economies. Madan, Desai, Kapadia, Karve, Nimkoff, Gore and Ross have especially contributed to the study and interpretation of the joint family in India.

Many sociologists and social anthropologists of the modern times have argued that the family type functionally adjustive to the modern, urban and industrial economy is the "Nuclear family", consisting of the husband, wife and their children. And, as societies get modernized in industrial and urban complexes, the "Extended" or "Joint" families gradually get replaced by this individual or nuclear type of family.

The concept of the traditional Hindu family has often been interchanged with that of the Joint Family though the two are not always synonymous. Early tradition has always emphasized joint living. It seems probable that in its earliest form, the Hindu family organization consisted of several lineages, making its structure joint. Right from the time of Manu the ideal of Joint Family was eulogized in Indian social thought. Thus the code of Manu was prescribed essentially in the context of the joint family.

Kapadia (1955) first studied the Hindu family organization in its traditional context. He traced the evolution and development of the Hindu family in India to the times of *Manusmriti.* Traditional Hindu marriage had been regarded as irrevocable and sacred, and could not be dissolved by individual will. Post-Vedic literature, such as the *Dharmashastra* and *Manusmriti* have in them references about the family organization then prevalent, as well as about the changes confronting it. The early joint family essentially patriarchal, was one in which the eldest male member usually held the highest authority. This joint family had property in common which was considered impartiable. The patriarch of the family had absolute authority over this property. But the trends towards individualism could not be suppressed for long and certain other devices had to be created to withhold them. The traditional joint family had something vital in its nature that prevented it from disintegration. The history of the Hindu family reveals at least one significant fact. Though there were trends towards individualism, the family constitution continued to be joint and essentially agnatic. This seems to be so because Hindu sentiments, from the beginning, were in favour of the joint family. Kapadia[1] maintains that the joint family has been featured since long as the base of the Hindu social organization. Even now, a kind of joint family is still, prevalent in India, though because of practical circumstances its structure has been affected and its function limited. K.M. Kapadia made a special study of the Hindu family in this context.

There has been a great deal of controversy about the usage of the term "Joint Family". Sociologists, anthropologists and Indologists in India have assigned it varied meanings.

M.F. Nimkoff and M.S. Gore have tried to analyse the term "joint family".[2] The feel that though term "joint family" is common in India, it has no significant equivalent in Hindi. This, author feels, is not wholly correct. The parallel term to "joint family" in the Hindi language is "*Samyukta Parivar*". It is a pity that Indian scholars themselves have not used this Hindi term and have preferred to use the equivalent in English, that is, the "joint family". The criticism levied against the usage of the term by the two scholars is thus not well-based. They also define and distinguish the "unitary" family, "nuclear" family and "extended" family and raise questions about whether the joint family is as popular as commonly believed. The authors quote a reference from a field study done in Kanpur by Tapan Kumar Mazumdar.[3] The urban position there is that the joint family and nuclear family ratio is found at disparity level; about 41.2 per cent are joint families, with an additional 8.1 per cent including those with relatives other than sons or daughters of the head being temporarily accommodated. This suggests that 49.3 per cent of the families have some kind of a joint living. Some 15.9 per cent live separately but maintain functionalties with their relatives by periodic remittances. These, can be said to be structurally nuclear though functionally joint.

What Nimkoff and Gore have included in the joint family, i.e. 8.1 per cent, author would have included in the "small joint family" of his nomenclature as adopted in the present study. It seems that to argue their own case more positively, Nimkoff and Gore have used this additional 8.1 per cent in their favour. In fact it should have been interpreted so as to suggest the link between joint family living and nuclear family living, the link which I have called the "small joint family". Thus author would have interpreted the data of Tapan Kumar Mazumdar in the following manner : 41.2 per cent "joint families", 8.1 per cent "small joint families" and 50.7 per cent nuclear families. What is surprising is that the eminent scholars have tried to derive functional interpretations from the data of Tapan Kumar Mazumdar's study (quoted by Nimkoff and Gore) which is a structural study.

Kapadia elucidates the point that the bases of the joint family are common values agreed upon and followed and which are often esteemed as ideals. Any accent on individual value leads to a strain and tends to break the joint structure. Nimkoff and Gore stress the fact that privacy is not a value in the Indian village as it is in the West. In author's opinion, this too, is not wholly true, in several aspects of family and social life privacy is not only expected but is also specially emphasized upon, and is thus expected as an obligatory value. One common value of the joint family is the occupation of agricultural farming which is considered as a non-individualizing enterprise. This situation is being gradually lost in Indian society with the change in the family organisation.

It is believed that accumulation of property, especially that of the land owned jointly by the family members promotes family unity. Land-ownership is also connected which prestige value. A cherished ambition of many rural immigrants is to return to soil on retirement. There are certain advantages of a joint household. It allows for a greater economy of expense than is possible in separate households.

This is because the members of the joint family have a comparatively greater economic independence. Two other economic factors bolstering the joint family to a certain extent are interest in "joint property" and the "economic need".

Nimkoff and Gore (1959) point out the fact that the joint family as a structure is found to be more frequent among higher castes which, in general, have a higher income. While this appears to be correct there also seems to be another side to the issue. Unfortunately Nimkoff and Gore seem to miss this point in their study. Mutuality of obligations is one of the main characteristics of the joint system that can apply equally to families of both the higher and the lower castes. It is these expected obligations that render greater possibility for the continuance of a joint family organization in the higher, middle and lower class income groups as well as in the higher and lower castes. Economic strains do caste their influence on the family but the tradition of joint living as an ideal always seems to over come the influence.

An important aspect of Hindu society which has, in course of history, helped the joint family to persist and which has also made it more intelligible and stable is its caste organisation, — one of the most complex systems in existence. Caste in India is, in fact, an extension of the joint family; it is an inclusive group of families having the same status and role. The two most important ties between the caste system and the family are the *Jajmani* system and, caste endogamy and village exogamy. Women were traditionally deprived of any rights of inheritance. A woman normally left her parental home to live with her husband after her marriage. This had made the disinheritance of woman functional in as much as it kept the ancestral land intact. The dowry for girls in marriage was believed to have compensated for this disinheritance in some way.

The Hindu Succession Act of 1956, however, now accords a daughter and her children equal rights with a son and his children to all the property of either parent. It is suspected that this legislature has tended to weaken the joint family. The criticism levied against it is that it hits at the base of the joint family spirit.

The traditional system of informal education indoctrinated then only aimed to lead the people to conform to accepted norms which never did value initiative and individuality. The only exception to this was the Brahman man.

The data quoted by Nimkoff and Gore suggest, that, with the increase of formal education, the percentage of joint families in urban areas have decreased. It is commonly believed that modern formal education has an individualising effect on personality and that it may have, in some cases, served as a probable cause of the disintegration of the joint family. Here Nimkoff and Gore seem to present education negatively. Education is in actual fact, the most potent and cognizable factor of change. It is also one of the greatest incentives to the individual and to the social group. It appears strange that Nimkoff and Gore did not see education though this perspective.

An appraisal of the relations between the Hindu joint family and other parts of the traditional social system shows that all its parts are essentially consistent with the joint family and tend to support it, though the contribution of these several parts varies and is not equal. The Panchayat, Hindu religion and traditional education seem to have a comparatively lower significance. The impact of modern schooling cannot be held to be important, not to much for its formal character as for the ideas it embodies, which usually emanate from many different cultures representing different points of views. Modern education teaches universalism and cosmopolitanism, ideas which are, said to be individualizing and liberating in their consequences.

Nimkoff and Gore maintain that the Extended family was common in the West 200 years ago before the onset of the Industrial Revolution which led to its transformation into conjugal units. As opposing this fact the joint family is still very widespread in India.

Nimkoff and Gore also believe that families may be structurally and residentially nuclear but functionally joint. For example, members of the unitary household in the city who usually make regular remittances to other family members in the native village are maintaining a functional tie with the joint family. This opinion is also supported by others, such as Desai, Madan and Kapadia. Author has also considered this an important factor in the continuance of the functional character of the Joint family over generations. But, author differs from Nimkoff and Gore from the point of trying to draw parallels between development of the extended family and the joint family. The extended family in Western society is the antecedent of the nuclear family born out of an industrial economy.

The joint family in Indian society is altogether a different type of institution, which has evolved out of cultural and ethical traditions and prerogatives.

From the analysis of Nimkoff and Gore it can safely be inferred that whereas the Hindu religion encourages marriage, it does not determine the form of the family. The link between the joint family and religion does not, therefore, seem to be very close.

It can also be concluded from this analysis that, while all the institutions of Indian society basically support the joint family, the indispensable basis for the joint family is a common agricultural and household economy, which emphasizes the accumulation of property on a joint or common family basis.

In the 50th Session of the Indian Science Congress Association at Delhi in 1963, discussions on the Family were held by participating sociologists and social anthropologists. A.A. Khatri attempted to develop a scale to measure the jointness and nuclearity of the Hindu family on the basis of living together or participation in ceremonies etc. It was suggested in the discussions that a clear distinction be made between "joint" and "extended" families, and also between "households" and families".[4]

B.B. Shah speaking about the "Youth and Joint Family", observed that the modern youth is changing fast and wants to break away from the traditional ties of the joint family. The validity of these statements for other parts of India, especially Bengal, was questioned in this paper.

Kapadia in his thought provoking address on the "Passing Away of the Traditional Society" observed that in Pre-British Indian Society, a self-sufficient village was breaking down gradually. Kapadia, however, had restricted his paper to only one aspect of change, viz., the occupational mobility in rural society of South Gujarat, and did not relate it to findings in other parts of the country.

The impact of industrialization and literacy was also discussed in the conference. It emerged from these discussions that industries become a potent factor of change only if local produce is used as raw material, and local people are employed as labour.

The concept of the joint family has been widely explained and interpreted during the last two decades, yet a slight confusion exists in several sociological and social anthropological circles about its actual usage in recent modern contexts.

The traditional Hindu family was essentially joint in structure. Mandelbaum believes that 'the classical form of the family in India is that of the Joint Family'.[5] Madan has tried to give a terminological clarification to the concept of the "joint family", by especially stressing the divergence implied in the connotation of the term.[6]

This joint family, according to Madan, normally consists of a number of married couples and their children living together in the same household, and related by blood, as a man and his sons or grandsons or a set of brothers and their wives, unmarried daughters, and perhaps the widow of a deceased kinsman. In a patriarchal family, a girl leaves her parental household after marriage and become a part of the joint family of her husband. Mandelbaum adds to this the features of holding all property in common.

Karve (1953) had earlier given a precise definition of the joint family. "A joint family is a group of people who generally live under one hearth, who hold property in common and who participate in common family worship and are related to each other as some particular type of kindred."[7] In my opinion, the definition given by Karve is more exact and applicable to the joint family still found to some extent in Indian society. It is more comprehensive and assumes all the factors that make up a joint family. Bailey (1960) feels that a minimal definition of a joint family should attempt to say how people are recruited into a group, and what they do together when we call that group a "joint family."[8]

Madan points out that two criteria seem to be in the minds of most writers, while mentioning the joint family. The first is the existence of a familial group larger than the nuclear family, and the second is the existence of some property relations, if not joint, coparcenary rights between all the members, or at least some of them. It seems that the major reason for the confusion in the connotation of the term, "joint family" arises from failure on the part of the concerned scholars to recognise that there is not any necessary connection between the existence of a familial group larger than the nuclear family and the existence of coparcenary rights and obligations among its members. Perhaps the confusion is created by using the term "joint family" and "extended family" synonymously. The term "joint family" should actually be used in connection with the ownership of joint property rights and obligations as the sole referent. Also a particular kind of composition of a familial group should not be considered as an essential criterion for it to be called a joint family. The etymological meaning of a joint family, as referred to by Madan, is "belonging to two or more persons etc., in conjunction, as joint of action, opinion, estate". In fact, with separation joint living eventually ceases, the daily round of interpersonal relationships is vitally affected, and may even be discontinued. But he also points out that the ties of relationship are seldom severed even in these circumstances.

Levi Strauss (1956) in his study objects to the usage of the word 'joint' to the family. He points out that it is erroneous to think of joint families as being made up of smaller (nuclear) families which are joined together, as it were, into a larger grouping.[9] Levi-strauss also disregards the usage of the term "extended family", instead suggesting the adoption of the term "restricted family" for the nuclear family to emphasize the fact that the so-called extended family is not made up of smaller units.

Cohn, taking his cue from Karve's definition, regards the latter definition as the standard definition and believes that cultural as well as structural criteria need to be adopted for obtaining an understanding of the joint family and the changes to which it is subjected. "Extended Families", which are the cultural ideal among the Hindus of northern

India, develop in response to specific conditions, among which are, a tradition of living jointly, an economic base to support a joint family, sufficient role differentiation within the family clear lines of authority among the generations, the need for a labour pool, and the longivity of the members of the family.

One of the qualities of the joint family more commonly agreed upon is its stability. Whereas Cohn has rightly referred to the joint family as a cultural ideal, he has not tried to emphasize the structural situation in which it is so. Madan's argument is that as we move from the parent-child (father-son) to the sibling (brother-brother and brother-sister), and to the cousin relationship, the ideal of the joint living gradually becomes weaker as cultural compulsive, personal interest and interests of those who are closer as against the interests of those who are remoter kin gain ascendance.[10]

Actually, Cohn failed to take note of the father-son coparcenary unit within the Hindu family. Savitri Shahani adopts the structural factor as the primary condition of the joint family, but lets in joint property by the back door as it were.[11]

Ross (1961) in her empirical study in Bangalore holds that the traditional joint family was a kind of entity of those related to each other in some way as some particular type of kindred. One common difficulty felt in studying family relationships in India is that the present families seem to have descended from two different lines, the patrilineal and the matrilineal.[12]

A common traditional joint family was the "large joint family", and the contemporary Hindu family, now more common than a typical nuclear family is a "small joint family". Whereas in the traditional joint family, three generations of close kin lived together, it is now more common to find only two or even only one generation of relations living in a small joint family. In his study, author has found this to be largely true. Also small joint families are more common in urban conditions than large joint families.

The large joint family fulfilled a large range of varied functions. It was more family-oriented and was characterised by intimacy and mutuality of interests. Also, control of the primary group was more effective. Members of the household tended to assist one an other in times of need and during crises.

Mandalbaum[13] (1949) had earlier characterised a joint family structure which, being essentially Hindu, is more of a rural type is his reference to the family is more pertaining to the upper strata of society, and to the orthodox sectors rather than to those who have been westernized.

In his opinion even urban and westernized Hindus, as well as some Muslim families, reflect patterns of interpersonal relationships set up by the joint family which do not yet seem to have been wholly ignored. The model of the orthodox, scriptural joint family is still popular throughout India. In the economic sphere the joint family is not considered a single consumer unit, but is, typically, a single producer unit as well.

The *Mitakshara* had codified the legal framework of the joint family around the eleventh century, and has, since then, served as a sole referent for the rights, duties and obligations of the members of the Hindu family.

Srinivas (1949) around the same time as Mandalbaum had given a reference of a typical South Indian Coorg Joint family, Okka in Mysore, primarily in the structural setting and in the sphere of roles and obligations.[14]

Invariably, a function of the traditional joint family was the arrangement of marriage for a son or a daughter by securing a suitable match through personal negotiations or family references. This continues to be a concern of the contemporary Hindu family even in urban areas and choice is seldom exercised by the boy or the girl. While most parents now usually concede that the final consent must be given by the the boy, a girl's opinion is not usually asked for, and even when it is known to be opposing, it is not paid much need to marriage is often ordained or circumvented by prior approval of parents and family considerations. It is perhaps only in the more urbanised and educated families in towns, that girls have now started stressing their own rights in making their choice for marriage and are able to make a discretionary choice in selecting their husbands.

The traditional joint Hindu family has been largely popular in the north. But there are instances of its existence elsewhere in the country. Jyotirmayee Sarma refers to the contemporary Hindu joint household in Bengal when she speaks of the formal and informal relations in a family.[15] The present joint Hindu household, normally of three generations shows its age-old basis in the past. Members of three and sometimes even four generations of the male line live together with their wives and children. The division of a large joint household into small joint families or individual families takes place mainly because of economic reasons. An analysis of the kinship behaviour of different members of a family shows that, apart from formal relationships in these groups, spontaneous relationships may also develop within the household. But such memberships are not very stable; they remain in a state of flux. Thus according to Sarma, friendship patterns are rarely stable within a joint household.

A typical example of the continued joint family are the Marwaris. They are spread all over India, but, invariably they pay a periodic visit to their native homes. Often, they even select spouses for their sons and daughters from either their native province or from native immigrant families.

The structural change that has occurred in recent years is mostly that from the large joint structure to the small joint household, and to a lesser extent from the large joint to the nuclear family of the western type. Even in instances wherein individual family is formed because of marriage or migration, it is largely due to circumstances. Moreover, kinship obligations are always accorded to the original family unit.

There is a great deal of controversy over the extent and amount of this change. Education has been an important factor in accelerating the change although its influence in India cannot be said to be to the extent of making people individual in their thinking. Highly educated societies, especially those in metropolitan cities, may be said to be an exception, but even there, family relations have not yet become too formalised.

Discussing the size and structure of families, Thomas K. Burch (1963), who studied the family through census data remarks, "A widely held generalization in the field of family sociology posits a close inverse relation between urbanization and industrialization on the one hand, and the "extended family" on the other. Within societies this is taken to mean that extended families are more prevalent in rural than in urban areas, cross-culturally, that extended families are more prevalent in underdeveloped than in developed societies."[16]

Clifford Kirkapatrick (1963) has shown that, as society develops, the extended family tends to be replaced as a model form, by the independent nuclear (or conjugal) family of husband, wife and their children. He stresses the fact that empirical research has documented the extent and significance of extended kinship relations for persons living in highly urban and industrial societies, such as England and United States.[17] It is also argued that in pre-industrial societies, the extended family was more common in urban rather than in rural areas. But it yet remains a matter of special significance to verify this fact because due to economic or demographic limitations, in no society so far, has the extended family become predominant in actual practice.

From a different angle, Burch argues that India is a case of particular interest as it is a nation renowned for its traditional extended family system. Though Burch has taken a broader view of the joint family structure, unfortunately he confuses it with the extended family system, which is not correct. He is perhaps under the same misapprehension common to many foreign scholars who fail to see that the joint family in Indian Society is a different type of family system which has evolved from different cultural conditions to those of the extended family which has evolved in western society.

I.P. Desai (1956)[18] has given a wider interpretation to the term 'joint family' and to its implications. In a symposium on 'Caste and the Joint Family', he led a discussion on the structure and directions of change in the Indian family. It was felt that, although with some modifications, the joint household still remains the basic family structure in India. R. Esterowitz (1957), remarking on the proceedings of the symposium, later wrote, 'The total number of persons living in the different types of households is a better index of the strength of the joint family, than the type of households, which is the index used by the Indian Census. The criteria for "jointness" consists of the "rights and obligations of the members of different units towards one another and in the feeling of oneness", rather than in the size of the units."[19]

Esterowitz, in his summary evaluating Desai's contribution "Interpersonal relations, affecting concepts of subordination and superordination and the inferior status of woman are being examined more critically. But the older family structure of sharing residence, kitchen, social functions and purse and property is still basically intact."[20]

Ross observes that the two ideal family types the Institutional and Companionship constructed by Burgess and Lock, serve as the basis for studying changes taking place in the contemporary Indian family. In her opinion, the transition from one type to another, implies a change in behaviour patterns as well as in the roles and role expectations of the individual. On the basis of a three-fold classification,—geographic, social and ideational mobility suggested by them, Ross feels that the Indian Family reveals a remarkable stability. The explanation for this stability may be found in the agricultural nature of economy, the caste system, the persistence of the joint family system, the laws of inheritance, diversity of language and culture and lack of education. This is because social mobility is limited to a considerable extent by the caste system and ideational mobility by educational limitations.

Ross concludes her discussion with the remark that the companionship family being more adaptable and flexible is more suited to the present, changing world.

Sociologists, social anthropologists and Indologists have given wider and more varied interpretations to the term 'joint family'. The implications differ from a truly large joint family consisting of three or four generations of the recognised line of relations (mostly patrilineal in India), as was popular in the past, to a small joint family of husband, wife and children living with some kin, as is found at present.

In his supplementary note to the criticism of the 'joint family' given in the symposium, Desai writes, "The prevalence of different types of families is important for understanding the social structure of Indian Society. In this context the number of different types of families is important."[21]

In my opinion, an appraisal of the different interpretations given to the 'joint family' concept suggest that the concept of the 'joint family' has developed more through the constant research made by various scholars. Sometimes it eulogizes the idealness of the joint family, and at other times it subdues the actuality.

In Desai's opinion, there are mainly two types of families in India, the patrilineal and the matrilineal, and although they differ in the matter of descent, they are basically similar in all other respects. Co-residence, common property and income, commensality, Co-worship and observance of certain rights and obligations are some of the essential criteria of joint family. It is, in fact, the relationships among the members of a household and those between members and with of a household with another household, which originally determine the family type of that particular household. A few relationships, such as kinship, generation depth, property, income and mutual cooperation are kept in view. In a nuclear family, a group of parents live with their unmarried children, are not related to other kin through property or income, or through rights and obligations pertaining to them and expected by those related by kinship. A joint family has greater generation depth, usually of three or more generations and its members are related to one another through property, income and mutual rights and obligations. The members of this type of household may be related either collaterally or lineally.

On the basis of empirical work done in the country by several sociologists, it appears that nuclearity is gradually on the increase. But, in Desai's opinion, this view is based on an improper definition of the nuclear and joint family. Such a view of the nuclearity and jointness is more apparent than real, Desai feels that the basic criteria of co-residence, commensality, size, composition and the number of dependents, as used by the Census authorities are not valid and the picture that we get from them is rather unreal. He questions how far it would be right in assuming the growth of the spirit of individualism. This approach of Desai seems to be more rational in understanding the joint family in its realistic and contemporary perspectives.

The joint family, has, thus, not totally disappeared, at though it has certainly passed through rigorous changes in its structure, composition, size and to some extent also in function especially during years after independence.

Jyotirmayee Sarma (1964), in her study of the Hindu family in West Bengal, observes that the Bengali Hindu Joint Family usually consists of three generations of persons in the male line with their wives and children, living in the same house, showing common income and expenditures, and under the leadership of one senior member.[21] Sarma (1964) has shown that a joint household cannot perpetuate itself after three or four generations at the most. This is because bears within itself the elements of conflicts and change. The word *nuclearisation* is meant to denote "the process of separation of a joint household into several family units", each consisting of parents and children.[22]

According to Mulla, who gives a legal interpretation to the joint family, "an Undivided Hindu Family is ordinarily joint not only in estate, but also in food and worship". Since Mulla's study was done in the sphere of law, he appears to have seen only the legal aspects of the joint Hindu family and seems to have omitted other social aspects.[23]

Every joint family has a history of growth and decline. New factors have brought about the break-up of the joint family into smaller nuclear households, but the tendency and fact of nuclearisation can be traced back to old times, as seen in old scriptures like the *Mahabharata*, which tells the story of the hostility between two sections of a large joint family, the Pandavas and the Kauravas. Folktales also corroborate similar facts. Yet, seems more probable that in the old days, there were not many true joint families as mentioned in literature but a greater number of small joint families consisting of the parents and some married, as well as unmarried children were certainly in existence. Instances of Nuclear families are also found in the old literature.

Kolenda (1968)[24] has suggested a baseline for the structure of Indian families in different parts of India. She structures this on the basis of data gathered by various sociologists and social anthropologists between 1949 and 1961. A sociological comparison of the 26 studies accomplished during this period reveals marked regional differences in the prevalence of various types of family. In another earlier study (1967)[25] she had also explored the cultural factors behind these regional differences.

At a still later stage Kolenda (1970) made an evaluation of her conceptual framework and remarked, 'While the baseline of our earlier decade may be useful to investigators of the future, the statistical data necessary for measuring change in a longer-range period are lacking. Clearly, the identification of variables and specifications of hypotheses relevant to variations in family structure are more advanced than the accumulation of factual evidence that might test the hypotheses. Given this state of affairs, Surgeon Coat's competent 1819 report for a Poona Village has a unique significance'.[26]

Observing the contemporary situation of the family structure in India, Kolenda remarks that it has been found that ever since the censuses made by the British Government in India towards the end of their regime, observations of the "breakdown" of the "joint family" have been avowed. In her opinion, there is not much precise statistical data that could perhaps support such claims. This is especially, so as censuses done up to 1961 did not mention in their records family structure, but only family size, and it still remains unclear as to what formula should be applied to the relationship between size and structure. A "joint family" may well consists of as few as four persons; for example, the parents with the married son and his wife, while a nuclear family may have from two to ten or even more members, depending upon the number of unmarried children present where the rate of fertility is rather high.

Author's own observations during the present study on family change make me believe that larger nuclear families are now gradually disappearing, especially, from urban upper middle and middle-middle class societies where family planning has been adopted practically and where couples are now not in the favour of having more than two or three children. This is largely due to the Government's family planning programmes which have made the upper middle and the middle-middle sub-classes of society adopt an enlightened outlook about family planning and are conscious about the size of their family and thus to restrict it to two or three children only. Correspondingly the size of the small joint family and the joint family has also been effected.

Orenstein (1961)[27] had briefly surveyed the statistics on family size and the number of persons per household, from the censuses made in India from 1911 to 1951, during which census operations were made. Orenstein suggests that, contrary to expectation, there is no sign of a decrease in household size in a period of five decades. Data for earlier years are sporadic, but a review of that offers little that may contradict this'. In a later study with Michael Micklin (1966), he examines the Hindu Joint family in reference to its "norms and "numbers".[28]

In author's opinion, these studies reveal one significant conclusion – that the recent changes in the Indian family in the context of Urbanization, Industrialization and Modernization have tended to break-up the joint family structure. Sometimes the break-up has been into individual, typically nuclear households, but quite often the joint family has split into a small joint family. Moreover, this break-up of a joint household is usually only a temporary change, as, after a period of residing in towns or industrial areas, members of the old family often return to their native homes and reunite with the joint family. This kind of change, thus, remains only structural; functionally, the members of such families remain joint and continue to discharge their role obligations through monetary remittances and periodic visits. Also, the feeling of belonging to a common home is seldom lost. It may, however, be, true that this functional discharge is not made regularly, and for the daily round of duties, a split family on migration to a town or an industrial centre works out its own independent set of duties.[29]

Till then the concept of the joint family was developed mainly through these studies done by early scholars then, A.M. Shah did a significant study on the Hindu family in Gujarat, and, through his brilliant review of other studies, developed a more precise concept of the joint family which is now acceptable.

A.M. Shah's[30] (1973) contribution to the sociology of the family in India has been spread over two decades—first when he had first worked in Gujarat to study the rural family in a Gujarat Village in 1955-1958, and later when he contributed in illuminating work based on his painstaking researches, *The Household Dimension of the Family in India.* This work presents his empirical observations of a field study done in a Gujarat Village, in a very systematic manner along with an exhaustive review of literature on the family in India.

It appears that originally, he had wanted only a village study, but later when he found the data too extensive he used material based on the family to give an analysis along the following lines : (i) The Household in a Gujarat Village, and (ii) The Study of the Household and Related Dimensions of the Family in India. Under these two titles, the material is organized into nine chapters and has such captions, (besides an introductory note to each), as Preliminary Considerations, Migrant Households, Complex Households, Simple Households, Conspectus; The Households, other Structure and Social change; Basic terms in the Sociological study of the Indian Family, The Indian family in Law and Jurisprudence, The Sociological and study of the Indian Family, and the Conclusion. The book is appended with a rich, annotated bibliography of studies made so far on the family in India. It covers a number of works, research papers, project reports, seminars, summaries and books which deal with various aspects of the Family in India.

His two other papers published elsewhere in journals, 'Basic Terms and Concepts in the study of family in India,'[31] and 'Changes in the Indian Family: An Examination of some Assumptions',[32] also seem to be the outcome of this original field work, to which he has added his own sociological observations.

In the introductory note to the first part of the book, Shah clearly mentions that the focus of his book is the "Household Dimension of the Family in India." He tries to define and demarcate the term "household." He also suggests that in its English usage, the term "family" has many varied connotations. It may be used for a "household". It may be used for a body of persons, "who live in one house or under one head, including parents, children, servants etc. It may also indicate, a group consisting of the parents and their children, whether living together or not; that is, in a wider sense, all those who are connected by blood or affinity. In a fourth sense, it may also indicate" those descended or claiming descent from a common ancestor; a house kindred, lineage. In such implications of the term "family", Shah seems to have followed the definition of a family laid down in the *Shorter Oxford English Dictionary* (1959) and also in some prescriptions laid down in *Notes and Queries on Anthropology* (1957). The four social units indicated by the four meanings are usually related to each other in Shah's opinion, but he also feels that they should be clearly distinguished from one other for sociological analysis.

At the very outset Shah remarks that a distinction between the terms "household" and "family" has become quite common in sociology and social anthropology, particularly since the publication of W.J. Goody's (ed.), *The Developmental Cycle in Domestic Groups* (1958). The "household" in Shah's opinion, is one of the several dimensions of the family and should always be viewed in relation with the other dimensions. He suggests that the term "family" refers to, on the other hand, genealogical models, without any definite indications of the persons composing the group, as in the family in the sense of a "household", and in the "joint family" in the sense of a property holding group.

Shah has thus made a departure from the conventional usages of the terms "elementary" or "nuclear family", "joint" or "extended family". This dichotomy has prevailed since long, and it still continues to do so, to some extent, in certain sociological and social anthropological quarters of India and the west. The superstructure of the entire study of the family in India has rested on these two concepts for more than a century. Shah has made certain terminological innovations in his study based upon his field study of the Gujarat Village.

Shah has made an attempt to show a developmental pattern in types, with the help of the concept of the developmental cycle of domestic groups, evolved by Fortes and his associates (Fortes; ed., Goody, 1958), although he modified it to suit his requirements. The pattern of interpersonal relations in each type of household has been described in considerable detail and has shown, in particular, the harmony and conflict among the general norms governing the formation of households and the norms of behaviour attached to the different roles in relationships within the household. He views the household pattern in relation with other structures in society, such as caste, kinship, and rural and urban communities and compares past patterns with the present.

Shah observes that it is necessary to pose the problems in the study of household dimension of the Indian family differently, in terms of the development process, the principle of residential unity of the patrikin and their wives, the extent of observance of the principle and of the various norms subsumed under it, the pattern of interpersonal relations in the various parts of households and a real rather than hypothetical view of the past. He remarks that problems posed should be studied in different sections of society in different regions of the country so that it may be possible to evolve an all India picture. He reiterates the view that it is also necessary to employ a variety of methods and techniques of investigation, although a concentration on micro studies and participant observation may have to be continued for some time. He remarks that when we think of past achievements and compare them to future tasks it seems as if we are only on the threshold of the study of Indian family.

This according to author, seems to be a valid observation. Author also believes that, on the basis of the present study, new areas of study have yet to be explored, and in studying these new areas of the family, we can discover new dimensions as well as new techniques.

As mentioned earlier, at the end of his book, Shah has given a large, annotated bibliography which is not only informative and systematic but is also brought up-to-date. In a conclusive review of Shah's work, it can be said that such an integral picture of the household dimension of the Indian family, does indeed make a positive contribution to the Sociology of the Family in India.

An important aspect of Shah's contribution is that he has tried to construct a theoretical model for the universal study of family in India.

Apart from the above major research studies on the Hindu Family, several small studies have been made in different parts of India. Most of these have been published in the form of research papers in journals or monograph. These are:

1. N.C. Desai, *Hindu Joint Family System* (1936).
2. David Kingsley (a) Changing modes of Marriage: Contemporary Family Type in eds., H. Becker and Hill, R., *Marriage and the Family* (New York : D.C. Heath, 1942) and (b) *Human Society* (New York: Macmillan, 1948).
3. B.B. Agarwal, 'In a Mobile Commercial Community', *Sociological Bulletin,* VI, No.2, September, 1965.
4. Ajit Ray, 'A Brahmin Village of the Sasna Type in District of Puri', *Man in India,* 36, 1956.
5. Sunil Sengupta, 'Family Organization in West Bengal; Its Nature and Dynamics', *The Economic Weekly,* X, 1958.
6. William A. Morrison, 'Family Patterns in Badlapur: An Analysis of Changing Institution in a Maharashtraian Village', *Sociological Bulletin,* VIII, 1959.
7. R.K. Mukherjee (a), 'A Note on the Classification of Family

Structure' in *Regional Seminar on Techniques of Social Research: Proceedings and Papers,* (Calcutta UNESCO Research Centre, 1959).
(b) 'On the Classification of Family Structures' in eds., T.N. Madan and Gopal Saxena, *Indian Anthropology: Essays in Memory of D.N. Majumdar* (Bombay, Asia Publishing 1962).
(c) *'The Sociologist and Social Change in India Today* (New Delhi, Prentice-Hall of India, 1965).

8. M.G. Kulkarni, 'Family Patterns in Golak Taluka', *Sociological Bulletin,* IX, 1960.
9. William J. Goode, *World Revolution and The Family Patterns* (New York, The Free Press of Glencoe, 1963).
10. A.B. Pose et al, 'The Size and Composition of the Households in dispersed Dwellings,' *Journal of Family Welfare,* X, 1, 1963.
11. Saroj Kapur, Family and Kinship Groups among the Khatris in Delhi', *Sociological Bulletin,* XIV, 1965.
12. Lalit Kumar Sen, 'Family in Four Indian Villages', *Man in India,* 46, 1965.
13. Milton Singer, 'The Indian Joint Family in Modern Industry', in eds, Milton Singer and Cohn, Bernard S., *Structure and Change in Indian Society* (New York: Werner-Gren Foundation for Anthropological Research, 1968.
14. George H. Conklin (a) 'The Family Formation – Process in India', *Journal of Family Welfare,* X, IV, 1968.
(b) 'Social Change and the Joint Family, The Census of Research Biases', *Economic and Political Weekly,* IV, 1969.
15. M.S. Gore, *Urbanization and Family Change,* (Bombay, Popular Prakashan, 1968).
16. M.S.A. Rao, 'Occupational Diversification and Joint Household Organization', *Contributions to Indian Sociology, New Series,* II, 1969.

It seems probable in the light of the above research and the evidence emerging from it that whereas a tendency of nuclearization seems more marked in recent years of the contemporary urban Hindu Family, the joint family still persists in some areas and in certain conditions, largely due to cultural traditions, as well as because of certain practical factors. The small joint family is now found to be emerging from special conditions of inspiration and employment and is also getting more popular in the urban areas. Practical considerations such as need of a helping hand in the family to assist in the stressed conditions of urban life are of no less importance for its continuance. The small joint family seems to be largely popular in today's modern age where crises of various types are becoming an order of the day and man is facing new challenges and strains.

Though the family has been treated at least to some extent, in all such village and community studies, there are a few studies devoted only to the study of family change with a reference to role dynamics. Most of the earlier studies provide only descriptions of the forms and structures of the different types of family in Indian Society. Though some discuss the relevance of the traditional, joint Hindu family in present society, we gain little insight of the functions of the family, or of the roles of family members and the various role conflicts and strains within a family group, whether it be joint, small joint or nuclear.

An appraisal of these multifarious researches made on the Hindu family in different parts of India, carried out in the six or seven decades also reveal that although various aspects of the Hindu family organization have been studied at length, there are yet several gaps in these studies. Most of the earlier studies have discussed the traditional Hindu family, emphasizing the change from jointness to nuclearity. Some have studied the Hindu family in the process of urbanization, and/or industrialization and have emphasized spatial mobility. The intra-familial role dynamics of the urban Hindu family has scarcely been studied so far.

The role dynamics of the urban Hindu family, had drawn author's attention, as it is an integrated study of this role dynamics that can help us to understand the process and trends of change in the contemporary Hindu family, as well as give us an insight to the understanding and interpretations of tensions, strains and conflicts in the family organization. Author has, therefore, concentrated more on these aspects and have made an attempt to fill in this major gap in urban Hindu family studies, by studying the role dynamics in the urban Hindu family. Role expectations, Role taking, Role playing, Role obligations and Role discharge have been studied extensively in the contexts of their traditional order as well as the changes which are now taking place in them.

This has enabled author to examine the variables of change in the role discharge on the one hand, and, on the other hand, which sets of roles, role expectations, role obligations and role discharge have actually undergone a change. Author believes that this is the first original study on the role dynamics of the urban Hindu Family and will, hopefully, inspire more original sociological research on similar aspects by other scholars.

NOTES

1. K.M. Kapadia, *Marriage and Family in India* (1955).
2. M.F. Nimkoff and M.S. Gore, 'The Social Bases of the Hindu Joint Family', *Sociology Research,* Vol. 44, 1959-1960, pp. 27-36.
3. T.K. Majumdar, *The Structure and Composition of the Urban Middle Classes in city of Kanpur* (1957), Mimeographed.
4. "Proceedings on Family, 50th Session, Indian Science Congress Association, Delhi, October 1 to October 10, 1963", *International Journal of Comparative Sociology,* Vol. V, 1964, pp. 118. 119.
5. David G. Mandalbaum, 'The Hindu Family', in ed., R.N. Anshen, *The Family: Its Function and Destiny* (New York: Harper and Brothers. 1949).
6. T.N. Madan, 'The Joint Family: A Terminological Clarification', *International Journal of Comparative Sociology* Vol. III, 1962, p. 7.
7. Iravati Karve, *Kinship Organisation in India* (Poona:Deccan College Postgraduate Research Institute, 1953), p.vi.
8. E.G. Bailey, "The Joint Family in India: A Framework for discussion", *The Economic Weekly* Vol. XII, No. 8, 1960.
9. Levi-Strauss, 'The Family' in H.L. Shapino ed., *Man, Culture and Society* (New York, 1956).
10. Op. cit., p. 15.
11. Savitri Shahani 'The Joint Family: A case study', *Economic Weekly,* XIII, 1961, pp. 1823-1828.
12. Aileen D. Ross, *The Hindu Family in its Urban Setting* (Bombay Oxford University Press, 1961).
13. D.G. Mandalbaum, 'The family in India' in ed., *The Family: its Function and Destiny* (New York, Harper and Brothers 1949).
14. M.N. Srinivas, *Marriage and Family in Mysore* (Bombay: 1942).
15. Jyotiramayee Sarma, 'The Formal and Informal Relations in the Hindu Joint Household of Bengal', *Man in India,* Vol. XXXI, No. 2, April-June, 1951 pp. 51-71.
16. Thomas K. Burch, 'The Size and Structure of Families: A Comparative Analysis of Census Data,' *American Sociological Review,* Vol. 32, No. 3, June, 1963, pp. 347-365.
17. Clifford Kirkapatrick, *The Family: As Process and Institution* (New York: Ronald Press, 1963).
18. I.P. Desai, 'The Joint Family in India, an Appraisal', *Sociological Bulletin,* Vol. V, No. 2, September, 1956.
19. R. Estorowitz, 'I.P. Desai' Symposium on Caste and Joint Family: an Analysis', *Sociological Abstract,* Vol. 5, No. 2, January, 1957, pp. 39-40.
20. R. Estorowitz., 'K.M. Kapadia: *Changing Pattern of Hindu Marriage and Family*; III, *Sociological Abstract,* Vol. 5, No. 1, January, 1952, p. 40.
21. I.P. Desai, 'The Joint Family in India — An Analysis', *Sociological Bulletin,*

Vol. V, No. 2, September, 1956, pp. 144-156.

22. Jyotiramayee Sarma, 'The Nuclearization of Joint Family Households in West Bengal' *Man in India,* Vol. 44, No. 3, July-Sept, 1964, pp. 193-206.
23. D.F. Mulla, *Principles of Hindu Law* (Bombay:1959) p 314.
24. Pauline Mahar Kolenda, 'Region Caste and Family Structure: A Comparative Study of the Indian Joint Family' in eds, Milton Singer and Bernard *S.Coh, Structure and Change in Indian Society* (Chicago, Aldine Press, 1968), pp. 339-36.
25. Pauline Mahar Kolenda, 'Regional Differences in Indian Family Structure in Robert Crane, *Regions and Regionalism in (ed.) South Asain Studies: An Exploratory Study* (Duke University Prog. Comp. Studies on South Asia, Monograph No. 5, (1967), pp. 147-226.
26. Pauline Mahar Kolenda, "Family Structure in Village Lonikand, India: 1819 and 1967, *Contributions to Indian Sociology, New Series,* No. IV, December, 1970, pp. 50-72.
27. Henry Orenstein; 'The Recent History of the Extended Family in India,' *Social Problems,* 8, 1961, pp. 341-353.
28. Henry Orenstein and Mickline, Michael, 'The Hindu Joint Family: The Norms and the Numbers, *Pacific Affairs,* 39, 1966, pp. 314-325.
29. Ibid.
30. A.M. Shah, *The Household Dimension of the Family in India*, 1973.
31. A.M. Shah, 'Basic Terms and Concepts in the Study of Family in India', *Indian Economic and Social History Review,* I, 1964.
32. 'Changes in the Indian Family: An Examination of Some Assumptions, *Economic and Political Weekly,* III, 1968, pp. 127-134.

3

THE STRUCTURE AND COMPOSITION OF THE URBAN FAMILY AND CHANGE

Family in India has been broadly classified into various types on the basis of the structure and composition, the situational condition and functions, with this base of classification, it can be further sub-classified with certain other variables. An effort in this regard is being made in this chapter while presenting a social picture of the urban Hindu family in Bhopal city.

The Social Structure of the Urban Family

On the basis of structure and composition we have the Joint Family with its two sub-groups, the Large Joint Family and the Small Joint Family. Besides these, there is the Individual Family or the Nuclear Family. On the basis of situational condition, we have the Rural Family and the Urban Family. Through my empirical observations in different parts of Northern India, I have discovered one more type of family in between these two types which could be most appropriately called the "Semi-Urban Family" that is the family which is living in those towns which have been under pressure of urbanization but have not yet been fully urbanised, that is, which is living on the fringes of the two processes, the rural and the urban and is still retaining some of their rural of Kasbaic cultural traits. The older part of Bhopal city falls much nearer to this category. On the functional basis there are Urban Joint and Rural Joint, and Urban Nuclear and Rural Nuclear families. We have seen in the earlier discussion that structurally a family may be individual while in function it may continue to be 'joint'. Functional jointness depends upon the 'joint ties' maintained with and obligations satisfied towards the joint family and from where these individual families may have branched out or family obligations may have been satisfied.

Conditions of urbanization and industrialization bring a change in the structure and function of the joint family. Besides this, there may be some imminent changes involved in the very dynamic nature of the society and which may also be influencing the urban Hindu family. Over and above these, normal processes of change, interaction of the family group with other culture family groups also bring some change in the family organization. Inter-caste marriage plays an important role in this cultural interaction.

On the basis of the different variables introduced to study functional change in the traditional family, a number of sub-types of the family can be envisaged, such as the "Educated Urban Joint Family", "the Educated Rural Joint Family," the "Educated Urban Nuclear" and the "Educated Rural Nuclear Family.

The social complex of Bhopal city mainly consists of the following basic types on the basis of this classification:

(1) The Urban Joint Family.
(2) The Urban Small Joint Family.
(3) The Urban Individual or Nuclear Family.

Cocklin's (1968, 1969) "transitional family" is akin to my "small joint family" (Type II) as this family suggested by Cocklin consists of husband, wife, unmarried children and assorted single relatives, such as father's mother.

Introducing the variable of education would not reveal much significance here as almost all the middle class families studies in the urban complex of Bhopal are also the educated families, though on the basis of the degree of education, a four type formulae can be evolved, the ordinarily educated the moderately educated, the highly educated and the advancedly educated or professionally educated, Education as a variable has therefore been analysed with the further four variables of education categories.

My observations in the area of my research reveal that the traditional large joint family comprising of three or four generations of people living together which was popular in former times and upon which sociologists and Indologists have built up their original formulations of "joint family" is hardly found in the city of Bhopal. I have, therefore, considered it unnecessary to classify the joint family in its two types, the Large Joint Family and the Joint Family. This "joint family" for purpose of all my references in this thesis would essentially mean to consist of two parallel or one parallel and one elder generation of people, living together in the same house, sharing a common kitchen normally though not necessarily, pooling their income in a common purse jointly, recognizing the authority of the head and meeting the family obligations jointly and under a family-feeling of common good, mutual trust and confidence among the family members.

As distinct from this, I have preferred to designate the "Small Joint Family" which consists of husband, wife and their unmarried children living with one or more dependent kin of an elder generation, that is to say husband, wife and unmarried children living together with a dependent uncle or aunt. But where both uncle and his wife are found to be living together with the nuclear composition group the two generations seem to be involved here, this immediately forms a joint family. The small joint family, for purpose of analysis of my empirical data in the universe of my study, is a middle category between the two generation joint family and the individual or nuclear family organisation. The small joint family involves only one additional kin of an elder generation living as a dependent upon the individual family, recognizing the supremacy of the head of the individual family, and meeting out all family obligations under him. This small joint family is a link to the two, the joint family and the nuclear family. My classification of the Urban Hindu Family, is, therefore, based upon a combined view emerging from conceptual thinking and my own empirical observations.

Similarly, two brothers living together with their wives and children and the third couple living by themselves without any children may also form a joint family. Husband and wife living with their unmarried children and one additional kin living with them as dependent form a small joint family. There is no definite attribute assigned to this "additional kin". This additional kin may be father, mother, father's brother, both elder and younger, or even some distant relative who comes to live with the family in its urban setting.

The members of small joint family share the family obligations jointly even through the additional kin lives here as a dependent kin. This dependent kind is also bound by family obligations.

Size has not been made a criterion in my study. An individual family can be as large as consisting of eight or ten members, whereas a joint family may only be composed of five or six members.

The size of the household does not affect the family type. The size of the household or numbers of people living in it may be important for economics or statistics, but not for sociological or anthropological researches as far as it only gives an indication as to whether the size of the household has undergone an expansion or contraction during the last one generation or so, or whether it has maintained its stability. But it does not influence the intra-generational relations or roles within the family.

The third category of my classification is the "Individual or Nuclear family", consisting of husband, wife and their unmarried children. It is thus composed of two generations, parents and their children. Normally both parents live here with their unmarried children but in some cases only one parent, father or mother may be living with a separated or a widower's status. This also forms the status in individual family. Practically for all reasons it can be further distinguished as a small individual family or one parent individual family.

In laying down the criteria for family types, I have considered permanent residence in the same family as an important variable. This means that the kin coming to live temporarily with a family, such as sisters or daughters coming to live with their parents during confinement, or uncles and other kin having come on transfer and during their temporary stay with their family for want of an allotment of a government quarter or suitable accommodation in the town do not affect the basic family structure. These are temporary situations and do neither influence the family group in its role functional discharge nor in meeting various family role obligations. The latter situation has emerged during the last two decades in the Bhopal town.

The small joint family discussed in my analysis of samples is somewhat different from Ross' small joint family classified under type B.[1] The small joint family defined by her is composed of a household in which parents live with their married sons and other unmarried children, or two brothers live together with their wives and children. She suggests that this type of family may be a temporary stage in the family cycle. It is usually formed when a son breaks away from his original familv on getting a job in another city and sets up his own small household there, one or more of his sons may then continue to live with him after marriage.

Desai also emphasizes the relationship bond in the family group when he says, "The residential joint family group is the three generation group. But functionally effective group is much wider".[2]

In may empirical study I have observed that the "small joint family" as treated by me in my analysis of data may either grow into a joint family of the first type, or may somehow get merged with the individual family, but it does not reflect a temporary stage.

In many instances I have found that the small joint family has maintained its continuity over two generations in an urban situation.

Many of the interviewees said that their father's family was a small joint family in their native place, while they are now actually living in an individual family. A third group of interviewees, though their number was small, consists of those persons whose father had lived in the small joint family and they are also now living in the small joint family, that is, there is a continuity of small joint family over two generations.

The composition of small joint family may also vary over a definite period or cycle.

The Complex of Bhopal Town

The Bhopal city chosen for purpose of studying changing trends in the Hindu family is the capital town of Madhya Pradesh and is situated in the north of the State. It has been a princely state before its merger with the Union of States in 1947 and later with the newly formed greater Madhya Pradesh in 1956. It was ruled in early history by the Hindu ruler and fell into the hand of the Muslims Nawab around the thirteenth century.

Because of its Muslim rule, the traditional Bhopal town has a bearing of the Muslim culture on it though the Hindu form a larger population. The older Bhopal is spread into different thickly populated clusters known as *mohallas*; there is a larger number of old buildings, lodging a large number of households, and some of the oldest houses are in themselves a more or less small *mohallas*, clusters of kin living together in vicinity.

The old Bhopal town has a mixed population of Hindus and Muslims. Sindhi refugees and Sikhs have also settled here after the partition and are having their business in the town. There is also quite a large number of Christians in the town. Only a few Marwaris or local Bania families in the congested old Bhopal may have retained the basic jointness to some extent.

The social complex of Bhopal includes the urban area of Bhopal, that is the population living essentially in the municipal limits of the Bhopal city, and comprises of those residents of the city who have been living here since their birth or those who have come to live here as emigrants. The joint, the small joint, and the individual families thus includes also those who have come to Bhopal from other states on appointment, or transfer in Government, Semi-Government services, autonomous organizations, firms and commercial concerns.

The complex of new Bhopal thus comprises of government persons' and semi-Government persons' households, that is, it forms those households whose head or some member of the family is working in the government, semi-government or autonomous organisation, such as the Madhya Pradesh Electricity Board, Bharat Heavy Electricals Ltd. Culturally we can classify these families as belonging to or coming from the following cultural zones; the North Indian cultural group comprising of families coming from Uttar Pradesh, Haryana, Delhi and Punjab; the Central Indian, that is of those belonging to Rajasthan, Bihar and the whole of the present Madhya Pradesh; the Western Indian, Comprising of families coming from Maharashtra and Gujarat: the Eastern that is families coming from West Bengal and Orissa and Assam, and the South Indian, that is families coming from Andhra, Tamil Nadu, Kerala and Karnataka.

Besides the main government colonies known as North Tatya Tope Nagar, South Tatya Tope Nagar, Shivaji Nagar, and Ravishankar, the New Bhopal is spread towards 74 Bungalows, the Arera Colony and the newly developing housing board colonies in the city called Kelendeo and Mahadeo Apartments. This provides a cross-cultural situation in the metropolis of Bhopal, and sample drawn from this culturally varied group has been changes. This sample represents the Hindu family not only in its urban, but also in its cross-cultural setting, or conveniently what can be called the cosmopolitan setting. The analysis of urban Hindu family in this context would thus provide a better understanding of multifarious factors behind the family change, as well as give us an insight into changing trends along with their different expressive forms and cultural variations within the family group.

The analysis of this study thus relates to the structural composition of the urban Hindu family and its functional roles in the joint, small joint and individual families. This analysis would thus include those structurally-joint families which are also joint in action, that is, those who are having joint obligations, are structurally nuclear though functionally joint, that is who have migrated from their native towns to Bhopal for sake of employment, but who are maintaining their joint family ties with their natal or parental joint family in their original town.

The sample, besides, these two main types also includes those families which have been small-joint in their native town and continue to be small joint in the new place, and those families which have been individual in their native places and continue to be individual in their new set up, though there may be a difference in their composition and size. The analysis of empirical data would indicate whether there has been a continuity in the family type over two or three generations, a variation from the larger type to the smaller type is marked, or a stability is maintained in the family type.

Type of Family related to Size of Households

The structure and composition of the families in the Urban Bhopal is presented in the Table 3.1 which shows the occurrence of a particular type of household, joint, small joint and individual in reference to the size of the household and sex distribution in the family and total composition of its members (Fig. 3.1).

TABLE 3.1: Distribution of Households by Type and Size of Family

Type of family	No. of families	Population			Average size of family
		Total	Males	Females	
1	2	3	4	5	6
1. Joint	17	191	101	90	11.2
2. Small Joint	49	350	189	161	7.1
3. Individual	156	800	405	395	5.1
TOTAL	222 100%	1341 100%	695 51.83%	646 48.17%	7.08

In the joint family of the sample representation, there were found 191 members, i.e., 101 males and 90 females thus bringing the average size of family to 11.2. In the 49 small joint families 350 members, i.e., 189 males and 161 females were found to be living, making an average size of family to 7.1.

In the individual family 156 households, there were 800 members living in, 405 males and 395 females, and the average size of family comes to 5.1. This suggests that the size of family gets gradually increased in the small joint and joint families. The present analysis indicates that an average size of 5.1 in the individual family increases to 7.2 in small joint and 11.2 in joint households. If we take an average view of the situation, we find that in the total composition of 222 families, the average size comes to 7.8. There are 51.83 per cent males and 48.14 per cent females in these 222 households of urban Bhopal.

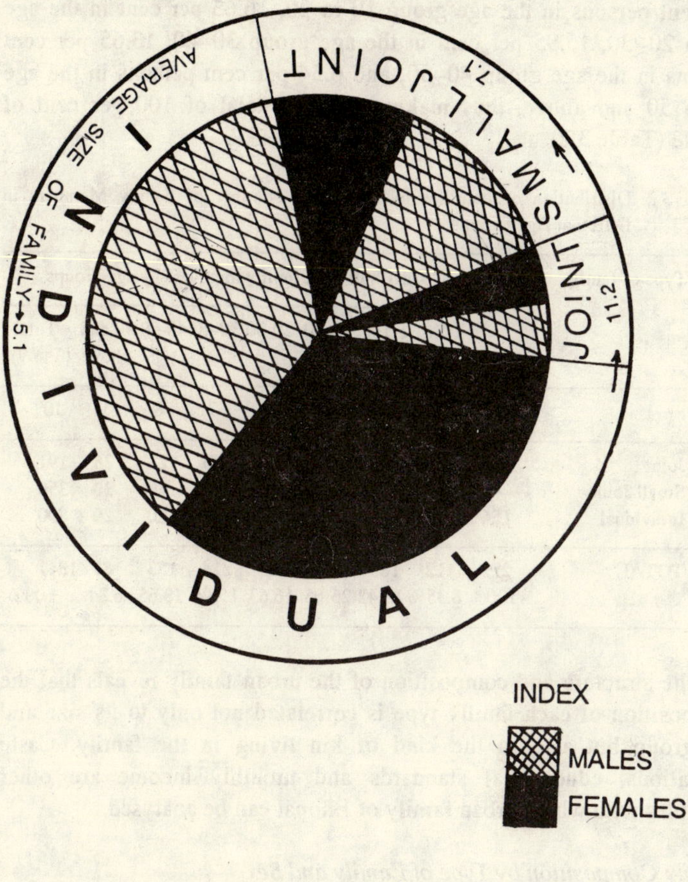

FIG. 3.1: Distribution of Households by Type and Size of Family.

Distribution of Families by Type and Composition of Age Groups

The total 222 families studied are found to be composed of 17 joint, 49 small joint and 156 individual families. When we break up these three types into age group compositions, we find that there are 8.35 per cent in the 1 to 5 age group, 13.42 per cent in the age group 5 to 10, 25.65 per cent persons in the age group 10 to 20, 16.63 per cent in the age group 20–30, 15.95 per cent in the age group 30–40, 13.65 per cent persons in the age group 40–50, and 6.34 per cent persons in the age group 50 and above, thus making a grand total of 100 per cent of sample (Table 3.2).

TABLE 3.2: Distribution of Families by Type and Number of Family Members in Different Age Groups

Type of family	No. of families	Distribution of family members by age groups							
		1-5	5-10	10-20	20-30	30-40	40-50	50 and above	Total (3 to 9)
1	2	3	4	5	6	7	8	9	10
1. Joint	17	15	21	31	44	23	23	26	191
2. Small Joint	49	35	40	80	66	59	40	30	350
3. Individual	156	62	119	225	113	132	120	29	800
TOTAL	222	112	180	344	223	214	183	85	1341
	100%	8.35%	13.42	25.65	16.63	15.96	13.65	6.34	100%

The structure and composition of the urban family reveals that the composition of each family type is correlated not only to its size and age-group but also to the kind of kin living in the family. Caste affiliations, educational standards and monthly income are other variables with which urban family of Bhopal can be analysed.

Family Composition by Type of Family and Sex

When we analyse each type of family from the point of view of the sex and major minor age group compositions, we get the following results:

Among 17 joint families, there were 32. 46 per cent adult males, 26.18 per cent adult females, 20.42 per cent minor males and 20.94 per cent minor females (Table 3.3).

TABLE 3.3: Family Composition by Type of Family and Sex

Type of family	No. of families	Adult Males	Adult Females	Minor Males	Minor Females	Total
1	2	3	4	5	6	7
1. Joint	17	62 (32.46%)	50 (26.18%)	39 (20.42%)	40 (20.94%)	191 (100%)
2. Small Joint	49	112 (32.00%)	96 (27.43%)	77 (22.00%)	65 (18.57%)	350 (100%)
3. Individual	156	214 (26.75%)	205 (25.63%)	191 (23.88%)	190 (23.75%)	800 (110%)
TOTAL	222	388	351	307	295	1341

Among 49 Small Joint Families there were 32 per cent adult males, 27.43 per cent adult females, 22 per cent minor males and 18.57 per cent minor females.

The comparison of male-female distribution in each type of family reveals that the percentage of adult males in the joint family comes very near to the percentage of adult males in small joint family, and percentage of adult females in small joint family comes almost near to percentage of adult females in joint family. There are less females living in both these types of family, the joint and the small joint, 26.18 per cent and 27.43 per cent respectively.

Similarly the percentage of minor males in the joint family is almost equal to the percentage of females 20.42 per cent to 20.94 per cent both the male-female sex ratio both in respect of adult and minor groups is almost equal in the 156 individual families, there were 26.75 per cent adult males, 25.63 per cent adult females, 23.88 per cent minor males and 23.75 per cent minor females. The family composition by type of family and sex is illustrated in Fig. 3.2.

When we analyse the ratio of sex, per thousand we find that for every 1000 males, there are 891 females living in joint family, 852 females in small joint family and 975 females in individual family.

This indicates that there are more females per 1000 males in the individual family (975) than in joint (891) and small joint families (852).

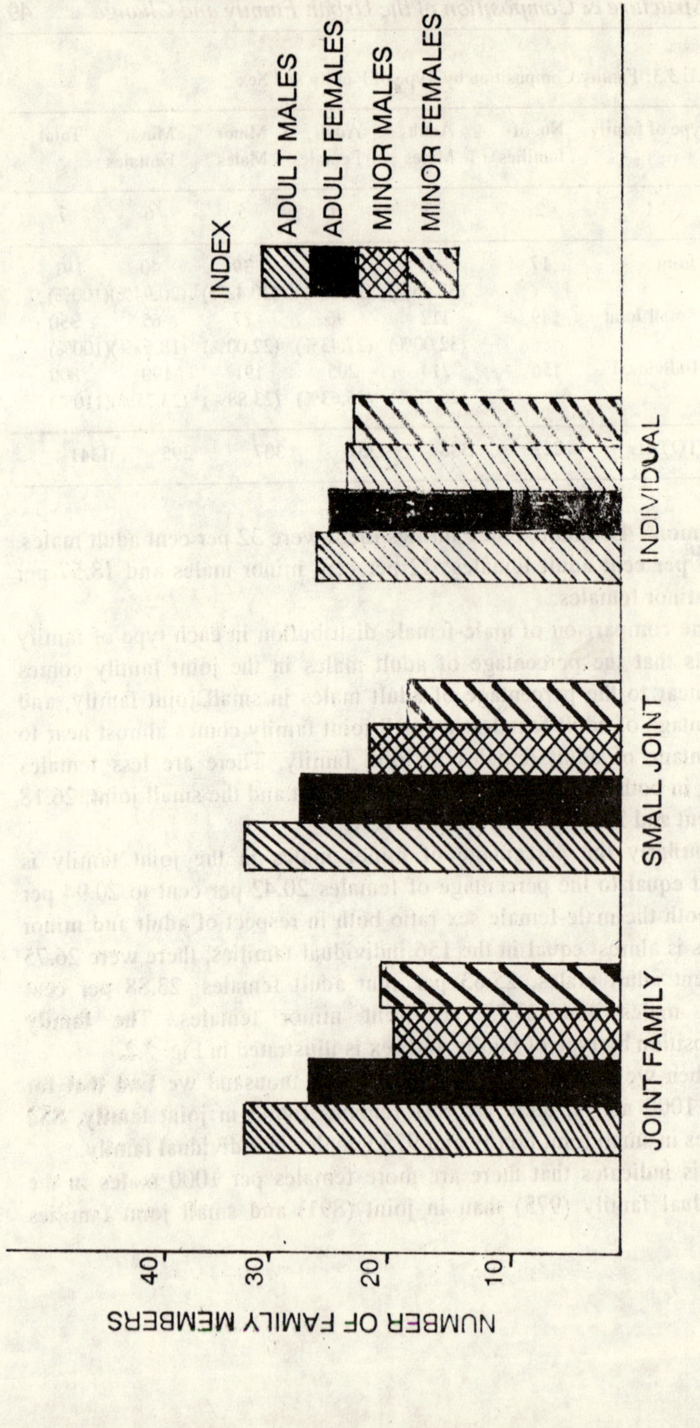

FIG. 3.2: Family Composition by Type of Family and Sex.

Caste Composition in Urban Bhopal

The urban population of Bhopal city is a mixed composition of many caste groups of Hindus, Muslims, Christians, Sikhs, Parsis and several other Anglo-Indian groups.

With this basic observation held for the urban Bhopal, let us now examine that form of classification of the Indian households had been followed by the Census of India so that we know how far our urban Hindu family agrees or disagrees to this structural criteria. The Census of India, 1951, has classified the Indian families into three types, according to the composition of number of household members. The 1961 Census has more or less followed the same pattern.

This classification suggests the large-size family as the first category of the census criteria falls parallel to our traditional large joint family (which is 17 in number) and 191 comes parallel to the second category of our small joint family (which consists of 49 numbers) and has 350 members living in it. And the third category of falls parallel to or traditional large joint family which is 17 in number and has 191 members living in it.

The medium-size family comes parallel to the second category of our small joint family which consists of 49 numbers and has 350 members living in it. And the third category falls parallel to our nuclear or individual family which is 156 in numbers and which consists of 800 members living in it. This appears a valid formula for census or for enumeration of households where classification is desired to indicate only certain broad types and does not have its correlation to other aspects of society. Sociologically this type of classification is only of a limited significance. The size of family does not provide any adequate basis for understanding the basic element of the family through all its dimensions. For this reason we do not accord much importance to this criteria adopted by the Census of India.

The Brahmins are found to be the dominant caste in the town. They are followed by Kayasthas and Viashyas who are almost equal in members. The latter include Agarwala, Gupta, Nagar, etc. who come under this wide Varna group of caste. The Kshatriyas or the Rajput occupy the third position (Table 3.4).

The Functional Composition of Urban Bhopal

The social complex of Bhopal is thus composed of the urban family which may be structurally local or emigrant, residentially individual, small-joint, or joint, and functionally joint or individual. This sample thus includes those families who are joint in action, though this action is discharged only occasionally when the members of the family visit their native home, and who share joint family obligations inspite of their living in the temporal and residentially nuclear or small joint families in the town. This joint obligation is fulfilled either by supporting some younger brother or sister in education, or by keeping him or her with them, or by remitting regular money orders. The sample drawn from my universe also analyses this aspect and indicates the nature of family obligations, the mode of meeting these role-obligations and relative changes within them with attributive factors and variables; all these taken together are indicative of trends of change in the urban Hindu family.

TABLE 3.4: Distribution of Families by Type and Caste

Type of family	Caste Groups				
	Brahmin	Kshatriya	Vaishya	Kayastha	Total
1	2	3	4	5	6
1. Joint	9	2	5	1	17
2. Small Joint	26	4	8	11	49
3. Individual	83	14	29	30	156
TOTAL	118 (53.16%)	20 (9.01%)	42 (37.83%)	42 (37.83%)	222 (100%)

The Hindu castes are dominant in the urban population. We had selected four Hindu caste groups in our sample of 222 families for our present study. When we look into our data from the point of view of caste composition, we find that the caste groups hold the following related order of preponderance in the three different types of family.

Among the 17 joint families, there are 9 Brahmin, 2 Kshatriya, 5 Vaishya and 1 Kayastha households. Among 49 small joint families, there are 26 Brahmin, 4 Kshatriya, 8 Vaishya and 11 Kayastha households. And among 156 individual families, there are 83 Brahmin, 14 Kshatriya, 29 Vaishya and 30 Kayastha households.

This suggests that Brahmins have the largest preponderance in the four caste groups. The Brahmins also holds a proportic.

preponderance in all three types of family. They form 53.16 per cent in our sample of 222 households. The Kshatriya hold the lowest order in this respect, forming only 9.01 per cent in our urban sample.

As the majority of this sample relates to service class families, this also indicates that Brahmins are the dominant class in all service occupations.

Continuity of Joint Family Over Two Generations

The observations on continuity of joint family type over two generations and its correlation with the present family type reveals that though there has been a structural change in the family type over a period of one generation, many of the urban families, whether they are at present residentially "joint family" or not, have shown a basic belief in the feasibility of the joint family type, and believe in the continuity of joint family over their generation.

The reasons for this belief in the traditional joint family as an ideal type of family may be various and many. One of the main reasons seems to lie in the "sanctity of the joint family". The Hindu Joint Family has been for a very long period of history a traditional form of family, on which the Hindu Social Organisation had laid its foundations. And the Hindu Families largely value the sanctity of the Hindu family as a part of the large tradition and show a kind of respect for the cultural tradition. The Hindu joint family is the most important part of this tradition. The opinion expressed about the continuity of joint family as "a feasible type" naturally falls within this purview and has this privilege in its favour. Many Hindu Family members would not like to break off completely from the traditional Hindu family mainly first by because it has been conventionally maintained for ages and their fathers had been living in it inspite of their individual discomforts, their own under privileged position, and the new strains on them. Thus in other words they want to adhere to the tradition, adherence is what most sociologists have called "continuity of joint family". I have tried to relate it to the continuity of conventional or traditional ideas and values.

This appears to be a universal situation with the Hindu joint family in India, and only some regional variations are marked. It is this sanctuous attachment with the joint family that enables even people of nuclear family in migrated places to maintain an emotional tie with the parental joint family.

The other important reason thus lies in the emotional bond with the joint family system. The classical Hindu sentiment has been in favour of the joint family and even a modern Hindu family member wants to maintain its continuity. He wants a change, a moderation but not a complete break off from the conventions, and though the joint family appears to be difficult institution and often an institution expecting a lot of family obligations from junior members, he cannot easily severe his relations. It also appears less pragmatic in the modern conditions, and the occupational mobility, combined with other modern conditions have limited the joint family. The modern Hindu while proud of his cultural tradition does not now probably want to adhere to the old conventions in an orthodox way and seems to seek a more rational approach towards his joint family in the native place.

Distribution of Families related to Monthly Income

The urban complex of Bhopal reveals that individual or nuclear family is growing more popular, smali joint family is still found in adequate proportion, but joint family with two generations is gradually showing a decline. When these three types of family are analysed in relation to the monthly income of the household, we find that the largest number of families, 110 or 49. 55 per cent belong to the middle income group having a range of Rs. 501 to Rs. 1000, 99 or 44.59 per cent belong to the higher income group of above Rs. 1000 while only 13 households or 5.86 per cent are found living under lower income group having less than Rs. 500 monthly income in all three types of family. It thus appears that the most common group in which most of the families live is the monthly income range group of Rs. 501 to Rs. 1000. This indirectly also indicates that there has been a rise in the monthly income of an average family in the urban situation, and that the middle-middle class has been rising slowly in predominance (Fig. 3.3).

Distribution of Families by Type and Occupation

When we classify the families by type and occupation of the Head of the Household, we find that in the total sample of 222 families, 151 individual families belong to the "Service Group", while 43 small joint and 10 joint families belong to this occupation group thus together forming a percentage 91.90 per cent. Only two individual families, and one joint family were found to belong to the "Profession Group", thus

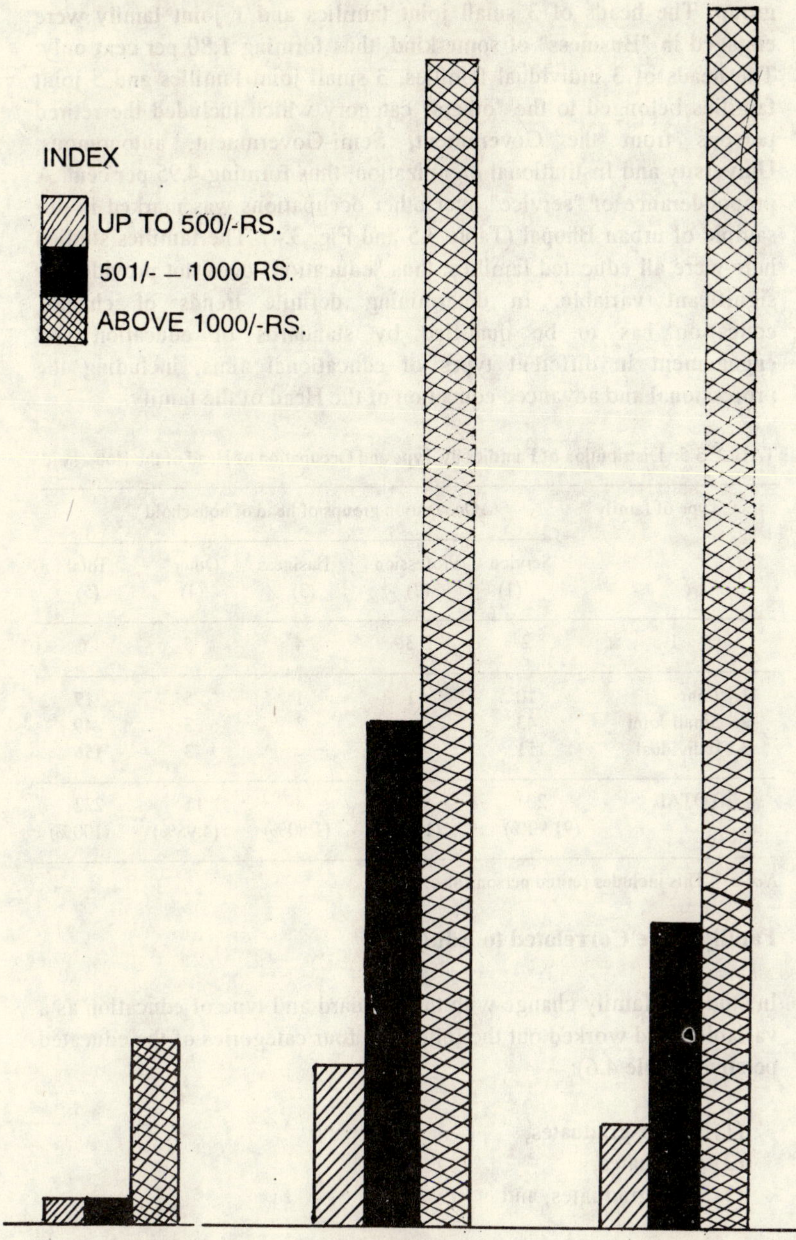

FIG. 3.3: Distribution of Families by Type and Monthly Income Groups.

forming 1.35 per cent none of the small joint families belonged to this group. The heads of 3 small joint families and 1 joint family were engaged in "Business" of some kind, thus forming 1.80 per cent only. The heads of 3 individual families, 3 small joint families and 5 joint families belonged to the "others" category which included the retired persons from the Government, Semi-Government, autonomous, University and Institutional organization, thus forming 4.95 per cent. A preponderance of "service" over other occupations was marked in our sample of urban Bhopal (Table 3.5 and Fig. 3.4). The families studied here were all educated families, thus "education" does not provide any significant variable. In determining definite trends of change, education has to be qualified by standards of education and engagement in different types of educational aims, including the professional and advanced education of the Head of the family.

TABLE 3.5: Distribution of Families by Type and Occupation of Head of the Household

Type of family	Occupation groups of head of household				
	Service (1)	Profession (2)	Business (3)	Other* (4)	Total (5)
1	2	3	4	5	6
1. Joint	10	1	1	5	17
2. Small Joint	43	—	3	3	49
3. Individual	151	2	—	3	156
TOTAL	204 (91.90%)	3 (1.35%)	4 (1.80%)	11 (4.95%)	222 (100%)

Note: * This includes retired persons also.

Family Type Correlated to Education

In studying family change with the standard and type of education as a variable I had worked out the following four categories of the educated persons (Table 4.6):

(1) Under-graduates,
(2) Graduates,
(3) Post-graduates, and

(4) The Professionals, or the Advanced educated, LL.B., LL.M., M.B.B.S., M.S., M.D.B.Ed., M.Ed., Ph.D., D.Lit., B.E., B.Tech., etc.

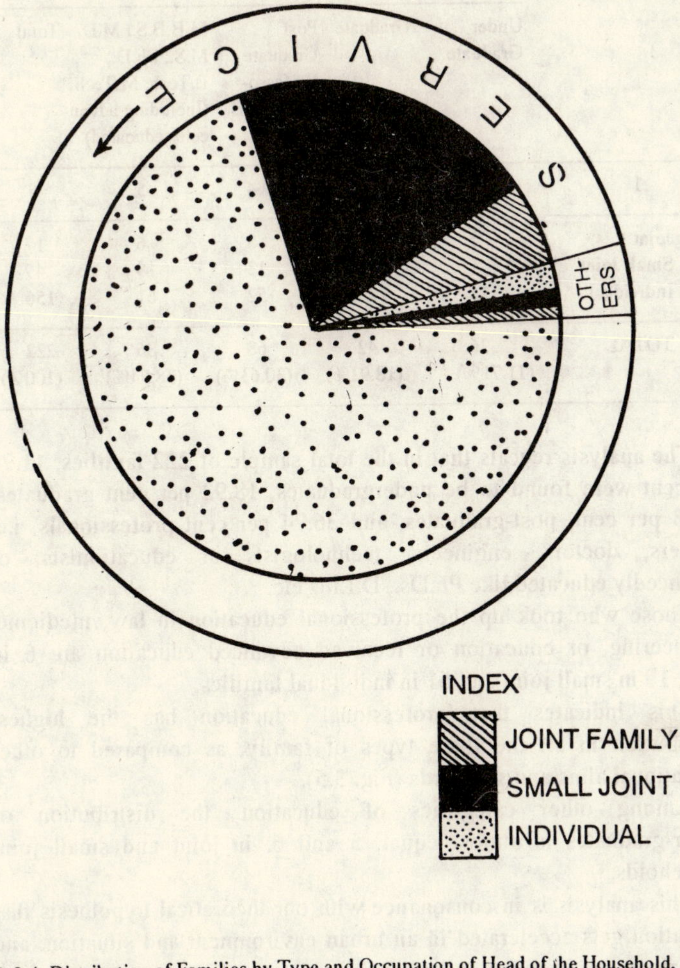

FIG. 3.4: Distribution of Families by Type and Occupation of Head of the Household.

TABLE 3.6: Distribution of Families by Type and Educational Standard of the Head of the Household

Type of family	Education Standards				
	Under Graduate	Graduate	Post Graduate Professo-nals: LL.B., LL.M.	M.B.B.S., M.D. M.S., Ph.D., B.Tech. M.Tech. (Including advan-celly educated)	Total
1	2	3	4	5	6
1. Joint	5	3	3	6	17
2. Small Joint	6	11	13	19	49
3. Individual	15	28	52	61	156
TOTAL	26 (11.71%)	42 (18.92%)	68 (30.63%)	86 (38.74%)	222 (100%)

The analysis reveals that in the total sample of 222 families, 11.71 per cent were found to be undergraduates, 18.92 per cent graduates, 30.63 per cent, post-graduates, and 36.74 per cent professionals, i.e. lawyers, doctors, engineers, technologists or educationists, or advancedly educated like Ph.Ds., D.Litts etc.

Those who took up the professional education in law, medicine, engineering, or education or received advanced education are 6 in joint, 19 in small joint and 61 in individual families.

This indicates that professional education has the highest distribution in all the three types of family, as compared to other educational aims and standards (Fig. 3.5).

Among other categories of education, the distribution of under-graduates is almost equal, 5 and 6, in joint and small joint households.

This analysis is in consonance with our theoretical hypothesis that education gets accelerated in an urban environment and situation, and specially where education was achieved in at least last one parental generation, the family shows a larger frequency of the continuance of education. This condition further provides an additional incentive to its follow up in the next generation. Besides greater the period of urbanization of a family the more emphasis is laid upon technical and profession-oriented education.

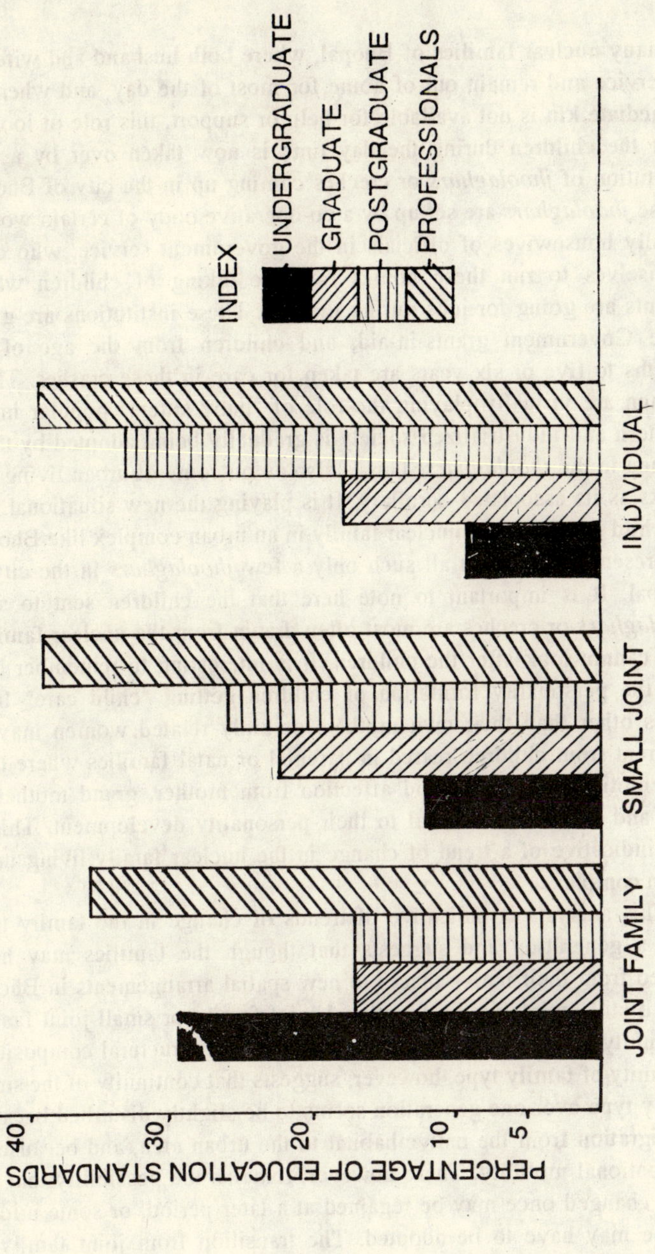

FIG. 3.5: Distribution of Families by Type and Educational Standards.

A New Urban Situation

In many nuclear families of Bhopal, where both husband and wife are in service and remain out of home for most of the day, and where an immediate kin is not available for help or support, this role of looking after the children during the day time is now taken over by a new institution of *jhoolaghars* or creches coming up in the city of Bhopal. These *jhoolaghars* are set up by a co-operative body of certain women usually housewives of officials in the government service, who offer themselves to run these homes for care taking of children whose parents are going for jobs during the day. These institutions are given State Government grants-in-aid, and children from the age of six months to five or six years are taken for care in these crashes. These women are virtually playing the role of "baby sitters" popular in the Western and industrialized society is gradually being adopted by these women in the *jhoolaghars*. This is also an outcome of urban living and works as its associated corollary. It is playing the new situational role of "child care", for the nuclear family in an urban complex like Bhopal. At present there are in all such only a few *jhoolaghars* in the city of Bhopal. It is important to note here that the children sent to such *jhoolaghars* or creches are most often drawn from the nuclear families who cannot look after the children. It is interesting to remember here that the personality formation of children getting "child care" from ladies other than their own mothers or kinly related women may be different from children reared in parental or natal families where they get emotional caressing and affection from mother, grand mother or aunt and which are so vital to their personality development. This is also indicative of a trend of change in the nuclear family living in an urban complex.

This analysis is indicative of trends of change in the family type over a generation and suggests that though the families may have moved from their native places to new spatial arrangements in Bhopal city, it still maintains the functional joint family or small joint family continuity over one generation. This analysis of structural composition and unity of family type, however, suggests that continuity of the small family type over one generation seems to be slightly disturbed because of migration from the native habitat to the urban area, and because of occupational mobility. There however, remains the possibility that the form changed once may be regained at a later period, or some middle course may have to be adopted. The transition from joint family to individual family and growing of individual family into small joint family in course of time is a clear example of the continuity and change that prevails in regard to the Hindu family and is thus quite significant for any study of family change.

NOTES

1. Aileen D. Ross, *Hindu Family in its Urban Setting,* Toronto, University of Toronto Press, 1962, p.35.
2. *Op. cit.*, p. 177.

4

THE INSTITUTIONAL SET-UP AND FUNCTION OF THE URBAN FAMILY AND CHANGE

Change is always a relative term and can be assessed in relation to the context in which it occurs and other correlated factors which work behind it, a few main ones figuring more prominently and others in a conducive manner. It can be well studied in an institutional set up of the urban family which is under process of transition and change. We can assess how far the structure of the family institution continues to function in the traditional pattern and how far it reflects change in different situational conditions. By institutional set up, we mean the social cultural order in which family organization expresses itself.

Change in family comes through several factors, break-up of the joint family into individual units owing to occupational mobility from native areas to towns and industrial centres, loss of faith in the traditional order and the old value system, growing sense of individualism and adoption of new ideas of modernism and technology, etc. But besides this, change can also come through the related institution of marriage. Marriage is a union of not only two opposite sexes but also of two different personalities who for the sake of founding a family meet, make adjustments and live in a cordial relationship with a definite objective of raising and rearing children. Whether this basic objective may be fulfilled or not, the marriage institution retains its validity.

The Marriage and Related Aspects

The form of marriage is important from the point of view of the relative change. It may indicate that the Hindu marriage has always been monogamous. Even though the ideal of *patrivartya* suggests one-sided emphasis for the morality of wife and absolves off the husband from any moral obligations towards his wife, it has indirectly promoted the unity of family. Except for certain kings and rulers who were given a special licence in the historical times, polygamy was never favoured by the Hindu social organisation. In the later period of cultural history monogamy was prescribed by law in India and the Hindu Marriage Act of 1955 makes legal provision of punishment for breach of monogamy.

In our universe of Bhopal town, monogamy was found universally. There was no deviation from this form with provision of the social or legal sanction. None of the respondent admitted such a deviation. It may, however, be pointed out that all such deviations are not expressively made in our Indian society and are nourished secretly and without assuming any institutional form. Change envisaged to be assessed in marriage form thus does not lie in determining whether monogamy prevails or not, but in seeing whether interest and love marriages are now accepted within this marriage form. The traditional pattern of Hindu Marriage has been the negotiated marriage by mutual arrangement by parents of the two parties within the domain of caste with sub-caste consideration and preference (Table 4.1).

Caste and sub-caste considerations still reign supreme above everything else in the rural as well as urban Hindu families. Not much difference is marked in their outlook towards rigidity of caste and sub-caste.

The conventional Hindu marriage by negotiation and mutual settlement is found to prevail largely in the Bhopal urban complex. There were found a few families who had accepted a love marriage of a son, daughter, brother, or sister in the family.

Where emphasis on suitability of match specially in terms of education, and suitable employment is getting more concern of parents in the recent days, the issues of caste considerations, regionalism and dowry still remain important. Dowry has not yet been replaced entirely by high education or a suitable employment (Table 4.2).

The Intercaste Marriage

If the age of girl or boy has surpassed the marriageable age, and there is little hope of getting a suitable match within the closed caste circle, there is sometimes a selection desired from the outside caste group. With hope of getting more opportunities for a better match, the group of selection is now made much wider. In this venture, however, caste considerations are limited to upper caste Hindus only. The normal

TABLE 4.1: Forms of Marriage by Type and Caste and Prevalence of Dowry

Type of family	Caste Group	Monogamous family	Nos. where Dowry prevalent	Nos. where Dowry taken	Nos. where dowry given in sister's marriage	Dowry given in daughters marriage	Question on dowry not responded
1		2	3	4	5	6	7
1. Joint	1.	9	2	1	5	1	—
	2.	2	—	1	2	1	—
	3.	3	1	—	—	—	—
	4.	3	—	—	—	—	—
TOTAL		17	3	2	7	2	—
2. Small Joint	1.	26	10	7	8	3	1
	2.	4	1	1	2	—	—
	3.	10	7	3	5	2	1
	4.	9	7	3	—	—	—
TOTAL		49	25	14	15	5	2
3. Individual	1.	83	42	16	24	7	1
	2.	14	7	6	4	1	—
	3.	29	13	9	10	3	1
	4.	30	13	—	9	3	—
TOTAL		156	75	31	47	14	2

TABLE 4.2: Opinion of Family Heads Regarding Dowry

Type of family/ Income group		No. of families	Dowry be taken as per will of the giver	Dowry be bargained according to the status of boy	Dowry is in perfect agreement with old customs & should not be broken	Dowry is essential for getting a suitable match	Dowry is a bad practice and social evil
1		2	3	4	5	6	7
1. Joint	1.	1	1	1	1	1	1
	2.	10	7	1	2	1	8
	3.	6	3	2	—	1	6
TOTAL		17	11	4	3	3	15
2. Small Joint	1.	1	1	—	—	—	1
	2.	30	22	6	3	11	24
	3.	18	17	2	2	7	16
TOTAL		49	40	8	5	18	41
3. Individual	1.	11	9	1	—	7	11
	2.	70	51	7	2	23	61
	3.	75	57	3	—	21	72
TOTAL		156	117	11	2	51	144

concession is made only up to one or two degrees of proximity. Normally the upper most castes, Brahmins and Kshatriyas have shown little relaxation in their attitude towards caste rigidity. The Vaishya groups have shown some kind of relaxation and are willing to marry outside their own caste group. The Kayastha group has not shown any relaxation in their outlook towards marriage. The increasing number of matrimonial advertisements in *The Hindustan Times* and some other newspapers and magazines indicate this change.

Attitude Towards Love Marriage

The other consideration affecting caste rigidity in the situation emerging out of love affair between the boy or girl of the family. Where it breaks off because of some reason or other, the question does not arise, but wherever either of the two parties exerts a pressure on the other family, and worked out a solution, caste barrier, if coming in the way, is usually broken and the pairs desiring to marry are given an approval. For such approval, the initiative is usually taken by an elder brother, uncle, or distant relative of the boy or girl, sometimes some close friend who may play this role. It is not only important to know how far love marriage are becoming accepted in the urban Hindu family, but also to determine what institutional roles are actually assisting this acceptance. Particular emphasis was thus laid up on this aspect and a question was posed on this particular issue: "acceptance of love marriage by the family," and whether caste restriction was thus usually broken and concession given in such circumstances. The responses reveal that it is rare to find a love marriage occuring with in the caste or sub-caste group.

Even where inter-caste marriage are accepted in such circumstances, this acceptance is never blind: it always keeps a due consideration for avoiding proximity in relationship and keeping emphasis on an equal initiative. In fact social status of the other mate whosoever takes inter-caste marriages are encouraged only where social distance between the two groups is not wide enough.

Inter-caste marriage otherwise is not encouraged. In some circumstances where it is not possible to get a suitable match for the boy or girl, his or her parents may advertise in newspapers for a suitable match even from outside the caste.

Inter-religious marriage is very much restricted and occurs only where there may have been an advanced love affair between the boy and the girl and one of them may be exerting pressure on the other group. But in such circumstances, the marriage is usually secretly so that criticism and ostracism are avoided, celebrated. In my sample of Bhopal, I have not found even a single instance of inter-religious marriage.

These are some of the trends which are being reflected in the marriage institution and are ultimately affecting the related institution of family. The Hindu marriage institution is under a nobel influence of these new trends, and though their form is less intense, trends of change, less intricate, and the tempo is not very fast, they have started influencing the institution.

The nature and extent of this influence is corroborated by analysis of my empirical data.

Acceptance of Inter-provincial Marriages

The feasibility of getting a suitable match depends upon caste and clan composition, social connections, qualifications, job at hand, nature of job, and future prospects expected from it. Property considerations tend to be unimportant now since most of the marriages arranged in urban areas are with migrant groups of people, who have come for employment from outside and do not have any property in the local town. And it is impractical and rather irrelevant to know about their parental property where the new couple may never go to live. The break up on joint family organisation has also effected the emphasis on property. Migrated families in the new place are not expected to have much property. Provincial barrier has also become less rigid now and there are few families who would not hesitate to marry their daughters outside the State if they get a really suitable match. Generally many of the marriages in urban areas are inter-provincial marriages.

Where the provincial barrier has been broken or ignored, the caste restrictions have not ceased. There are a few families who would like to marry their sons or daughters with another caste member willfully and by open negotiations. There has, of course, been some liberalising of attitude in regard to sub-caste, marriages where relaxations are being made for caste, they are generally under pressure, either from the prospective matches or from other kinsmen or friends.

Acceptance of Love Marriage by the Parental Family

As love marriage is supposed to indicate a change in the conventional system of marriage, acceptance of love marriage by the parental family was examined through a set of questions. It was found that love marriage has occurred to a very small extent among the families but the cases where it was found had given varying opinions on the manner of acceptance of love marriage by the parental family or by the joint family.

These have been analysed with variables of cultural zones, income groups and educational groups.

Permissibility to love marriage has been expressed in varied forms. These are analysed in the following tables separately given for the joint family, small joint family and individual family (Table 4.3).

The head of one of these families in which love marriage was accepted was a graduate and the other a post-graduate.

One case related to a son's love marriage and the other to a brother's love marriage in the family. This indicates that love marriage was acceptable by parental family or by family of the same generation and in the second generation. Both these love marriages were accepted by the joint family. Both were performed through the traditional Hindu marriage system (Table 4.4).

When we compare the date of these two types of families which indicate some kind of jointness with individual families, we find that not only the total cases of love marriage are more in number here, but also they come from four different cultural zones, though here also maximum numbers come from the central zone.

The analysis of individual family indicates that love marriage is found in the parallel generation and not in the parental generation. Most of these love marriages were resented by the parental family, a substantial number (27) of love marriages were performed through the traditional Hindu marriage system and the rest were performed through the registered marriage system (Table 4.5).

This kind of change in the family marriage system can be further understood through other related aspects by examining how far these love marriages are inter-caste and inter-religious marriages too, that is, how far they have broken the barriers of caste and religion in marrying (Table 4.6 and Fig. 4.1).

We also wanted to know further that in helping these love marriages who from the family actually took the initiative in getting the love marriage consummated, and whether prior consent was sought by boy or girl from their parents or generations. The replies that we got from these sets of questions have been correlated to residential

TABLE 4.3: Permission to Love Marriage in Joint Families

Cultural/Income/ Educational groups		Occurrence of love marriage-type					Love marriage accepted by family	Love marriage resented by family	Form of love Marriage		Total
		Sons	Daughter	Brother	Sister	Self			by Hindu method	by legal court method	
1		2	3	4	5	6	7	8	9	10	11
1. Cultural	1.	—	—	—	—	—	—	—	—	—	—
group	2.	1	—	1	—	—	2	—	2	—	2
	3.	—	—	—	—	—	—	—	—	—	—
	4.	—	—	—	—	—	—	—	—	—	—
	5.	—	—	—	—	—	—	—	—	—	—
TOTAL		1	—	1	—	—	2	—	2	—	2
2. Income	1.	—	—	—	—	—	—	—	—	—	—
group	2.	—	—	1	—	—	1	—	1	—	1
	3.	1	—	—	—	—	1	—	1	—	1
TOTAL		1	—	1	—	—	2	—	2	—	2
3. Education	1.	—	—	—	—	—	—	—	—	—	—
group	2.	—	—	1	—	—	1	—	1	—	1
	3.	1	—	—	—	—	1	—	1	—	1
	4.	—	—	—	—	—	—	—	—	—	—
TOTAL		1	—	1	—	—	2	—	2	—	2

Index for codes for cultural groups: Northern Zone — 1. Central Zone — 2. Western Zone — 3. Southern Zone — 4. and Eastern Zone — 5.

TABLE 4.4: Permission to Love Marriage in Small Joint Families

Cultural/Income/ Educational/ groups		Occurrence of love marriage-type					Love marriage accepted by family	Love marriage resented by family	Form of love Marriage		Total
		Sons	Daughter	Brother	Sister	Self			by Hindu method	by legal court method	
1		2	3	4	5	6	7	8	9	10	11
1. Cultural group	1.	—	—	—	—	—	—	—	—	—	—
	2.	—	—	5	1	1	4	3	4	3	7
	3.	—	—	—	—	—	—	—	—	—	—
	4.	—	—	—	—	—	—	—	—	—	—
	5.	—	—	—	—	—	—	—	—	—	—
TOTAL		—	—	5	1	1	4	3	4	3	7
2. Income group	1.	—	—	—	—	—	—	—	—	—	—
	2.	—	—	2	—	1	1	2	2	1	3
	3.	—	—	3	1	—	3	1	2	2	4
TOTAL		—	—	5	1	1	4	3	4	3	7
3. Education group	1.	—	—	—	—	—	—	—	—	—	—
	2.	—	—	—	—	—	—	—	—	—	—
	3.	—	—	2	1	1	2	2	2	2	4
	4.	—	—	3	—	—	2	1	2	1	3
TOTAL		—	—	5	1	1	4	3	4	3	7

TABLE 4.5: Permission to Love Marriage in Individual Families

Cultural/Income/ Educational groups		Occurrence of love marriage-type					Love marriage accepted by family	Love marriage resented by family	Form of love Marriage		Total
		Sons	Daughter	Brothers	Sister	Self			by Hindu method	by legal court method	
1		2	3	4	5	6	7	8	9	10	11
1. Cultural group	1.	—	—	—	—	—	—	—	—	—	—
	2.	2	2	9	3	—	14	2	14	2	16
	3.	—	—	6	1	2	8	1	8	1	9
	4.	—	—	2	2	—	—	4	4	—	4
	5.	—	—	—	1	—	1	—	1	—	1
TOTAL		2	2	17	7	2	23	7	27	3	30
2. Income group	1.	—	1	—	1	—	1	1	2	—	2
	2.	2	1	6	1		8	2	8	2	10
	3.	—	—	11	5	2	14	4	17	1	18
TOTAL		2	2	17	7	2	23	7	27	3	30
3. Education group	1.	1	—	2	2	—	5	—	5	—	5
	2.	—	—	—	2	2	3	1	3	1	4
	3.	1	1	7	2	—	9	2	10	1	11
	4.	—	1	8	1	—	6	4	9	1	10
TOTAL		2	2	17	7	2	23	7	27	3	30

TABLE 4.6: Relation of Love Marriage with Intercaste/Inter-Religious Groups

Type of family/	Caste Group	Love marriage is an inter-caste marriage	Intercaste love marriage is also an inter religious marriage	Boys of the superior caste	Girls of the superior caste	Equal Caste	Question not responded	Total Number of love marriages
1		2	3	4	5	6	7	8
1. Joint	1.							
	2.	1	1	1	—	—	—	1
	3.	1	—	—	—	—	1	1
TOTAL		2	1	1	—	—	1	2
2. Small Joint	1.	—	—	—	—	—	—	—
	2.	3	1	1	1	—	1	3
	3.	4	1	1	1	—	2	4
TOTAL		7	2	2	2	—	3	7
3. Individual	1.	1	—	—	—	1	—	2
	2.	8	2	3	2	—	3	10
	3.	10	2	4	1	4	1	18
TOTAL		19	4	7	3	5	4	30

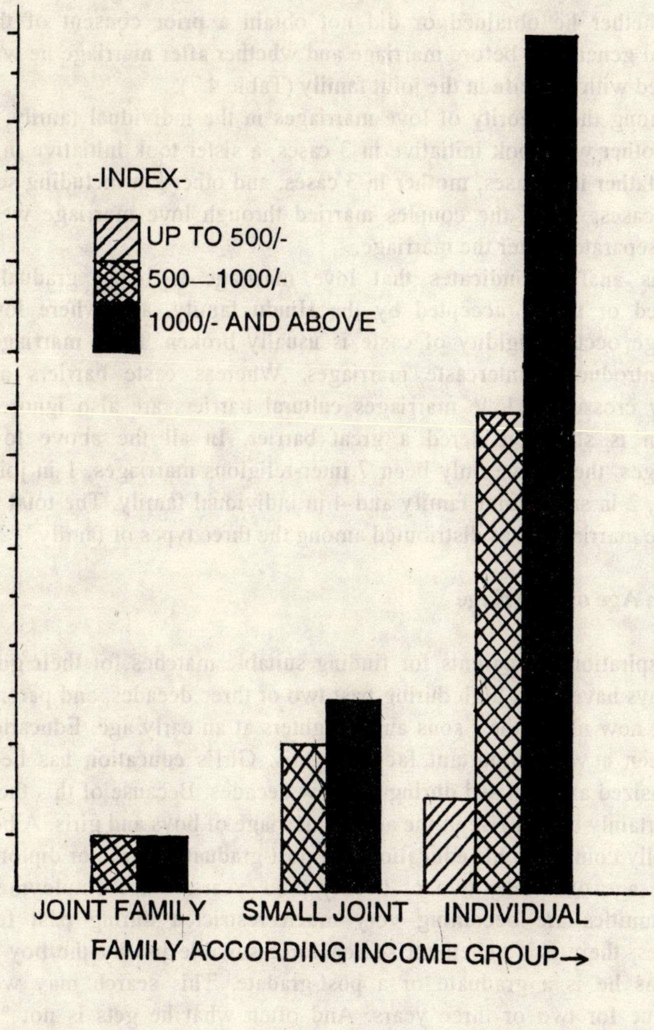

FIG. 4.1: Relation of Love Marriages with Intercaste and Interrelations.

acceptance of the married couple by the parental family, that is whether the boy of the family was married through a love marriage, and whether he obtained or did not obtain a prior consent of the parental generation before marriage and whether after marriage he was accepted with his wife in the joint family (Table 4.7).

Among the majority of love marriages in the individual family, it was brother who took initiative in 3 cases, a sister took initiative in 2 cases, father in 5 cases, mother in 3 cases, and other kin including self in 17 cases, 26 of the couples married through love marriage were living separately after the marriage.

This analysis indicates that love marriage is being gradually tolerated or tacitly accepted by the Hindu family, and where love marriage occurs, rigidity of caste is usually broken. Love marriages thus introducing intercaste marriages. Whereas caste barriers are usually crossed in love marriages cultural barriers are also ignored, religion is still considered a great barrier. In all the above love marriages, there have only been 7 inter-religious marriages, 1 in joint family, 2 in small joint family and 4 in individual family. The total of 30 love marriages was distributed among the three types of family.

Rise in Age of Marriage

The aspirations of parents for finding suitable matches for their girls and boys have risen high during past two or three decades, and parents do not now marry their sons and daughters at an early age. Education has been a very important factor in this. Girl's education has been emphasized and realised during last few decades. Because of this there has certainly been a rise in the age of marriage of boys and girls. A boy normally completes his education at a post-graduate degree or diploma by the age of twenty two or twenty three years. Since employment opportunities are becoming very much restricted during past few decades, there is a vehement search for a suitable job by the boy as soon as he is a graduate or a post-gradate. This search may well continue for two or three years. And often what he gets is not "an adequate job" for him, as he thinks it, and plans to leave it sooner he gets the next better. This keeps his mind in a stage of disengagement and incertitude about his future. He does not feel settled in his life and postpones his marriage till he gets settled to his satisfaction. This normally he is able to marry at or around thirty. The prospects of marrying at a proper age between 25-30 becomes limited for a boy

TABLE 4.7: Love and Intercaste Marriage in Relation to Initiative and Acceptance in Parental Family

Type of Family/ Income Group		Prior consent sought by Boy/ Girl	Initiative taken by				Other kins including self	No. of couples living separately	No. of couples forced to live separately number NR		Total number of love marriage
			Brother	Sister	Father	Mother					
1		2	3	4	5	6	7	8	9	10	11
1. Joint	1.	—	—	—	—	—	—	—	—	—	—
	2.	1	1	—	—	—	—	1	—	—	1
	3.	1	—	—	—	—	1	—	—	—	1
2. Small Joint	1.	—	—	—	—	—	—	—	—	—	—
	2.	1	1	—	—	1	1	3	—	—	3
	3.	3	1	—	1	—	2	3	—	1	4
TOTAL		4	2	—	1	1	3	6	—	1	7
3. Individual	1.	1	—	—	—	—	2	2	—	—	2
	2.	9	2	—	2	—	6	10	—	—	10
	3.	14	1	2	3	3	9	14	—	—	18
TOTAL		24	3	2	5	3	17	26	—	—	30

Grand Total of Love marriages : 39

belonging to service class. On the other hand, a girl now gets her education up to twenty or twenty two years. Though her parents are normally anxious about her marriage even while she is in college, her marriage does not materialise till twenty five, or twenty six, in some cases even up to thirty. The very fact of boys' deterring their marriage till thirty or thirty five has ultimately affected the girl's marriages. Dowry considerations continue to be important and thus indirectly affect the issue, even though dowry is not legally banned. The girl's age of marriage has thus normally risen from twenty four to twenty six in normal circumstances and to thirty in some cases.

Aileen D. Ross (1961) in her interesting study of the changing urban Hindu family in Bangalore probably the only exclusive study of Hindu family in the context of change observes while discussing the "changing marriage patterns", that the age of marriage of both men and women in India has varied from time to time and region to region as well as with religion, caste and language differences. Even when the age was supposedly set by custom, it varied in practice not only from place to place but much according to the convenience of the families. Famine, pestilence, harvests or a rise in prices also affect the size of the household. In determining the cultural factors behind the emphasis for early age of marriage; she remarks that the main consideration which determined the girl's age of marriage until recently was that she was supposed to marry before she attained puberty. This custom was due to high regard for the chastity of woman which was assured by her marriage before she could lose her virginity or be suspected of having lost it. This seems to have remained a cultural tradition for long in the Hindu family but it is now losing significance under other challenging factors, such as education of girls, new employment opportunities and employment conditions of girls. In my opinion, though this may still be a consideration in South India which is highly traditional, my observations in Northern India amplify that this does not wholly stand as a valid reason behind the late marriage of girls.

Ross supports the dictum of upward trend of marriage in India when she mentions about the age at which her interviewees wished to marry. But she admits the missing point in her study as she says that since no comparable studies seem to have been made for men, it is different to know whether their age of marriage has changed as radically as that of women, though many indirect references of bridegroom by women respondents suggest that it has also risen.

My own observations in my universe of study as well as evidences drawn from other sociological studies conducted elsewhere in India reveal that the age of marriage for girls has again been coming down slightly during last some years. One of reasons for this seems to lie in the growing emphasis on emotional stability of the girl. The common belief is that emotional adjustment is possible before the girl attains maturity, and that adjustments before twenty five become more easy. Many educated parents show much concern over the future of their educated daughters and since they are well aware that men still command authority in the family in spite of enlightenment and modern ideas now popular in their society, they want to provide better ground for adjustibility by making their daughters marry early and preferably before they are twenty five. Moreover with the growing stress in the modern society: the parents are now anxious to provide economic security to their daughters at an early date.

Many parents prefer to marry their daughters before they are twenty and though a vehement search starts at a much earlier age of her, while she has hardly passed her higher secondary examination in many regions and castes, she is not usually married before twenty. In many cases marriage of girl is performed around the age of twenty five. As the conditions are becoming hard and competitive, it is becoming tough to marry her early, and many factors are at play behind the rising age of marriage of girl now than ever before, the age of marriage of girls has certainly risen during past ten years.

The age of boys has also shown a relative rise, during past ten years though it is affected by some other factors, such as difficult conditions of employment, insecurity of job, insecure service conditions, frequent transfers, family responsibilities etc., because of which the boy does not feel stability in his life and goes on postponing his marriage. This so-called stability is not attained now usually before thirty five or so, consequently the normal age of marriage of boys has risen to about thirty five years.

It seems tangible to conclude tnat there has been an overall small decline in the upward trend in the age of marriage of both, boy and girl, during the last ten years or so. The curve which may have risen during past three or four decades is now showing a decline (Fig. 4.2).

The Institutional Set-Up and Change

The advanced education and enlightened views of the highly educated have motivated them to accept the need for equal participation of

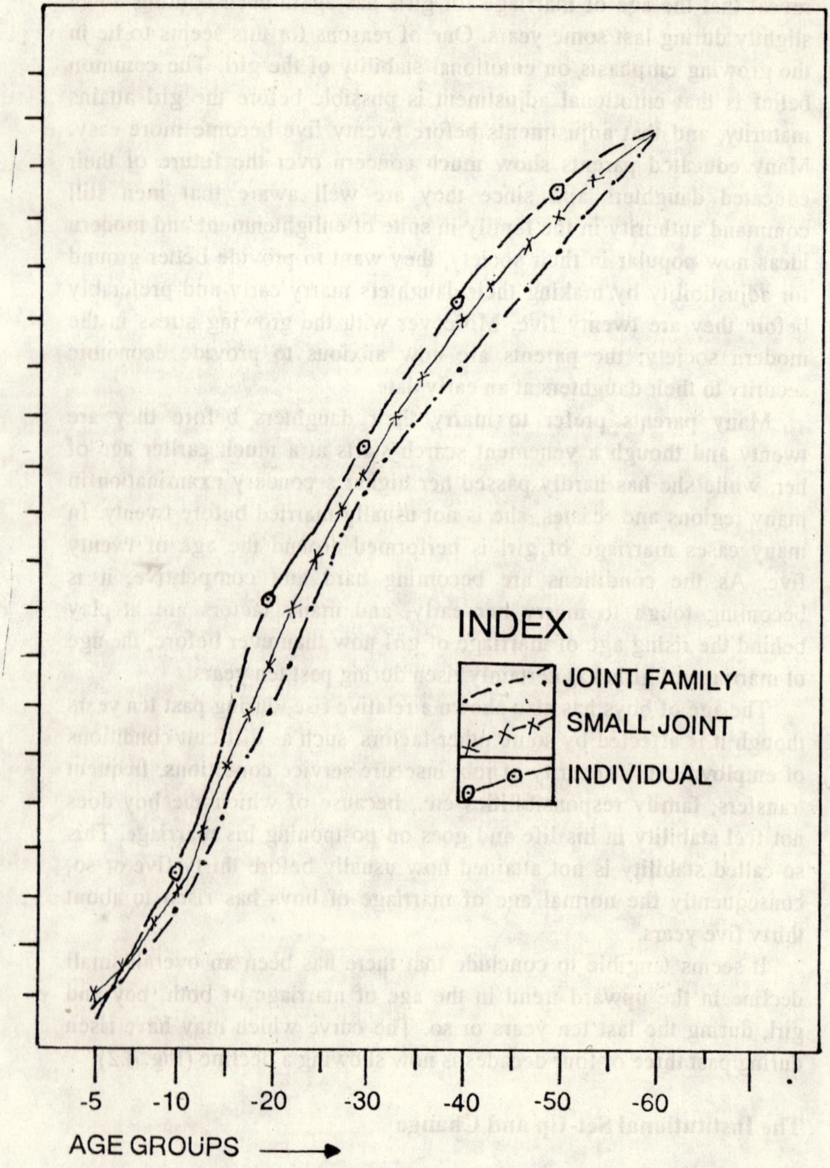

FIG. 4.2: Cumulative Percentage Distribution of Family Member in Different Age Groups.

woman with man in this modern era, and in response to this motivation the first concession that they have given her is 'the freedom of learning'. But in relation to her marriage, there has been marked little change. The parents still feel it their fundamental duty to marry her to the best possible match. She is allowed education to the best of her desire and she is permitted to accept job of her choice. But she has not been given the freedom of searching a companion for herself.

Discretion of Girl in Her Arranged Marriage

The parents still believe that it is their primary responsibility to marry their children at a proper time. The change that has come in relation to daughter's marriage is in raising expectations for prospective matches. Some fifty years ago, girls were married with optimum expectation of the suitability of the match. A girl with matriculation or intermediate could be considered happily married to an under-graduate or graduate clerk. There has now been a remarkable change in this sphere. Girl's education has been given maximum encouragement and it has become now common to find a graduate or post-graduate girl waiting to be married till later twenties or even middle thirties. Extended employment has whereas opened new facilities for job opportunities and it has indirectly postponed her age of marriage. At the same time it has also raised aspirations for prospective match. A post-graduate girl in an educational career, such as a lecturer in a degree college, now cannot be easily married to a match less qualified than herself and she awaits her fortune indefinitely. With keep competition growing more acute day by day among educated elite in the urban areas, possibility of getting suitable matches is becoming more difficult. Even the more qualified girl finds that the centre of authority still remains concentrated in her father, her prospects of getting a suitable match out of her own choice thus remain limited. Moreover she has to be essentially married under the traditional arranged marriage system. The father depends much upon his conventional system searching match through the help of relatives and friends, or now also through matrimonial advertisements in the newspapers like *The Hindustan Times*, *The Times of India* and *Sarita* (Hindi monthly). If these negotiations are not fruitful up to a reasonable time, or if the parents are not able to meet the high demands of dowry expected by what they consider a prospective match, the educated-employed and prospective girl may remain unmarried for a longer period of for whole of her life. If she would have been conceded the maximum freedom of selecting her companion from among her acquaintances in her circle or whom she has a greater opportunity to meet and understand, this unhappy situation would have probably been averted.

This suggests that the traditional attitude in regard to arrangement of daughter's marriage still persists even in the educated urban families. Even where both father and mother are educated and are in higher services, there has been little change in this attitude.

One of my interviewees in Bhopal city, who was a senior Reader in Regional Collage of Education around fifty, at the time of this study emphasized that the authority for selection of a suitable match for a daughter should always be exercised by the father. Who is the best custodian of the family. He said with confidence that he is giving his daughter best of education, and she is doing very well in it. "I have high ambitions for finding a suitable match for her", he said. He was specially interrogated on the point that would he not like to give her the freedom of selecting someone from among her companions which could approve on the basis of merits, he declined positively, and affirmed that "this is not very right approach. The girls have little experience at this young age and are likely to err".

The prevailing view even in such highly educated, upper caste urban Hindu families is that it is the responsibility of the father who has more experience of the world. When the above respondent was asked whether he would not like to provide a guided selection by her which implies that he may keep a watch on her movements and developments and provide a necessary guidance whenever possible so that she makes a proper and meritorious selection of her companion, he again said," "No", and repeated his original view in other words by saying, "I don't think, that this can be of any avail. The best way is for the father to search the best possible match for her."

This traditional attitude seems to be related to the conventional role of father in the Hindu family. It can be safely said here that even the educated father's adherence to this traditional role is because of the deep impact of this traditionally expected role of father in the Hindu family which seems to be culturally ingrained in him, and which he is obliged to discharge to the best of his capacity. And this expected role of father is closely associated with the "role of authority" discharge as the head of household. He is not prepared to transfer this role to his son or daughter because that would amount to his own failing in his conventional " role-discharge".

One part of the cultural tradition always demands that it be not broken without logic. The daughters are, however, given a consideration in their opinion in most of the urban educated families. they are usually consulted whether they like the proposal or not before it is finalised. Many parents even take their free opinion and would not hesitate to abandon a current proposal if their daughter totally disagrees to it. Another anomaly in this situation is that many girls in the Hindu families who are asked their opinion would not normally express it, except saying that whatever is arranged by their father, would be acceptable to them as it would have been done with best consideration, and is thus acceptable to them. The freedom to dissent is not yet granted even to the educated girls. In this circumstance the freedom to express opinion becomes only a freedom to agree, and never to disagree.

The same traditional attitude prevails in regard to the marriage of the son. The son's marriage is mostly arranged traditionally by negotiations. The settlement is reached by the parental authority with a view to ulterior considerations though the boy is now normally consulted before finalisation of his marriage proposal. As compared to this the boy's opinions play an active role in this matter. It is true that the status of male is not alone responsible for casting choice, there are other factors, like their education, jobs secured or expected to be secured which make the boys assert their views before their parents.

But again this privilege is given to them in case of arranged marriages. In exceptional circumstances the boys can insist upon their own choice or discretion about love marriage. In such circumstances, relative and friends of the family may make them somehow agree to the proposal. In other circumstances it depends much upon the issue and the manner in which it comes before them.

This suggests that though there seems some difference in the traditional attitude towards sons and daughters in regard to conceding them the freedom of choice, the cultural tradition so much persists here that the rigid rule is hardly broken. The authoritative role still persists almost in a conventional manner even among the educated urban families.

The only important change that appears to lie in the context of arranged marriages is that other social connections or considerations of being "Well-connected" which were once upon a time an important criterion in selection of the mate are now of not much importance. Few parents bother about these. The pragmatic view of match making now lays more emphasis upon the qualifications and present status of the prospective match, his job and future prospects in it, other considerations such as background of good or noble family, high connections of family and property etc. are also now becoming less important in making a choice of marriage.

This indicates that the conventional arranged marriage system still remains the most popular system of marriage even now.

In my sample from the universe of Bhopal city almost all marriages in the surveyed families were enlisted to be the "arranged marriages", that is, these were actually performed traditionally by the Hindu method of *Saptapadi* and oath taken before the sacred fire, only a very few, 39 love marriages, were found to have been performed in this conventional system.

Two of these were found in joint family, seven in small joint family and 30 in individual families. All these 39 love marriages were intercaste marriages. The position of arranged marriages can be better understood if we correlate it to different caste compositions and family types.

It we retrospect on our sample we find that the distribution of family types, is 17 joint families, that is, these couples are still living in joint families, 49 in small joint families, 159 in individual families 'love marriages' hold a small percentage in the total marriages performed in these families. All these marriages which were results of prior love or courtship between the couples and were performed through individual will, or and mutual consent of the boy and girl, and did not depend upon the discretion of the parents have been grouped under 'Love marriages'. All these love marriages are found to be related to the dependents, a brother in most cases, or a son as in some cases sister or daughter. It is found that of the total 39 'love marriages', only two were living in joint families, seven in small joint families and 30 in individual families.

It is evident that almost all the arranged marriages are performed with the members of the same caste. None of the arranged marriage was performed in another caste. It was always within the same caste, while some of the love marriages are found to be performed through the traditional Hindu system.

It is the 'love marriage' that normally breaks the caste barrier as well as the traditional order though sometimes love marriages do occur within the same caste, we may now correlate these love marriages to the five cultural zones, that we have evolved in this study and to the education and income groups.

Inter-provincial and Inter-religious Marriage Relations

The discussion on marriage in its different dimensions warrants that an in sight is also made into the issue whether the marriage are also "Inter-provincial" and "Inter-religious" marriages. Therefore, a pointed question was posed to our interviewees on this issue. The responses suggest that arranged marriage in all types of families are generally caste marriages, that is, they are performed within the prescribed fold of caste or sub-caste. Inter-provincial relations in marriages are now usual order of the day and no one brothers about the fact whether one belongs to his own province or not while selecting a marriage partner for his son or daughter. In fact occupational mobility has given rise to a situation of greater cultural interaction in most of the urban areas and there has been horizontal mobility of caste in these areas. Aspirations for highly prospective matches have broken the provincial barrier in respect of marriage relations. Still some lingua-cultural considerations are there. For example, a Brahmin can agree to marry his daughter to a Brahmin in Uttar Pradesh, Bihar, Rajasthan and sometimes to Delhi, as there are cultural and language similarities. But he would avoid marry his daughter to a South Indian or Kashmere Brahmin family whose culture and language are altogether different.

Cultural considerations are, thus, maintained, there are certainly some broad cultural areas in the country which are normally not crossed by different caste groups. For example a Kanyakubja Brahmin may find it most convenient to have marriage relations with Kanyakubja Brahmins of Uttar Pradesh who are residing there; he may also feel it convenient to marry those who are residing in the same province like him as emigrants. He does not mind entering marriage alliances with persons of the Saryupari Brahmin group, with whom formerly there was some hesitation. He also concedes now in exceptional cases to marry a locally resident Brahmin of Madhya Pradesh or an emigrant from Rajasthan or Bihar for in all these provinces, there prevails a broad cultural similarity, there may be, of course, some regional variations such as in certain marriage customs, or socio-religious rites associated with the marriage but they are not so very different and opposite that adjustments may not be possible. But a Kanyakubja or Saryupari Brahmin would refuse to marry a Kannada, Mysorian, Tamil, Malyali or Telugu Brahmin even though he may be holding an equally comparable social status in his own group.

Social status in Hindu society is more or less a relative term which is understandable in the context of a particular culture in which it is used or meant. Every culture has its own social system predetermined by its own cultural tradition.

There are five such cultural zones operative in India according to Iravati Karve. Broadly basing my observations on that model here, I find that there can be found five cultural zones in the social complex of Bhopal. 1. The North-Indian Cultural Zone, 2. The Central Cultural Zone, 3. The Western Cultural Zone, 4. The Southern Cultural Zones and 5. The Eastern Cultural Zone.

Thus whereas there has been enough provincial mobility in the present era, cultural mobility has not been much marked. There are some practical considerations in the modern era which are also influencing the flexibility of caste marriages. The old considerations of property and land are now not given any importance in the marriages being performed or negotiated. This is perhaps because of two things: firstly, because of break up of the joint family into individual units, which severed most of the property claims, there is a growing awareness among the educated urban families that the people in jobs in urban areas find it difficult to maintain a regular contact with their native families in villages or other towns, and thus their parental property there is of little help to them moreover, there is an emphasis on the more practical aspects like the qualifications, the present job, the nature of job and total emoluments of pay and socio-economic status of the prospective match. If these requirements satisfied few parents, would now hesitate to marry their daughters to other sub-castes, even if they fall a degree or two lower in their social caste status. For example, an educated Kanyakubja Brahmin would not mind marrying his daughter to any respectable Saryupari Brahmin of Madhya Pradesh, provided he is well qualified and has a stable job. Whereas caste considerations are still maintained, sub-caste considerations are not much bothered for and are often overcome if there is a proper balance of some of these expectations in the prospective match. These are some of the urban strains which have affected the flexibility of caste marriages. Whereas intercaste marriages have been possible to a limited extent, as we have discussed above, it may be pointed out that they are not actually inter-caste, but inter sub-caste marriages which have become some what more popular during past ten or fifteen years due to impact of urbanization, spatial mobility and enlightenment.

Inter-religious marriages are not possible easily and occur only sporadically in cases of prior love. Only love marriage are in very few cases found to lead to inter-religious marriages. There can be envisaged no direct correlation between the inter-religious marriages and education, social status economic standard or family type. They are much dependent on coincidence, choice and decisive will of the individuals.

Participation in Decision About One's Own Marriage

The modern trends in marriage have come in a number of ways, and while these cannot be classified easily, some of them can be marked out in the various spheres of activity connected with the marriage institution.

Education which has set in the upper strata of Hindu society has made people about their rights. It has opened before them the new area of rational thinking and rational behaviour which emphasize that problems of life should be tackled with the help of rational approach and not through sentiments and emotions. Thus the educated sons and daughters in the urban families are becoming aware of their right of choice in marriage. They want to maintain their family obligations towards their parents and do not want to defy their will. But in the meantime, they want that they should be given full freedom in rationally thinking as to who would suit them best as a mate. Most of the young people now want that they should be given a free choice in selecting their marriage partners and for this reason would seem to favour "love marriage". But many young people do not stress this much and would seem to be contented if they were only given right of participation in the decision about their marriage by their parents. This decision sharing has expressed itself in various forms in the Hindu families. This participation in decision about the marriage has been increasing during last few years. This is mostly because of conflicting views of the parental generation and the younger generation about various social matters and privileges among which marriage is an important one. The young boy, for example, may like to marry an educated girl with some training or diploma in teaching or in other specialized branch of education so that she could be useful to him as an active partner in life, the father, if he is of orthodox views, may attach too much emphasis on family connections and money. In such cases there is likely to emerge a conflict between the two. The younger generation has, therefore, started emphasizing upon their own role in selecting a marriage partner even where marriage is being arranged traditionally. The older generation seems to be more considerate towards their younger generation as they have now started conceding to their demands slowly, though often there is a resistance from their side and younger generations: even though in a silent manner, they are now coming up gradually to assert their rights and are thus providing resistance to authority.

It is little strange though true that there has not been much opposition or conflict over the demand of dowry; the dowry is demanded by the parents under various excuses and one major excuse is that there has been elaborate expenditure upon son's education. Often some fathers-in-law may even try to help their son-in-law to an extent that he earns more or attain a stability in job so that their daughter lives more comfortably in her husband's family.

This appears a paradoxical situation which has ultimately helped the dowry system to continue in Hindu society in spite of law made and social antipathy raised against it. One obvious reason for its continuance lies in the fact that the quarter from which it needs to be resisted most itself has been feeding it some way.

Institutional Functions of Urban Family and Adoption of New Approach Towards Children

Change in the urban family can also be examined by seeing whether the members of the family adhere to their family conventions, or their views and opinions suggest some deviation from the norm, what do they feel towards some basic functions of family. In other words, we wanted to examine whether their views remained conventional or they reflected some change.

We provided a set of questions on the essential functions of family from the head of the household, to the respondent giving him a series of such functions, as 'emotional, economic and educational'. The respondents answered these questions expressing their consent or dissent on each issue. The essential functions outlined were:

(a) Rearing and shelter of children;
(b) The economic function meant for sustenance of family members;
(c) The educational functions comprising of informal education of the child in home, what is called "enculturation", and

formal education of the child in school; and

(d) Socio-religious functions.

The respondents answered these questions expressing their agreement to one or more of these functions. We also wanted to examine change in the family by seeing whether the head of the household is acquainted with the modern approach of child development which recommends an altogether constructive approach towards the child as compared to the old punitive and corrective approach. Our purpose was to assess whether educated heads are getting familiar with such trends of child development approach. Familiarity with and adoption of such approach is considered as an indication of such change.

The respondents expressed their consent or dissent to this query. We also tried to know who introduced such and approach in the family father, mother, elder brother or elder sister.

The data on the expressed opinions of the heads of households on the essential functions of family and adoption of child development approach has been correlated to caste and education with a view to have some analysis on family change through this dimension.

Opinion Regarding Functions of Family in the Joint Family

Table 4.8 provides the analysis for the joint family.

Of the 9 Brahmin families among 17 joint households, 4 Brahmin heads considered all four, emotional economic, educational and socio-religious functions as essential functions of family, 1 Brahmin head considered emotional, economic and socio-religious functions as essential functions of family, 1 Brahmin head considered economic, educational and socio-religious functions as essential functions, not mentioning the very basic emotional function as essential function, 1 Brahmin head mentioned only any two of the functions as essential functions of family. Two of the Brahmin heads did not reply.

Five of the Brahmin heads said that children in their families were reared with conscious child development approach and that such an approach has been introduced by father; in one case it was introduced both by father and mother. Out of 2 Kshatriya heads of households, one considered all four functions as essential functions of family, while one considered only economic, educational and socio-religious functions. Both of these Kshatriya heads said that children in their families were

TABLE 4.8: Opinion of Family Head Regarding Functions of the Family and Parental Approach to Children; Caste and Education as a variable: Joint Families

Caste/Education Groups	No. of families	Essential functions of the family							Not responded	No. of families where children are reared with conscious child development approach	No response	If yes in col. 11 who has introduced such approach		
		All	1+2+3	1+2+4	1+3+4	2+3+4	Any two	Any one				Father	Mother	Elder brother
1	2	3	4	5	6	7	8	9	10	11	12	13	14	15
Caste Groups														
1	9	4		1		1	1		2	5	3	5	1	
2	2	1				1				2		2	1	
3	6	4							1	4	1	4	1	
4						1								
TOTAL	17	9		1		3	1		3	11	4	11	3	
Education Groups														
1	5	3		1		1				2	2	2	2	
2	3					1			2	1	2	1	1	
3	3	2							1	3		3	1	2
4	6	4				1	1			5		5	5	2
TOTAL	17	9		1		3	1		3	11	4	11	9	4

Codes:
Rearing and shelter of children — 1
Economic function — 2
Educational function — 3
Socio-religious function — 4

reared with conscious child development approach, and one said that such an approach was introduced in the family by father, and one said that such an approach was introduced both by father and mother.

Of the 6 Vaishya joint families, 4 heads of households considered all four functions as essential functions, one did not respond this query. All these 4 Vaishya heads of households said that children in their families are being reared with conscious child development approach, 1 did not respond this. This only one Kayastha family head among the joint households said that he considered economic, educational and socio-religious function as essential functions of family. But he did not mention whether children in his family are being reared with conscious child development approach.

Thus we find that among 17 joint household, 9 heads of households considered all four functions as essential functions, 1 considered emotional, economic, and socio-religious functions, as essential; 3 considered economic, educational and socio-religious functions, as essential; and 1 considered any two of the functions as essential. Three did not respond this question.

Of the 17 joint households, 11 mentioned that children in their families are being treated with conscious child-development approach, and all these 11 said that this approach has been introduced in the family by father, while of the rest 2 said that it has been introduced both by mother. Three did not respond.

When education is used as a variable, we get some different results.

Of the 5 undergraduates in joint family, 3 believed that all four functions are essential functions in the family, one believed that only emotional economic and socio-religious functions are essential, and one believed that only economic, educational and socio-religious functions are essential.

Of these 5 undergraduates 2 said that children are reared in their family with child development approach. They said that both father and mother have introduced this child development approach in the family; 2 heads did not respond.

Of the 3 graduates, only one said that he believed in economic. educational and socio-religious functions as essential functions, the rest of 2 did not respond.

Of these 3 graduates only one said that children are being reared with conscious child development approach. And he said that this approach has been introduced in the family by father as well as by mother. The rest of 2 did not respond here too. Of the 3 post-graduates

2 said that they believed in all four functions, while one did not respond. These three also said that children are being reared with conscious child development approach, and that it has been introduced by father, one of these gave the credit for it to mother also besides recognizing fathers, contribution.

Of the 6 professionals, 4 believed that all four functions are essential functions of family, one believed that only economic, educational and socio-religious functions are essential functions, while another one said that the two are important.

Five of the these professionals mentioned that children are being reared in the family with conscious child development approach. All these wanted to acknowledge father's and mother's role in family in introducing this approach in the family. While 2 of these acknowledged elder brother's role as well.

Summing up the whole situation, we can say that in the 17 joint families, heads of 9 joint households believed in all four functions of family. One believed only in emotional, economic and socio-religious, functions, while 3 believed in economic, educational and socio-religious functions, and one believed in any two of these functions. Three did not respond.

Eleven of the 17 joint household heads said that children in their families are being reared according to the conscious child development approach and they attributed credit for this to their fathers. Among these 9 wanted to recognise mother's role too in this and 2 of these included brother's role in this. 3 of the heads did not respond this query.

The Small Joint Family

In the 49 small joint households, there were 26 Brahmin families. The heads of 12 small joint families among these believed in all four functions of family, viz. emotional, economic, educational and socio-religious, 2 believed only in emotional, economic and educational functions. While 1 believed in emotional, economic and socio-religious functions, 2 believed in economic, educational and socio-religious functions, and 1 believed in any two 2 believed in any one of the functions, 5 did not respond.

Eleven heads said that children in their families are now being reared with the conscious child development approach. Nine of these further said that this new approach has been introduced by father while

6 said that it has been introduced by mother, and one attributed credit for this to elder brother.

Of the 4 Kshatriya families, head 2 said that all four functions are essential for family, 1 said that only emotional, economic and socio-religious functions are important. One did not respond.

Of these 3 said that children are being reared with conscious development approach and they said that this approach has been introduced by father while 1 mentioned mother and another 1 mentioned elder brother besides father, 1 did not respond.

Of the 8 Vaishya heads, all believed in all four functions, 1 believed in economic, educational and socio-religious functions, 2 believed in any two, and 1 in any one of the four functions. Two did not respond.

Four of these heads said that children are being reared in their family with conscious child development approach. Two did not respond here too.

Four of these said that it has been introduced in their family by father, according to 3 by mother, and according to 1 by elder brother who have also played their part in introducing this approach.

Of the 11 Kayastha heads, 5 believed in all four functions, and one believed in economic, educational and socio-religious functions. All these 11 heads believed that children are being reared with conscious child development approach, 6 of these said that the approach has been introduced in their home by father while 5 said that mother has done it.

Summing up this analysis, we find that of the 49 total small joint households, 23 believed that all four functions are essential functions of family, 2 believed that only emotional, economic and educational functions are essential, 1 believed that only emotional, economic and socio-religious functions are essential, while 3 believed emotional, educational and socio-religious functions to be essential, another 3 believed economic, educational and socio-religious functions, 3 believed that any two of these functions and another 3 believed that one of these functions are important. 8 heads of families did not respond.

Of the 49 heads of small joint families, 29 said that children are being reared in their family with conscious child development approach, 22 said that their fathers have introduced this approach, while 14 attributed this credit to mother, and 3 to elder brother (Table 4.9)

TABLE 4.9: Opinion of Family head Regarding Functions of the Family and Parental Approach to Children: Caste and Education as a Variable: Small Joint Families

Caste/Education Groups	No.of families	Essential functions of the family					Any two	Any one	Not responded	No. of families where children are reared with conscious child development approach	No response	If yes in col. 11 who has introduced such approach		
		All	1+2+3	1+2+4	1+3+4	2+3+4						Father	Mother	Elder brother
1	2	3	4	5	6	7	8	9	10	11	12	13	14	15
Caste Groups														
1	26	12	2	1	2	1	1	2	5	11	7	9	6	1
2	4	2			1				1	3	1	3	1	1
3	8	4				1	2	1	2	4	2	4	3	1
4	11	5				1				11		6	15	
Total	49	23	2	1	3	3	3	3	8	29	10	22	14	3
Education Groups														
1	6	3	1				1		1	5	1	4	2	
2	11	4		1			2	2	2	6	2	4	4	2
3	13	8	1		1	1	1		1	9	2	6	3	2
4	19	8			2	2	2	1	4	8	5	6	5	
Total	49	23	2	1	3	3	6	3	8	28	10	20	14	4

Codes: Rearing and shelter of children — 1
Economic function — 2
Educational function — 3
Socio-religious function — 4

While caste as a variable has shown these results, let us see what results are derived from the data when we introduce education as a variable.

In the 49 small joint family households, 6 families heads were found educated up to under-graduate level. Of these 6 undergraduates, 3 considered all four functions of family to be essential functions, 1 considered emotional, economic and educational functions to be essential functions, 1 believed in any two of the four functions. One did not respond.

Five of these 6 heads of small joint-families said that children in their families are being reared with conscious child development approach; 4 of these further said that father in the family has introduced this now approach in the family while 2 said that mother in the family has introduced the approach. One did not respond here too.

Of the 11 heads of families who are graduates, 4 said that all four functions are essential functions for the family, 1 said that emotional, economic and socio-religious functions are essential functions, 2 mentioned any two of the four functions, and 2 mentioned any one of these. Two did not respond.

Of these 11 heads, 6 said that children in their family are being reared with conscious child development approach, 4 said that father in the family has introduced this approach, 4 mentioned about mother and 2 about brother, besides father. 1 did not respond.

Of the 13 post-graduate heads, 8 considered all four functions as essential functions, 1 considered only emotional, economic and socio-religious functions, 1 considered only emotional, educational and socio-religious functions, another 1 considered only any two of the four functions. One head did not respond.

Of these 13 post-graduates, 9 said that children in their families are being reared with conscious child development approach, 6 of these attributed the credit to father, and 3 to mother for introducing this new approach, while 2 wanted to give credit to elder brother. Two did not respond.

In the 49 small joint families, 19 heads of households were found to be professionally educated, that is they had a professional degree in medicine, engineering, technology or law. Eight of these 19 heads considered all four functions to be essential functions, 2 considered only emotional, educational and socio-religious functions, 2 considered economic, educational and socio-religious functions, 2 considered any two of the four functions aat children in their families are being reared with conscious child development approach. And of these, 6 said that father in the family has introduced this new child development approach, while 5 said that besides mother has also introduced it.

It is thus seen that out of 49 small joint families, 23 heads of households considered all four as functions of family, 2 considered only emotional, economic and educational functions, 1 considered emotional, economic and socio-religious functions, 3 considered only emotional, educational and socio-religious functions, 3 considered only economic, educational and socio-religious functions, 6 considered only two and 3 considered only one of the four functions of family. Eight did not respond on this.

Out of these 49 heads of households, 29 said that children in their families are being reared with conscious child development approach. 20 of these further said that father in the family has introduced the new approach. 14 said that mother and 4 said that elder brother have to be acknowledged for it (Table 4.9).

The Individual Family

The castewise analysis among these 156 individual households reveals that 83 belonged to Brahmin caste, 14 to Kshatriya caste, 29 to Vaishya caste, and 30 to Kayastha caste among the four castegroups selected for the study.

Of the 83 Brahmin heads of households, 48 believed that all four functions of family enlisted in schedule are essential for family. Seven believed that emotional, economic and educational functions are essential, 4 believed that emotional educational and socio-religious functions are essential, 1 believed that emotional economic and socio-religious functions are essential, 1 believed that economic, educational and socio-religious functions are essential. Ten believed that any two and 5 believed that any one of these four functions are essential. Seven respondents did not reply.

Of these 83 heads of the household, 45 said that children in their families are being reared with conscious child development approach, and 35 of these further said that father in the family has introduced this approach, 17 gave credit to mother and 4 to elder brother for introducing this new approach in the family.

Of the 14 Kshatriya households, 6 believed that all four functions are essential, 3 believed that only emotional, economic and educational functions are essential, 1 believed that economic, educational an socio-religious functions are essential, 2 believed that only two and 1 said that only one of the four functions are essential. One did not respond. Of these 14 Kshatriya heads, 9 said that children in their families are being reared with the new approach. Three did not respond.

Of these 8 said that father in the family has introduced the new approach, 3 said that mother has introduced it while 2 said that brother has done it. One did not respond here.

Of the 29 Vaishya caste group heads, 26 believed that all four functions are essential, 4 believed that only emotional, economic and educational functions are essential, 3 believed that only emotional, educational and socio-religious functions are essential, 1 believed that economic, educational and socio-religious functions are essential, 10 believed that any two of these and 6 believed that any one of these functions are essential 3 did not respond.

Of these 20 heads of Vaishya households, 32 said that children in their families are being reared with conscious child development approach, and 27 of these further said that the new approach has been introduced by father in the family, 7 said that mother has introduced it, whind 1 considered any one of these to be essential functions. Four did not respond.

All of these 8 professional heads of small joint families said that children in their families are being reared with conscious child development approach. And of these, 6 said that father in the family has introduced this new child respond here.

Of the 156 heads of individual households, 90 said that children in their families are being reared with conscious child development approach, and 72 of these attributed the credit to father in the family for introducing this new approach, 30 said that mother and 7 said that elder brother has introduced the approach in the family.

The analysis of different caste groups shows that most of the heads of households have admitted that they have now adopted a new modern approach of child development in their dealing with children. This suggests that new ideas and innovations are being accepted by different caste groups living in urban environments. When this analysis is compared with education-wise analysis, some more revealing findings are discovered (Table 4.10).

The education variable applied to family shows some different analysis than that drawn form the caste variable for individual family.

TABLE 4.10: Opinion of Family Heads Regarding Functions of the Family and Parental Approach to Children: Caste and Education as a Variable: Individual Families

Caste/Education Groups	No.of families	Essential functions of the family								No. of families where children are reared with conscious child development approach	No response	If yes in col. 11 who has introduced such approach		
		All	1+2+3	1+2+4	1+3+4	2+3+4	Any two	Any one	Not responded			Father	Mother	Elder brother
1	2	3	4	5	6	7	8	9	10	11	12	13	14	15
Caste Groups														
1	83	48	7	1	4	1	10	5	7	45	13	35	17	4
2	14	6	3			1	2	1	1	9	3	8	3	2
3	29	26	4		3	1	10	6	3	32	6	27	7	1
4	30	3				1	2		24	4	1	2	3	
Total	156	83	14	1	7	4	24	12	35	90	23	72	30	7
Education Groups														
1	15	12	1			1		1		11	2	9	7	1
2	28	12	5		2	1	4	2	2	18	2	12	7	4
3	52	25	5	1	2	1	11	1	6	30	8	22	11	2
4	61	34	3		3	1	9	8	3	31	11	29	5	
Total	156	83	14	1	7	4	24	12	11	90	23	72	30	7

Codes:
Rearing and shelter of children — 1
Economic function — 2
Educational function — 3
Socio-religious function — 4

In our sample, we had found 15 heads of households who were educated up to undergraduate or intermediate level, 28 were graduates, 52 post-graduates and 61 professionally and/or advancedly educated.

Of the 15 under-graduates, 12 believed that all four classified functions are essential functions for the family, 1 believed that emotional, economic and educational functions are essential, I believed that economic, educational and socio-religious functions are essential and 1 suggested any one. Of these 15 individual family heads, educated up to under-graduate level, 11 said that children in their families are being reared with the conscious child development approach, and 9 of these eleven heads further informed that the new approach has been introduced by the father in family, 7 however wanted to include mother and 1 elder brother.

Of the 28 graduates, who can be termed as moderately educated, 12 believed that all four functions are essential functions for family, 5 believed that emotional, economic and educational functions are essential, 2 believed that emotionle 1 mentioned brother.

Of the 30 Kayastha heads of Households 3 said that all four functions are essential functions for family, 1 said that only economic educational and socio-religious functions are essential and 2 said that any two of these functions are essential. Twenty four did not respond.

Four of these 6 heads further informed that children in their families are reared with conscious child development approach. Two of these said that the father in the family and 3 said that mother in the family has been responsible for introducing this new approach. One head did not respond here.

Taking an overall view of the analysis we find that 83 heads of individual households believed in all four functions, 14 believed in first three of these functions, 1 believed in only emotional, economic and socio-religious functions, 7 believed in emotional, educational and socio-religious functions, 4 believed in economic, educational and socio-religious functions, 24 believed in only two and 12 believed in only one of the four functions, 35 did not respond here.

Of the 156 heads of individual households, 90 said that children in their families are being reared with conscious child development approach, and 72 of these attributed the credit to father in the family for introducing this new approach, 30 said that mother and 7 said that elder brother has introduced the approach in the family.

The analysis of different caste groups shows that most of the heads of households have admitted that they have now adopted a new modern approach of child development in their dealing with children. This suggests that new ideas and innovations are being accepted by different caste groups living in urban environments. When this analysis is compared with education-wise analysis, some more revealing findings are discovered (Table 4.10).

The education variable applied to family shows some different analysis than that drawn from the caste variable for individual family.

In our sample, we had found 15 heads of households who were educated up to undergraduate or intermediate level, 28 were graduates, 52 post-graduates and 61 professionally and/or advancedly educated.

Of the 15 under-graduates, 12 believed that all four classified functions are essential functions for the family, 1 believed that emotional, economic and educational functions are essential, I believed that economic, educational and socio-religious functions are essential and 1 suggested any one. Of these 15 individual family heads, educated up to under-graduate level, 11 said that children in their families are being reared with the conscious child development approach, and 9 of these eleven heads further informed that the new approach has been introduced by the father in family, 7 however wanted to include mother and 1 elder brother.

Of the 28 graduates, who can be termed as moderately educated, 12 believed that all four functions are essential functions for family, 5 believed that emotional, economic and educational functions are essential, 2 believed that emotional, educational and socio-religious functions are essential, 1 believed that economic, educational and socio-religious functions are essential, 4 believed that any two of the four while 2 believed that any one of the four functions is essential. Two did not respond.

Of the 28 graduates, 18 said that children in their family are being educated with modern child development approach; of these 12 said that this approach has been introduced in the family by father, 7 said that mother has done it and 4 said that elder bother has been responsible for it.

Of the 52 post-graduate heads, 25 believed in all four functions of family, 5 believed in emotional educational and socio-religious functions, 1 believed in emotional, economic and socio-religious functions, and 2 believed in emotional, education and religious functions as essential. One believed that economic, educational and socio-religious functions are essential while 11 believed that only two of the functions, and 1 believed that only one of the enlisted functions are essential. 6 did not respond.

Out of these 52 post-graduates, 30 said that children are being reared in the family with conscious child development approach, and 22 of these 30 heads further said that the new approach has been introduced by father, 11 said it has been introduced by mother, while 2 said that elder brother has introduced it.

Of the 61 professionals and the advancedly educated, 34 believed that all four functions are essential for family, 3 believed that emotional, economic and educational functions are essential, another 3 believed that emotional, educational and socio-religious functions are essential, 1 believed that only economic, educational and socio-religious functions are essential, 9 believed that any two of the four functions are essential, while 8 believed that any one of the these is so. Three professionals did not respond here.

Of these 61 professionals, 31 informed that children in their families are being treated with modern child development approach, and 29 of these informed that father and 5 informed that mother in family has introduced this new approach; none of these suggested elder brother. Eleven did not respond on this issue.

Taking an overall view of this analysis of individual family, we find, that among total 156 households, 83 heads of households believed that all four functions are essential for family, 14 believed that emotional, economic and educational functions are essential functions, 1 believed that emotional, economic and socio-religious functions are essential. Seven believed that emotional, economic and socio-religious functions are essential, 4 believed that economic, educational and socio-religious functions are essential, 24 believed that only two of these four functions are essential and 12 believed that only one of these is essential. Eleven heads did not respond this aspect of enquiry.

Of these 156 heads of households, 90 informed that children in their families are being reared with the new child development approach, and of these 72 further informed that this new approach has been introduced by father; 30 said that mother has introduced it and 7 said that elder brother has done it (Table 4.10).

The analysis thus suggests that both caste and education work as important factors in introducing new ideas and innovations in the urban Hindu family. The greatest number of those who opted for all four essential functions of family and who said that they had accepted the new child development approach in their rearing of children, came from among the upper castes, and from the more educated class – the post-graduate and professionals and advancedly educated. This proves the general thesis that higher caste groups and the elite accept change and get the first advantage in accepting new innovations, and taking a lead for any new change in their society; the rest only follow them. The data from all three types of family, joint small, joint and individual families correlated adequately proves this thesis.

It appears probable that in family change, as in social change, the elite class plays a major and leading role.

5

ROLE PLAYING AND ROLE TAKING IN THE UNIVERSAL HINDU FAMILY

Roles in society are culturally prescribed and obligatorily expected from different members having different statuses. These roles are acted functionally by them according to the role expectations and the related ascribed or achieved status. These functional roles have a direct bearing and influence on intra-personal and inter-personal relations in the family. In the present chapter we will discuss how the traditional roles have been operative universally in the Hindu family and how they are now getting changed because of various processes of social change, modern pressures and strains on the Hindu family and new conditions and emerging crises.

The traditional family roles in the family were organised largely on the basis of authority, or what Mandelbaum (1970) calls more appropriately hierarchical authority, age, sentiments, feelings of filial love, bonds of fidelity of husband — wife etc. The hierarchical authority was centralised in the eldest male of the Hindu family who also had the decisive authority in matters of family as well as inter-family relations. Age and sex are the main ordering principles in family hierarchy.

"The men have the more decisive authority in the traditional Indian family as compared with women and elders have greater authority as compared with young persons."[1] He suggests that difference of a year or two in age is sufficient to establish firmly who is the formal superior. As between the authority of an elderly woman and a younger man, sex is the more important determinant. Men used to have the formal property rights, and so the formal authority of a younger man, not necessarily his actual influence is higher than that of his elder sister, though he is expected to respect and cherish her. The Hindu Code Bill with its recent amendments has introduced a basic change in the property rights in which the girls of the family are also now authorised shareholders. It is, however, a different question that in practice, few married daughters may be asserting this right. Influence of tradition and convention still governs feelings of Hindu girls who are encultured not to seek their fortune in their father's family. The common notion prevalent in the traditional Hindu family has been that girls take their share in the property in dowry paid for their marriage, and are thus not legally entitled for any share with their brothers.

A woman in the traditional Hindu family was not deferent as wife, but as mother. Children were expected to owe permanent deference to both parents. Parental authority was unceasing as an ideal and was much sustained, though the actual duration and degree of this authority were affected by economic circumstances and *Jati* Tradition, (Mandelbaum; 1970).

Within the family son and daughter were expected to be devoted to their parents, respect their will, provide obedience, and avoid hurting their feelings. In this too, they were supposed to care more especially for their father's will and orders.

If grown-up sons do not wish to follow a parental mandate, they usually find ways to circumvent father than to contradict it. A widowed mother may wield considerable influence on her son and his family. Ross cites a case of an educated family in this connection from her study in Bangalore, "When I was growing up, father was the chief authority in the house on all official and financial matters. He was a district commissioner and practically ruled the district like a king, and yet he would always go to his mother, who was nearly illiterate, for her final decision on any important family matter. Grand-mother was the authority too in all household matters and father left everything to her.

Age and sex have been the two basic determinants in organizing various family roles in the traditional Hindu family. The spheres of man and woman were clearly demarcated in the family and they were expected to perform their roles within their own prescribed sphere. These roles were also governed by certain values', value systems were devised to keep women's contact within the family or kinship circle and to prevent any outside contacts. *Purdah* was one such system which was borrowed from the Muslim society and adopted first by the North Indian Hindu Society, particularly of Uttar Pradesh to keep the women of the family restricted within the household.

A husband is expected to be his wife's superior and as such expected to receive symbolic and actual deference from her. There is not great expectation that the couple should share common thoughts and tastes. This, however, does not undermine the importance of conjugal love between them, but it prescribes utter devotion on the part of the Hindu wife under the value-ideal of *Pativratya,* literally meaning following of husband's will with absolute faith and without any doubt or demur, and recognizing husband's supreme authority. These conventional prescriptions only segregated the wife's role from her husband's role in which she was not expected to be a sharer but only a devout assistant. In all such matters as setting weddings, father and mother did the preliminary choosing, then father would ask Grandmother for her final approval" (Ross, 1961, p. 96).

The ideal of deference to parents is seldom questioned and in practice it endows elders with an authority that is not lightly ignored by their children. Among siblings too the role differentiations were made on the principle of sex and age in the traditional Hindu family.

Among brothers, status was determined on the basis of age, the eldest son received greater respect from all his younger brothers and sisters. The authority used to rest with the elder. Younger brothers were expected to give some of the same respectful compliance to their elder brother, at least in formal term that a son gives to his father. When an eldest brother succeeds as head of the joint family, his younger brothers and their wives and children are supposed to give him the kind of allegiance and obedience that the father commanded in his time. Within the realm of women's activities, a woman's authority usually depends on the position of her husband in the family. The wife of the senior man is the paramount authority in women's affairs subject only to the presence in the household of his mother, who must be heard out patiently and respectfully (Ross, 1961, pp. 55, 132).

As in any human relationships, the weight of influence in a family may be wielded by a forceful personality, say youngest brother, even though he does not have an acknowledged position of power in the family structure (cf. Sarma, 1951, p. 52). The formal hierarchy is, however, clear and influential. A man is expected to have his natural authority over his wife and children and it could not be questioned in the traditional family. A woman is expected to exert control over her unmarried daughters and daughters-in-law. A senior brother has legitimate authority over his younger siblings. Each person's dominance yields to the presence of higher family authority (cf. Mandelbaum, 1972, p. 40). The eldest brother should give ear to the wishes of the mother, the mother should defer to the wishes of the father; the father should give way in family affairs if he is over-ruled by his own father, or by the senior male of the joint family.

With the family authority is enjoined responsibility. The superior is also obliged to look after the welfare of his charges so that they will not suffer, either by his own misjudgement or because of untoward circumstances.

A villager of Poona District in Maharashtra said that the general ideal is that a man should respect and obey his elder brother as his father and should treat his elder brother's wife as an elder sister. Orienstein (1965, pp. 47-48), remarks on the basis of his own observations of Indian society that the oldest male of the highest generation is supposed to receive the most respect and obedience, the female as the opposite pole, the most protection and care.

The authority has its various dimensions in the traditional Hindu family. T.N. Madan who studied the family and kinship pattern among the Rural Pandits of Kashmir writes about the Kashmiri Pandits, "What strikes the observer is the extreme restraint which characterizes relations between adult men and women in Pandit Society."[2]

Adrian C. Mayer (1960) who studied the Hindu caste and kinship in a Malwa village in Dewas — District of Madhya Pradesh observers: "The dominant note in the formal pattern of relations in the household is that of restraint. There is restraint between people of different age and restraint between those of opposite sex."[3] Mayer adds that while his characterization may make the household appear, particularly to one from a different tradition of family life, as a place full of restrictions and autocratic authority, it is not really so, the net work of authority is knit so well in the obligation and cultural norms of the family that the members seldom feel its burden. Mayer himself observed that yet in a happy household this is patently not the case. Authority on the one hand, and respect on the other, mix, in an easy carrying out of duties, and the reliance of the women is one of modesty not fear. 'Restraint and hierarchy are also characteristics of relations among peoples of different *jatis* as well as within the family' (Mandelbaum, 1972, p. 41).

Family roles are important for proper functioning of the family. Some features in these roles are biologically given to an individual. As in all other human societies, the most important roles in the Hindu family are roles of husband-wife, mother-son, father-son, mother-daughter, father-daughter, brother-sister, brother-brother and sister-sister relationships. People use generally broad stereotypes of proper family behaviour to guide and judge family conduct.

The family roles significant in the functional order are first those of a boy and a man, then comes those of a girl and a woman. Mandelbaum (1972) remarks in this connection that not every family has full complement of members and roles but there is a strong tendency to fill in a missing major role.

The major role sets in the urban Hindu family in reference to interpersonal relationships are husband-wife, parent-child and brother-sister. I have, therefore, purposely selected these role-sets for analysis in the present discussion.

The Role of Son or the Role of Love, Devotion and Feelings

A person enters a family as a body and lives in it for a major span of his life as a man. His role as a boy and man thus becomes one of the most important roles in the family. As boy and man, he is expected to treat both parents with great respect. This respect also entails obedience and the avoidance of any behaviour that might indicate a contrary will or wayward desires nourished under not so strong parental authority.

Every young man is expected to show utmost respect and devotion towards his parents, and try to have a special regard towards their feelings. In practice and action this may not be very much ensured, but this is what forms the expected role of a son towards his father and mother. The urban situation has certainly made a change in this as in the individual family commonly found in towns and cities, parents are usually not staying with them. The role that would be performed for them in their presence gets a change now. In feelings and sentiments they may continue to have some regard for their parents, but occasions for their strife and tension on account of failures or short comings are usually avoided. Role of filial love and feeling is changed in its behaviour pattern in the urban individual family.

Parents also owe a certain respect from their children. They are expected to command natural respect from their children by virtue of their ideal performance. They should behave not in such a way that it becomes difficult for the children to respect them. This is even more important when a son grown-up and his parents are, or may soon be, dependent upon him.

Father-Son Relationship and Behaviour Pattern; Role of Obligatory Duty, Authority and Guardian Companionship

Father-son relations are governed by filial feelings, affection and guidance. Mandelbaum (1972) remarks, 'Between father and son relations are supposed to be formal and restrained and are often so in reality. Each may have great affection for the other, but after the boy becomes adolescent there should be little familiarity, intimacy, or demonstrativeness between them. This holds especially true among landowners of high ritual rank.'

Among the upper caste families, especially those who are economically well-off, sons depend upon father during his life time and they do not normally bother much for their responsibilities. It is the father who has to give a good deal of attention to his sons in their early childhood, as specially studied among the Brahmans of a Tanjore village in Southern India. Later when a boy is eight or nine, he comes under stricter training, and he and his father are now expected to keep physically more distant from each other. The boy does not touch either parent and he should prostrate himself in obeisance before each of them daily. After the son's marriage, he may be given some economic responsibilities to share with his father or other earners, if he lives in a large joint family, or is expected to independently maintain his own family, if he lives in a small joint family.

Rural situation is slightly different from the urban. In rural families a son may continue to enjoy his parental patronage even after his marriage. Kathleen Gough (1956)[4] who studied some Brahmin families in a Tanjore village cites an instance from her own observation. One of her respondents, an adult of thirty-five was a husband and a father, when interrogated about his responsibilities replied to her surprise, "I am only a young boy, Madam : My father is alive. What is my responsibility?" This suggests that because of father's filial love and affectionate patronage, sons feel little responsibility and obligation to discharge their expected roles so strictly in the family. The imperative need for sons and the long dependence of a son on his father is sanctioned and sanctified in scriptures. The father-son relationship and duties constitute the essential legal bond of the classic Hindu family (Kapadia : 1947, p;. 83-92 Derrett: 1960, p. 311).

The father-son relationship has been very much idealized in the classic Hindu family. The father-son relation is not without personal strain even among those who extol the ideal. Carstairs (1957) reports from his study in a Rajasthan town that the men of the high jatis insisted to the inquirer that it was unthinkable to disregard a father's command, but they also gave him reason to think that the tension between father and son was very strong.[5]

Adult son may resent father's strong authority or aggressive nature, but traditionally open defiance has been prohibited. But whenever occasions for such defiance arise, the son can stand on his legal right and demand partition and his equal share in the family property.

Ross (1961) had studied family relations in the urban Hindu family in Bangalore and distributed a questionnaire to 157 men and women mainly educated and belonging to upper castes. She observes that many of her respondents said that they lived in a relation of affection with their father, they mentioned that they did not feel any kind of dislike and hostility. Only 16 of the respondents expressed some antagonism against father. Several respondents noted that there was a marked drawing apart of the two when the son was a young man but was not yet independent. In the words of one respondent. 'The father is always a little like stranger to the son and the mother acts as intermediary between them (Ross 1961, pp. 101, 137, 114).

This suggests that an attitude of formalism prevails between father and son when the latter grows-up and disparity of age is bridged-up by experience of life or educational attainments while relationship between mother and son is one of close intimacy and confidence.

Mother-Son Relations : Role of Motherly Feelings, Affection and Possessiveness

Mother-son relations are the central point in the family organization of a joint family; mother has naturally more affection for her sons than for daughter. According to the notion prevalent in the classic Hindu family that it is the son who repays his father's debts and the daughters are born to be out to other homes, between mother and son there is everywhere in India, a strong, tender, unchanging dependable bond. 'The bond is celebrated in sacred writings, romanticized in popular tales, upheld in actuality of family life' (Mandelbaum; 1972: p. 62). The mother is naturally revered for her motherhood. The sons give abundantly of the tokens and substance of esteem to their mother. Unlike her husband who is often considered the aloof person by sons, she is everlastingly loving and caring, certainly in ideal, often in reality. This is particularly true of a woman in a wealthy family who has little more to do than to care for her children, and in that care lies her greatest fulfilment as a person. And her authority over her son does not cease at his marriage. Her exclusive possession is now shared by someone who is a stranger and comes from another family. Her identity takes time to be adjusted to the new condition. There is natural jealousy, therefore, in the first instance. In the second instance, she admits the facts of life, but still would not like to surrender her authority. An equilibrium has to be maintained between her feelings for her son and those of her son's wife. If this is not ensured, conflicts are likely to emerge between mother and wife and emerging tensions thereof may often threaten the peace of the family. The principal strain on her comes generally when the son's wife feels secured enough in the household to assert for her own independence. Dube (1955)[6] suggests that if quarrels burst forth at this, a man generally feels himself torn in between irreconcilable adversaries between his mother whom he cannot cross and the mother of his sons whom he really does not want to make unhappy.

Agarwala (1955) in his study of the mobile commercial community of Agarwala and examined this situation and distributed a questionnaire to the 590 Aggarwal men and women. Each man was asked whether he was closer to his mother or to his wife or equally close to both. A majority of men, 56 per cent, replied that they were closer to their mothers; only 20 per cent said that they were equally close, and 5 per cent gave other replies. However, the picture emerges a little different when examined from the point of view of 'wives'. Only 17 per cent of the wives of these men thought that their husbands were closer to their mothers; 57 per cent said that their husbands were closer to them. At another place reviewing the whole situation she comments; 'It seems obvious that men's own experience of their relationship to mother and wife is different from the image the women have of these relationship'. The majority of the men in this sample followed the traditional pattern in the questionnaire reply at least holding maternal bond above the marital one.

Mother's authority over her son gets more exerted when his son falls in love with some girl and wants to marry her out of his own choice. The very idea of the decision of marriage being taken by the son or daughter provokes enough reaction in the minds of parental generation, and they usually react strongly against such an action. If the finance proposed belongs to some other caste the reaction is still strong. An if the girl belongs to some other caste lower than their own, they find the situation irreconcilable. It largely depends upon the son how far he can mould the opinion of his parents in his favour. And here the son often takes help of his mother. Mother's reactions often sublimate in her motherly feelings for her son.

Brother to Brother Relations : Role of Fraternity and Competition

In interpersonal relationships of the family sibling relations do not seem apparently to be playing such an important role as father-son, mother-son and husband-wife relations, but they are significance in understanding the behaviour patterns of all the family members. Sibling relations are guided primarily by filial love and a unity bond of the parental family.

Among these brother-to-brother relations, the ideal of unity, solidarity and mutual support is better realized when brothers are under the firm authority of their father, or when they deal against a threat from outsiders. But when parallel authority is weak or absent and when they are not defensively united, grown-up brothers often reach each other the wrong way and find reasons reach for argument. However, as one brother is considerably older than another, their relationship is less likely to be strained. The the elder one more easily assumes some of the responsibility and respect that the father commands. Often the eldest brother takes up the responsibility of bringing up his younger brothers and sisters. When the father is not living the eldest brother's relations towards his younger brothers become a strange mixture of brotherly, paternal and filial feelings.

Caste feelings still prevail, particularly the difference of upper castes and lower castes is still important for many upper caste Hindus. The change that seems to have come in the past three or four decades, and more especially in the post-independence era, is that people have become a little liberal about sub-caste considerations. For example, a Kanyakubja Brahmin would not now mind marrying a Saryupari girl, and even *vice versa* relations are not out of consideration now. Similarly among Kayasthas, Dusre and Shrivastava relations are now possible. Kshatriyas or Rajputs have become liberal in giving-up preferences for highly connected families or families of royal blood, higher status than their own and sub-caste rigidities and sultry considerations. Mother-son relations which are disturbed in such cases of love marriages are repaired either by son's initiative of apology and more care and consideration for mother, or mother's pardon for her son's mistakes. Where both of these are in want, time comes as "the best healer", old things are forgotten or repaired.

Mayer (1960) who studied the rural people of Ramkhari village in

Dewas says that all agnatic relations tend to be formal and this holds widely true about the rural Hindu family at large. A major ambiguity and common sense of strain in the fraternal relationship is that brothers are equal and yet they are not equal. Mandelbaum has analysed this dilemmuratic inequality and says, they are all equal in property rights, all equally representative of the family, all equally bound with the family's social status and fortunes. Yet an elder brother is also vested with some authority over a younger brother, and the younger brother should, in some degree, be submissive to his elder brothers, but sooner or later the question arises of the degree and nature of deference. The uncertainty as to when equality should prevail tends to rile their relations. Brother-to-brother relations show a cultural variation more than the parent-child relations. Brother-brother relations and behaviour are naturally different where fraternal polyandry prevails, such as among Noyars of Kerala till recent past. Since that does not relate to a large area, but only to a very limited cultural area there is little need to deal with it here.

The bond between brothers is taken ideally as a durable and cohesive relationship for co-operative action and falls second to the father-son relationship. But in practice this is very much limited. In actuality the fraternal bond tends to become unstable in time, and various challenges of life affect it from time to time. Occasions of jealousy; misunderstanding, malice, ill-feelings against each other arise as they live their life. Occupational mobility and urbanization are, however, averting such occasions, as their different families live in different towns. Distant living and lesser chances of meeting often provide a healthier feeling with the large family group.

Estrangement among adult brothers has been noted as a salient feature of the joint family such as one that develops in a Kashmiri rural Pandit family which Madan (1968) has pointed out.[7] Feelings of rivalry are also not uncommon, particularly after father's lifetime.

Orienstein (1965),[8] who studied conflict and cohesion in an Indian Village of Maharashtra, suggests that brothers commonly quarrel after their father's lifetime, each viewing the other as rivals. Their quarrels sometimes assume a vindictive character. The same fraternal conflict is reported from a village near Bangalore in Mysore whom Beals and Siegel[9] studied in 1966. The incidence of brother's quarrels is not a large proportion of all village conflicts but "it is the most shocking kind of conflict and the most contrary to traditional values". On the contrary in many places and castes, brothers are expected to be allies:

they are exhorted by parents, kin and neighbours. But as they become husbands and fathers they tend to change and become in course rivals within one household and they may be abetted in this by their wives. They usually want to be friendly and mutually supportive, yet the younger ones may find themselves irritated by the elder's flaunting of unwanted independence.

Family roles and behaviour achieve a special meaning and purpose when they function in a coordinate manner. This coordination is not only ensured by direct roles but also by some other operative roles in family which are related to the main role set. These roles which express filial love and feelings in the family institution play an equally important role as the roles which are directly concerned with the fundamental behaviour of authority, sentiments, emotional support and companionship. Among these brother-sister relations are more important than brother-brother relations are that feeling of innate jealousy and rivalry is conspiciously absent here. No such uneasiness mars the usual relations of brother and sister which then become typically more stable, durable and affectionate. Mandelbaum (1972) who has tried to interpret various institutional behaviours in Indian society in his remarkable study, *Society in India* remarks, "A man can be giving and protective to his sister, open-handed, without formal reserve or inward calculation. He gives more to her than he receives from her and feels rewarded just to do so. He keeps up the relation after his sister has married and left her original home. This entails special responsibility toward her husband and particularly to her children and the relationship is of major importance for the individual and for the jati. So in acting as brother to his sister a man also assumes the duties of brother-in-law and of mother's brother. In discussion of the one role, it is well to consider the extensions of that role as well".

Another link in brother-sister relation comes through the latter's marriage, She now leaves her parental, or what has been called "institutional" family and enters her husband's alien family to live there most of her life. Her parents are always anxious to know particularly during the first few years of her marriage, as to how she is received in her new home, what is her in-laws' behaviour towards her, how the mother-in-law treats her, while these may be feminine quarries, the father particularly wants to know whether there is any fuss over her dowry. And here the brother plays a special role. He acts as an emissary to his mother. Should she need help and protection in that house, he tires as best he can give it to here. He can be frequent traveller between the two families. A number of sociologists and social anthropologists have analysed this aspects of brother 's role in relation to his sister in the family.

Dumont (1957)[10], Carstairs (1957)[11], Karve (1965)[12], Ross (1961)[13], Mayer (1960)[14], Sarma (1952)[15], and Rowe (1960)[16] are a few important ones among these.

Feelings of rivalry between brother and sister are rare, nor is there any rivalry between mother and daughter for sharing the affection of son and brother. Interests of brother and sister are different in the Hindu family. The girl right from her early age knows that she is going to leave her natal home in a couple of years, therefore, she does not have jealousy against her brothers which is characteristics of his brothers. A natural attachment, therefore, develops between them. The tradition of *Rakhi* (tieing of a cord) to brother at an annual festival and a cotton thread on the second day of Holi and Diwali as a token of her deep feelings for her brother have cemented the bond between brother and sister very much during the last many centuries of Indian tradition. The brother accepts the *Rakhi* and *Dora* with a genuine feeling of filial love and affection for his sister and as a token of great affection and bond of fraternity for him. He truly honours such feelings and gives some presents or money as a gift to her, where he is unable to do so because of circumstances he feels belittled within himself though his sister may never mind, be tolerant enough or may not at all expect anything from him. The acceptance of this threat meant an unexpressed protection to sister in times of personal crisis to her in the traditional family. In fact, in the Rajput history, there are many recorded episodes where *Rakhi* was sent by a Rajput princess in distress to seek helping hand of a foreign Mughal ruler. Humayun, is a "recognised" brother for her protection against the invasion of Shershah Suri. The Mughal ruler, Humayun had duly respected the extended offer of the affectionate bond of Rani Padmavati, in spite of alienity of any such custom in the Muslim culture and had come forward to her rescue. A boy's elder sister may be his special childhood companion, as Mandelbaum (1972) points out. Though just barely a couple of years' older, she may caress the boy child, lugging him about on her hip and treating him as her playmate as well as her main chore. If all others in the household are too busy or too constrained to look after him with a continual loving care, at least she is neither distracted nor infuriated from treating him as a real person rather than as a container of urgent biological needs or a carrier of future social stakes. A younger sister does not tend him in the same way but she may also be more companionable and relaxed with him than a pre-occupied adult man.

Mandelbaum (1972) also refers to this ritualistic recognition of a special bond between brother and sister in this annual tieing of cord observed in northern and western India. He fails, however, to take note of the fact that there has been a cultural dispersal of this *Rakshabandhan* ceremony almost throughout India. In his opinion the sister gives her brother a charm, often a thread which she ties around his wrist as symbol of solicitude for him. He gives her in return, a token of his a role-gift as benefactor. Where brothers have now been going out for jobs in other towns, or where sisters are married in other places, the *Rakhi* is sent by post and the brother acknowledges it by a gift in return or money-order sent in lieu of it to his sister living in some remote town.

Brother-sister relations are thus very much cemented by feelings of attention and personal confidence. And this relationship persists even after her marriage in another family. Her husband finds his wife's brother to be the only kin with whom he can be informal. Thus a girl's brother becomes a more natural link between the two families. Often he also falls nearer to the generation of his sister's husband; therefore, there is little generation gap and communication gap between the kin. A boy's elder sister may be his special childhood companion.

The girls in the family are given an early training in child-care, tendering children, and be more responsible in their domestic duties by their mothers. This is part of a girl's informal education in her natal family which equips her to become a good housewife. Though there has been some change in the aspirations of girls, with higher education and career, they do not now necessarily look forward for becoming the housewives and playing an ideal role there; many girls with higher education are now choosing their professional career out of their deliberate will in preference to a choice for marriage and have been denying the domestic role of house wife in some recent years. But even this does not free them from their earlier cultural upbringing, and informal education which aims to make them more proficient to play their expected womanly roles in the family.

There has, however, also been a change in the role playing of child care by a girl in her earlier life. A study in child rearing by Minturn and Hitchcock (1963)[17] had found among the Rajputs of Khalapur, a village in Uttar Pradesh that there has been some change in the child rearing pattern and in the basic attitude towards child care and that girls do not now usually take care of younger children. Minturn and Lambert (1964)[18] suggests that this may be exceptional. Certainly it has been quite conventional to see in villages even small girls taking care of small tots. Carstairs (1957)[19] had specially observed this in a Rajasthan town. He adds further that a growing child experiences a continuity in physical and emotional contact with his sisters of a kind that is denied to him by his parents. Even his mother is constrained with the child when the mother-in-law is about and she also is engaged in other work. A sister's care, he observes, is thus not diminished for these reasons.

When a man's sister marries, he too takes on a new and different set of relations. Over such of northern India he becomes inferior to his sister's new family. To her he remains one of the closest of the dearly beloved in her childhood and to her new family, he becomes one who by definition is to be taken lightly. As in the traditional Hindu family she becomes subordinate to her husband, so her whole natal family falls subordinate to that of her husband. According to the Hindu convention, a family that takes a girl as bride considers itself superior to the family that gives her in marriage. Her family acknowledges this subordinate status though sometimes grudgingly. There has, however, been some change in this attitude owing to education and other advanced ideas now growing popular in the Hindu family. Educated and enlightened families are now refusing to accept this subordinate status for themselves, and are now emphasising a new attitude of equal status for themselves.

In South India, this kind of rank differential is not very much marked. In some time groups, as Dumont (1953) points out, the difference in rank at the marriage ceremony fades away in time, so that there is no suggestion of the wife coming from a lower ranking lineage. The superiority of one family line over the other is continued only if matrilateral cross-cousin marriages are consistently made between the two.[20]

One basic observation in regard to brother-sister relation, however, remains valid almost throughout India. Whatever formal status may be applied to each family, a brother throughout most of India is expected to keep giving gifts and ritual services to his married sister, perhaps also to her husband and certainly to her children. His benefactions are not required in any equal measures. There is little calculation of reciprocity and the giving is supposed to be its own reward. Because of this he also gets little glory for his benefected gifts. Since he is chief link between his family and his sister's conjugal household, he bears the brunt of their superior airs. And it is because of this inferior feeling shown towards him by his sister's conjugal family, which he learns to tolerate that the derogatory usage of his relation is equalled to an abusive term of *'Sala'*. The word *Sala* denotes a kinship relation of a wife's brother, perhaps coated with a tinge of amusement, but in popular usage it is adopted for a kind of mild abuse. Nicholas (1965) points out that in North India and Bengal, the very word for wife's brother is a common term of abuse which a man flings at a cursed ox, which he uses for a shaddy tool, and by which he refers to the affinal kinsman who periodically appears bearing gifts.[21] Yet this does not flinch him away from his duty towards his sister and whenever she needs him, he is always at her disposal without little regard for his respect or honour. And of course, he often gives the same kind of treatment to his own wife's brothers and to all the brothers of his brothers' wives. Receiving such treatment to his own wife's brothers and to all the brothers of his brothers' wives. Receiving such treatment does not sap a man's regard for his sister nor does it block a real, as well as ritual, devotion to her children.

In many South Indian castes brother and sister usually arrange each other's children's marriages.

In some cases brothers-sisters also play an important role in each other's marriages. In some of the South Indian castes, where the custom of cross-cousin marriage prevails, an elder sister is expected to urge her younger brother to marry her own daughter (Karve, 1953, p. 233). But this is only a preference and not any prescription. Nevertheless, a sister in these villages is generally expected to have the right of first refusal for her child in selecting a spouse for her brother's child. A brother has a similar right which in some castes is a formalized ritual.

What McCormarck (1958) has observed in her study about the brother-sister relationship, that the brother-sister relation is the main basis for cordial relationship among relatives, seems largely true about filial relations in the Hindu family at large in India.[22]

Role of Husband: The Role of Possessiveness Guidance, Companionship and Conjugal Love

The role of husband can be considered the most positive role in the Hindu family. It is more particularly so because of the patriarchally organized Hindu social organization where the person playing the role of husband also coordinates the role of head of the family which goes coterminous with the role of authority. His wife besides playing the role of wife and more specially "role of housewife" may often be also playing the role of mother in the family for her own children or children of her husband's younger brother.

Besides, the man playing the role of husband may also be combining in himself the role of son, role of father and role of brother in interpersonal sphere while in the socio-economic sphere of the family he may be playing the role of authority and the role of earner. These challenging roles put a strain on his personality, and even though there is no contradiction involved between his different roles, he often also faces conflicts in some of his discharged roles. A man may be affectionate and dutiful or even devoted to his mother while he may be also loving, considerate and loyal husband. He may continue both sets of his role concurrently for sometime when he finds that he is some how involved without his will or pre-imagination in a situation of conflict in role of husband. And the situation which prompts this conflict may be big or small one, may be supporting economically his aged mother, out of his inborn sense of duty as well as his natural feelings, without reducing his concern for his wife. To a period, when there are no children born to her wife, he may tacitly accept this role of devoted son towards his mother. But as soon as children are born to them, his wife may find it difficult to cope up with the increased expenses of the family and may wish that her husband stops or largely curtails his monthly contributory remittances to his mother who lives in his native place with other brothers. The husband may find in this unwarranted situation a challenge to his role, and this may easily precipitate into tension and continued conflict between his role of son and role of husband.

Similarly, the wife may be a working woman and may not be able to discharge many of her family obligations, mainly because of her having remained out of her home for most of time of the day such as her job in kitchen or housework. The burden of these left-back roles may ultimately fall upon mother of her husband, who may find difficult to cope-up with all these roles. She may grumble and try to obtain her daughters'-in-law co-operation, either out of physical pressure of work and her utter inability, or because of her own attitude of authority.

The husband exercises a difficult role in the family. In his role as husband, a man is expected traditionally to be always the superior, initiator, decisive, authoritative as well as the receiver of deference from his wife. A rural or an orthodox wife never flouts these expectations openly. Commonly she renders her best co-operation to his playing these roles by being submissive tolerant and adjustive. She is expected to show her gestures freely, spontaneously, and in full, as part of her womanhood, not out of feelings of duress. A man is expected to make clear demonstration of his unspondly authority at the beginning of a marriage and never to relinquish it, at least not publicly. In his privacy, he may be otherwise, but in appearance he has to behave authoritatively in true manner of tradition. Moreover, a young husband's personal, conjugal interest in his wife should in no way interfere with his duties to his parents, his siblings or to other elders of his household (Mandelbaum, 1972, p. 74).

This formalism between husband and wife was a little lessened on the birth of a child. The idea dominant behind this seclusion during day time seems to be largely connected with a sense of duty and loyalty to the parental generation as well as to consciousness of sexual intimacy between them, an issue tinged with so much sense of grace that he wants to avoid it in public.

As time passes, this expected behaviour between husband and wife became a part of the value ideal of the Hindu family. The ideal husband was expected to be one who would show little concern to his wife and children and more concern to his parents and his other elders in the parental joint family. His first duty lay towards his parents, then towards his brothers and sisters, and then his paternal Kinsmen. The wife and children came in the last of the order. This did not mean that the wife and children were neglected. On the contrary, they were expected to be looked after well by the father or elder brother of the man, who were expected to discharge their role of affection, passion and emotional care, usually expected from father. This was not exactly a transfer of the role, but in fact, it was a role culturally taken-up from father. It would perhaps be more right to believe that this role gradually became a part of their own role-set because of the joint living. The husband could also discharge this role a little secretly, or with some consciousness. This role-playing by father has been mobilised more by occupational mobility. When the family moves to the urban areas on employment or on profession, this role gets transferred essentially to the husband and father-man. The parental family can continue now sentimentally performing the role in the natal place and whenever the son gets back there occasionally, but the actual functional role in the individual family in the new setting is discharged by the husband and the father.

Mandelbaum (1972) remarks in his study of Indian Society that the prescription of the husband's role are laid at almost all social levels and in all regions. A husband's authority is more durable imperative among the higher and wealthier *jatis* than among the lower and poorer, where women can earn on their own and, therefore, are less dependent upon men. This seems to be corroborated by studies among higher castes and higher class groups, in different parts of India. The educated employed women in the large towns are also now not accepting absolute make authority as Promilla Kapoor (1972)[23] suggests on the basis of her empirical study. But this authority is also upheld among the lowest *jatis*, as Fuch's study (1950) in Eastern Mandla in Central Madhya Pradesh reveals.

T.N. Madan, who studied Rural Pandits of Kashmir in the perspective of their family and kinship behaviour, observes that husband-wife relations are marked by an apparent formalism. He illustrates this by citing an example from his field study. When a Pandit Brahmin returns to his native village after sometime, the man, women and children of his household block around him to greet him warmly. Men and women embrace him, kiss his forehead, the women weep with joy, the children run about and shout while his own wife stands mute at a corner and does not speak a word. She continues to do whatever she was doing before the commotion beings. She may go into the kitchen or engage herself to do any other domestic job, but she in not expected to show any concern in her husband or give vent to her feelings.

One significant reason for this formal aloofness, Madan explains, is that any display of special interest between the two is taken as a sign of a bond that may disrupt the man's filial and fraternal duties, and so is highly disfavoured. The precaution taken to regulate this behaviour is so severe that a young wife may not even prepare any food especially for her husband. If she wants to do some household task for him, she must do it for the whole family. Another reason for the display of indifference lies in the elder's view which holds that a young couple should have only one interest of their own, apart from the rest of the family, that is in sexual relations and with the primary motive of getting children. Consequently there is a sense of shame which surrounds the wife-husband relationship for many years after marriage and sexual drive is held to be the main interest which a man and his wife have in one another (Madan, 1965, pp. 134-135). This appears in my view, the outcome of the extraconsciousness about sex in the Hindu society which is often ambivalent; it on the one hand makes a segregation of men and women, but on the other hand tolerates all frivolities and hypothetical or real scandals in the name of sex even within the family circle.

The adoption of the role of husband on marriage is a great experience in itself for the young man. Though little seems to be altered in his daily life, he lives in the same house and family and acts in much the family roles, his inner self almost gets dynamically changed. The marriage typically makes a difference in his social potential and in his concept of himself. He now has a woman of his own, whose whole being is directed to him even if she must not show it openly. She has entered his life and has become a part of his life. He knows for certain that he is receiving an intensity of attention and emotional support from her that he may not have experienced since infancy. His social potential has greatly enhanced; an unmarried man in most cultural groups of Hindu society is not recognized or considered to be a complete person, and does not become capable of ritualistic rights.

The personal impact of the marriage on the young man is dramatically begun with the wedding century. He become practically a king in his family for those days, a being so exalted that everyone in the household, even his elders show deference to him. That lofty feeling usually coming at a time of adolescent restiveness is awakened daily by her covert ministrations as his wife. Her presence thus assures him of a superiority of being a superior individual, no matter to what *jati*, rank or personal capacity he may be belong to.

Wiser who had studied a Hindu village in Mainpuri district of Uttar Pradesh called Karimpur, in 1963, gives an appreciable account of the husband's position in his own family. He becomes a personage, when he enters his own courtyard his wife is ready to greet him and do his biding with head bowed and voice subdued and so are other women juniors to him. A young husband finds this most pleasant act after his long dependence on others, he has for the first time become independent in a real sense, he has a person who has grown into his command. He is now able to have a control over his wife.

Wiser tells at length her own amazement at witnessing a behaviour of wife and husband, a man almost abusing her in presence of many others, and she returning all his rude behaviour in rile. 'He had shown that he was a proper husband, and she that she was a proper wife, both were satisfied' (pp. 79-81).[24]

Dube (1955)[25] gives a different account of another kind. The reality of family life is not quite as the ideal formula would have it. The husband is without doubt superior and has, in most families, the upper hand; but practically nowhere do we find him a completely dominant, authoritarian, and patriarchal authoritative head.

The husband-wife relations get a ground foundation by mutual understanding and cooperation. This means that the wife should not only be expected to discharge her duties but should also be having some rights and prerogatives. One great prerogative that was given to her traditionally was her power of domestic ritual purity. To enable her to maintain her ritual purity was to bar her from much movement outside her home. Her Interactions with external world might defile the sanctity of her person and thus also contaminate food of the house. She need not go to the length of traffic with other men, she need not only be a bit lax about her menstrual seclusion. The socio-ethical code of the family warns that a respectable wife of husband's family can be an active temptress for outsiders.

To maintain her ritual sanctity, a housewife is expected to have a number of such prescriptions. This gives on the other hand more chances for conflicts and tensions in the family. The rhetoric of marital quarrels in a Mysore village has been critically observed by Alan R. Beals (1965, mimeographed). Certain actions, such as "salutary beatings" lend to reconciliation, others quite surely to divorce.[26] Similar patterns of domestic discord prevail in other villages and cultural regions of India. Generally the elders and kinsmen who are most closely related to the quarreling couple try to resolve their conflicts and prevent a serious break. This is with a conscious effort for maintaining stability of the family and preventing the most unwanted and unpleasant situation of a break or a series of continuous conflicts and bad will. Divorce was not traditionally allowed by the Hindu society, but there was always an impending danger of a woman going to her parent's family after a discord and remaining there indefinitely till her husband, his brother, or some close relative did not go to bring her back after patching up the differences. The Hindu Code Bill and its related amendments now make provisions for a divorce and the latest amendment of 1975 makes a further relaxations in the conditions, yet it is very much regulated mere quarrels and rhetorics of the unpleasant dialogues between the husband and wife are not enough to ask for exercising this right. Moreover, divorce affects social prestige of the couple and people are not prepared to endanger their positions in society and close affinity of kinship groups. Divorce is thus avoided as far as possible among the upper caste Hindus.

Husband's role in relation to his wife is thus the most critical and challenging role in the Hindu family.

The husband's role in the family, it appears, has been made formal by the convention, right from the very old times, and most of inter-personal relationships in the family almost ensure this in some way or the other. This is so much conventional that this form of apparent formalism between husband and wife seems a part of the large culture tradition of the Hindu social organization.

On marriage, the newly-wedded wife enters her husband's family, she is almost a stranger to the new house. Her family background may be different from that of her husband. Since her position in her husband's family is a subordinate position to practically all elders in the family, besides her own husband, she owes her dutiful allegiance to all of them and in return can expect only a mild gesture of affections or goodwill. This behaviour of members of the family towards her is a little different from reciprocal relationship normally expected in social interaction.

She and her husband, as the newly wedded are the most junior couple in a joint family, who have to live in complete obeissance to all elders in the family.

As the youngest members of the family they have to abide more by the familial and social norms and ethical code of behaviour.

The newly-wed husband is expected to be wearing a spectable of grave serenity and formalism towards his wife in the presence of other members of the family. He is expected not to show any personal intimacy with her. It is in private and when alone together that he may be playful, passionate, argumentative, affectionate. The physical arrangements in a traditional Hindu family are usually such that privacy can be attained only briefly, hurriedly and in darkness. In rural areas in fine weather, the fields offer some heaven. But in the presence of other persons, especially elders of the household, the two must keep their distance, and the husband's aloofness must prevail (Dube, 1955, p. 148, Mayer, 1966, p. 220, Sharma, 1956, a,p. 278).

Some other Associated Roles of the Husband

The husband besides playing this role towards his wife also plays some other roles in his family. These are his institutional roles in respect to consanguinal kin, but when he marries, he acquires through his wife also a set of relatives who may be his wife's close kin and who become his affinal kin, he is a much respected person, the recipient of their goodwill and gifts. Among the upper caste Hindus these affinal kin try to oblige him to their most by discharging many of their important responsibilities, sharing an affectionate attitude and consideration for his ambitions and proving themselves as his well-wishers and sympathisers. This initially may be an extended behaviour of courtesy and goodwill because of the fact that their own girl has been married to him, but in course of time it becomes an integral part of their kinship-behaviour.

Madan (1965) has specially observed this kinship behaviour of affines among the Pandit Brahmins of Kashmir. In the early years of a Pandit Brahmin's marriage, his relations with his wife's kin are not close, but when his children are growing up they induce closer ties. He adds that a men's affines typically support him both in word and in substance. Their gifts are for his entire household as well as for him personally, given partly for their daughter's benefit to help better her lot in her husband's family and also as a means of building and maintaining their own family's status in the caste. The tradition still accords an exalted status to affluence. The families rated highest are thus those who are lavish in their gifts to their daughter, not only on her marriage, but even all through her marital life in her husband's family and these gifts are also extended to her husband's family. In fact they are often made to the husband's family and are expected to reach her through the former only. What Madan has observed in relation to Kashmiri Pandit Brahmin holds largely true about upper caste Hindus, especially the Brahmins and Kshatriyas, throughout northern and central parts of India, in the northern cultural zone. Mayer (1960)[27] and Harper (1963)[28] have also suggested similar kinship behaviour prevailing in their areas of study. In Madhya Pradesh too the Hindu families originally migrating from Uttar Pradesh and Rajasthan as well as the native residents of Bundelkhand, Baghelkhand, and Malwa regions have similar tradition of kinship patterns of behaviour towards and on the part of wife's kin.

Madan invites our attention to another important aspect of

husband's role in the Kashmir village which seems to be of common occurrence in his opinion, though we do not have as yet wider empirical evidence from other parts of Hindu-cultural India. Madan suggests that a man with adult children is rather a lonely person in his household, his sons must keep a respectful distance from him and their wives do even more so. A woman in her old age can more easily shift her interests to others in the household but the older a man grows the more dependent he is on his wife since he cannot readily be on familiar terms with the younger people in the household (1965, p. 137). Apparently the pivotal, mediating role a mother often takes between her husband and her sons when they are adolescents and continues even when they are matured men with children of their own.

In his own family the husband man has to play some more roles of obligation. He has to teach his children to show more respect and obedience to his own father, that is to the children's father's father. They are trained in the agnatic discipline and recognition of paternal authority while they are in his presence, but levity, house-play demonstrations of parental affection are unsuitable. this situation has, of course, relatively lesser occurrence. Few grand-fathers live to enjoy this privilege for considerable length of time and those who do so are often in their native or separate households from their grandchildren, and in any case, they may be enfeebled or reviled. Mandelbaum (1972) remarks while critically appraising this situation the retirement of an elder from paramount influence in a household occurs at all social levels. In Driver's sample of 2314 multi-couple families in Nagpur district of Maharashtra, the elder couple occupied a subordinate position in 26.3 per cent cases.[29]

In the joint families of the traditional type and especially among the high-ranking land owners, the paternal grandfather is, however, often a figure of some consequence to his grandchildren, and the father of the children has to play an important role in ensuring cordiality in the relationship between two different generations. He is expected to exert his authority in instructing and disciplining this children and so he should be strict and authoritative to them. Hence among the Pandit Brahmins he does not favour frequent visits by them to their mother's natal family and frowns on the loving attention they are likely to get from the mother's parents and brothers there. This reflects the basic difference in the kinship behaviour towards two different sets of kin, the agnatic and the affinal. The fear behind that is that the children may get spoiled by extreme affection and extra care. Madan remarks, 'They complain that children get spoiled during such visits and by the time they return, they usually become undisciplined' (Madan, 1965, p. 212). It appears a little paradoxical, but is strangely enough true that the same man who may be making such a complaint about his son's children may now well act as the benevolent admirer of his daughter's children whey they come to visit him. This appears a typical feature of the Hindu kinship behaviour pattern.

A child's attitude towards his two sets of grand mothers in an upper caste Hindu family seems similarly divided. He may sense some of the characteristic strain between his mother and his father's mother. But his mother's mother welcomes the child most fondly as the darling son or daughter of her beloved daughter whom she has so sorely missed. An upper caste Hindu's ties to his mother's first family are most important to him when he is young, and it continues to be the chief source of his affection.

Madan stresses this when he says, after he marries and especially after his mother is no longer living, his principal love of affection is with his wife's rather than his mother's natal family. (Madan, 1965), Sarma (1951), Mayer (1960) and Ross (1961) have also made more or less similar observations from their own areas of study.

This thus makes the general theme in the family roles of the man whom we can call for sake of convenience "the Multiple Role Man" at most social levels and cultural regions of the Hindu society. He works with the other men of the household, as their assigned life partner, to achieve many vital purposes of life; food, shelter, procreation, socialization, defence. With them his roles are cost largely as a member of a co-operating group. Co-operation among men is continuous in daily tasks and ground events but commonly an element of rivalry or strain in these relations is also marked.

A man's relatives through his mother and wife do not directly contribute much to the maintenance and cohesion of the family group, but they are a fundamental resource of affection, goodwill and sympathy for him. Mandelbaum suggests that men who are related through women need not deal with each other as responsible members of a group but more as persons worthy of support. A man gets respect, affection, and sympathy from his mother's family as well as from his wife's natal family, and he gives off the same supportive currency to his sister's and daughter's conjugal family. In his roles as an agnate, a man supports the residential household group and the local lineage, but in his relations through the women of his family he also contributes to identification and co-operation within the caste. These individual, affectionate, affective aspects of a man's family roles do much to foster the cohesion of the larger social group, the *jati*. The Hindu family can hardly ignore its bond with the caste group. These expected family roles of man thus serve multifarious purpose and ensure a larger coverage of family obligations.

Woman's Multiple Roles

The interpersonal relationships in the Hindu family depend much upon the fact, how different members discharge their respective roles. The roles are divided among the family-members according to responsibilities expected from them and their ability to discharge these expected obligations. The question of ability to discharge a function or assumed responsibility is linked invariably to one's capability. The expectations culturally raised from different members of family are not dependent upon their individuality but rather on a basic diachotomic divisions of sex. It also seems to be based on some governing principle which holds that by nature, men can do certain things which women normally cannot do. Women are endowed with certain capacity by nature which men are utterly incapable of conception and child bearing are the main ones; nursing and tolerating during their infancy are others. And alongwith this biological capacity certain traits of character are also formed, such as endurance, patience and tolerance. Therefore, the role expectations in the family are different for men and women, if man's roles are of a boy and man, woman's roles are of a girl and woman. The expectations from each kin group of people have to be different first on the basis of sex, then on anything else. I have discussed man's expected roles in different situations of life, that of a son, a brother, a husband and a father, I shall now discuss family roles of woman, as a girl, a daughter, and a sister, and as mother and as wife. The break between being a daughter and sister in one family and becoming a wife and daughter-in-law in another is rather sharp and solely difficult in Mandelbaum's opinion (Mandelbaum, 1972, p.82). He suggests that women's recollection of the sweet joy of girlhood is not merely a construct of nostalgia; girls are commonly under less stern discipline than are boys, especially as their puberty and time of departure for husband's home approach.

Role of Daughter, Role of Tender Feelings and Affection

Participant in Cultural Training

Woman's roles in family begin with role of daughter as a girl. Her assuming the roles of a girl in her natal family are preparatory of her expected roles in her husband's family.

The traditional Hindu family has a conservative attitude towards girls. Formally and manifestly the birth of a daughter was considered a much less auspicious event than birth of a son. The sons usually got better treatment than daughters. And this resulted in an inferiority complex in girls, when it gets perpetuated in them generationally. The discrimination between brothers and sisters also basically causes jealousy between them. The sisters always felt a kind of partial treatment being meted out to them by their parents and other members of family but they had to repress their feelings. This often caused a bad misunderstanding between siblings and though formal cordiality was not lacking, genuine affection was rare. Madan (1965) describes in his study of Rural Pandits of Kashmir, how girls are given a differential treatment in a Hindu family but now these girls do not themselves feel resentful of any such discrimination. Their parents admit and justify the discrimination but they in the meantime also insist that they do not love their daughters less than their sons. An attitude of favouritism towards sons prevails in other parts of India too. There are different factors which have influenced the position of woman in the later half of the twentieth century. Girl's education, emancipation of women, movements for rights of equality and the provisions for equal rights of property to daughters in the Hindu Code Act have helped to improve the basic attitude towards woman. The educated and enlightened parents now do not find enough reason in giving a differential treatment. This change is certainly being reflected more in the urban families. It was with this purpose that I had tried to know specifically on this point through one of my questions in my schedule, whether the sisters find that they are being given a different treatment than their brothers in the family. I will be examining this in course of my analysis in the later parts of the book.

The daughter's position remains precarious where this differential attitude between brothers and sisters prevails. Studies in different parts of India, representing different cultures have been conducted from time to time by scholars of disciplines of sociology, social anthropology and social psychology which reveal interesting findings on this aspect of the family roles. A study was conducted on child-rearing among Rajputs of Khalapur village in Uttar Pradesh which contains a kind of clue to the reason for this response. Minburn and Lambert (1963) who conducted this study observe in their monograph that Rajput mothers of this village were less warm and more hostile to their sons than to their daughters. They particularly emphasize that this hostility to boys is particularly interesting in view of the fact that these Rajputs, like most Indians, want to have sons rather than daughters. And they offer a possible explanation that women prefer daughters on emotional grounds, partly because a woman must never directly express hostility or resentment of her husband. These emotions are generally expressed in the coldness with which these women treat their sons.[30]

It seems possible that these Rajputs may be exceptional among Indian villagers and their girls are given less work and responsibility for domestic chores than are those in many other castes and regions. Nevertheless, it appears quite typical that a girl's place in her original family involves less restraint and permits more open affection than she enjoys after her marriage. Her father usually sees little reason to assert strong authority over her.

Mandelbaum (1972) quotes an instance from the Naik Brahmins of a Mysore village. A girl is supposed to be "like a flower" which needs to be cherished and cared for because she will soon marry and come under the stern discipline of another family (Harper 1963). Madan (1965) and Gore (1965) also corroborate more or less these or similar observations.

The girl in the family as a daughter usually gets a fooding from her father who is often less stern, less concerned about her discipline in the home, though he is more attentive about her outside activities, the main purpose behind which is to keep her secluded from her contact with members of opposite sex.

But when a girl enters her husband's family, her roles get remarkably changed. Such fond relations cannot well be carried on after the daughter goes to her new home. He role expectations first get changed on her entrance in her husband's family. A father, in North Indian Hindu family is hardly expected to visit her daughter after her marriage. His position in that household becomes on ambivalent one. Traditionally as an elder he should be respected and given food, but at the same time, he should not expect anything from them. He is expected not to take his food there, not even a cup of tea. The convention prescribes that the donor of a bride must not take anything at all from these who have taken his daughter. Karve (1953) and Dumont (1961) both have amply emphasized this familiar code of conduct of the father of Hindu girl.

Yet, in spite of such ambivalence, a father feels himself benefited from his daughter's marriage. According to the traditional most concept, daughters are considered to be a kind of an old debt remaining to be paid through parents, particularly, the father who is obligatorily expected to get it paid by marrying her into another family. It is this attitude towards girls which has been culturally perpetuating in the minds of the Hindu men. It was with this conscious or subconscious motive in his mind that he wanted to demonstrate his power and enhance his family's status by arranging a prestigious marriage for his daughter. She thus helps to translate his secular gains into the more durable and desirable gain of higher status within his caste.

But the difficult role of upbringing a girls right from rearing her in the childhood to culturally training her into her expected roles of girl-hood, and later moulding her into a proper social person to be extremely adjustive are the most important roles of wife and mother. And this responsibility now rests with her mother, her father has little to do here. The father may pamper or remain aloof, but her mother must train and discipline her. That training is mainly arrived at turning her into a good daughter-in-law obedient, skilful, demure. It is commonly believed in the Hindu family that a girl's chances of a fine marriage are much improved if she gives evidence of these qualities. And the family's prestige is enhanced if she demonstrates these virtues after she is married, and her own happiness hinges on making the best of her roles as daughter-in-law and as wife. As the role of mother towards her daughter is so exact, so well defined and so certain that as a daughter approaches her puberty, her mother tends to draw closer to her and remembers poignantly that this child of her will soon be cast beyond her help. Srinivas (1949) and Rose (1961) stress the fact that this view softens discipline and leavens training with material compassion.

Role of Wife: The Role of Subordinate Duty Houswifeship, Conjugal Love and Companionship

The role of wife in the family is the most critical one of all family roles. It is a transition from role of daughter in her natal family to the role of woman in her husband's family. Not only the form, role obligations and role expectations are changed but also the area of operation changes, when the girl and her sphere gets spread wider and finds herself faced with a number of challenging problems and in a new environment where expectations from her are more and different than what were when she was a girl in her parental family. Her role there was exclusively governed by role expectations from a girl. Her new role here is now of a woman who is entrusted new responsibility. She does not have any experience in her new role though she may have well received her cultural training for this anticipatory role in her girlhood as a daughter in her natal family which tries to make a girl a successful housewife in future.

The transition from an unmarried girl's role to a wife's role is itself a great mark in a woman's life history. The nuptial rites mark the great event in a girl's life. She is physically transferred from the familiar intimacy of her childhood home to a strange place and new people, some of whom are, by reason of their roles, either distant or disciplinary. The transition is not so easy, and the bride has been prepared from her earlier age to find that is not easy. Her difficult position during this transition has been evaluated in several studies of sociologists and social anthropologists.

Opler (1985) who studied that Hindu families in a different ritual context, observers: 'In story, proverb, and song, the society has from her earliest years reminded her of the sharpness of the transition at marriage, and of the possible hostility of the mother-in-law and sister-in-law'.[31]

The departure of the Hindu bride from her father's home to new abode in her husband's family has been described pathetically in the classical as well as in later writings.

The said parting scene when the bride is taken away from her parent's home touches onlookers' hearts, when it is enacted in reality as it does when described over and again in drama and story. Irawati Karve (1953) even goes back to Kalidasa to illustrate the classic version of this scene. The situation is depicted in the fourth act of Kalidasa's drama, *Shakuntala*, written around the fifth century A.D. where the poet will portrays the usual situation in every Hindu household, which prevails even today. The parents are happy about the match, yet apprehensive about their daughter's future which remains uncertain in their minds. The girl is eager to join her husband but tremulous about leaving her beloved family and friends. Even now, the father gives his matured advice to his daughter, now he should behave in her new home, towards her husband, mother-in-law, father-in-law, sister-in-law and brother-in-law. Her mother gives some other instructions and her brother's wife often theoretically equips her with knowledge about woman's relations with man. In fact she brings with her a kind of orally prescribed code of conduct from her parent's family for her behaviour in her husband's new family. There has been little change in this situation for it has been culturally based deeply. Some fourteen centuries later, an educated Brahmin woman of western India, Mrs. Ranade recalls her father's advice when she was about to leave her home as a bride. He told her to endure silently whatever trouble might come to her. She was prescribed extremely restricted behaviour with kinsmen and even with her servants. Her father warned her that he expected her behaviour to enhance his family's name and that if it did not, he would never allow her to visit her mother's house. She writes, "Already I was beginning to sense that the discipline in this new home would soon make my carefree life in my mother's home seem like heaven itself".[32] This was the plight of a Maharashtrian Brahmin woman in the nineteenth century urban Poona. Writing in the mid-twentieth century about the plight and destiny of some regional Maharashtrian women, Mrs. Irawati Karve depicts a similar atmosphere in which a contemporary bride of North India finds herself. When affinal kin take their first look at her face, she must keep her glance demurely lowered or her eyes entirely shut. After marriage she must be self-effacing, neither seen, nor heard too much. Whatever misfortunes come to the household within a year or so, her arrival may well be attributed to her inauspicious qualities.[33]

The young wife, on her entry into her husband's house first finds herself stranger, she then finds her position precarious. The people in her husband's new family expect altogether different roles of behaviour, then what she discharges in her parents' family. And she finds herself at a loss to act in accordance with these new expected modes of behaviour though in her parent's family too, she was all the time being equipped theoretically for playing these expected roles well. But her informal training only presupposes her to be prepared in multifarious roles, and not the psychology associated with them.

The great event in the girl's life, expected for so long, is ceremonised well for sometime. But soon this ceremonial phase is over, the routine of home life surrounds her. She is burdened with some new responsibilities which she is expected to discharge effectively as a wife and more as a housewife. There is usually little consideration for her lack of experience in the new jobs or her unfamiliarity with a new set-up. Along with these responsibilities put upon her, there is also a prescribed code of behaviour awaiting her in the new household. The young woman is expected to keep out of the way of the male elders. Communication with her husband's father and elder brothers is minimal, highly restricted, and in some regions and castes strictly prohibited. The father-in-law's and elder brother-in-law's sudden encounter is supposed to be signalled by making a sound of coughing by them. This is their usual expected behaviour, but the responsibility to honour that gesture and evoke an avoidance falls ultimately upon her. She is expected to ensure this avoidance either by putting a veil over her face by her *sari's anchal*, or simply covering her head by her *sari*. One of the usual ways to avoid such encounters is to leave the room. Sarma (1951)[34], Karve (1953)[35] Dube (1955)[36], Fukutate et al (1964)[37] have all pointed out towards this avoidance behaviour of the Hindu wife.

Soon after the adjustments in the husband's family are made, which now for all theoretical and practical purposes becomes her own family, the wife is expected to bear a child soonest possible by the family members in general, and her mother-in-law in particular. The members of the family have curious anxiety to have a child, and because raising of children has for long been considered a social function, there is an apprehensive fear in the minds of family members whether the woman brought as wife is able to bear a child at all. Bareness in woman is a reproach and a curse. Because of this, they anxiously wait for the woman to conceive. The first pregnancy is usually celebrated in many regions in Hindu castes. First few years of marriage are those which are usually expected to become years of rejoice and marry-making for the husband and wife, these also often become strenuous months of borrowing and torture for her. There is on one hand, her own individual demand to spend her company with her husband in enjoyment and care-free expression of her wants, on the other hand, she is under a strain to remove the suspicion of her family members, or to cover her own inner desires. Srinivas (1942) observes in his study of Mysorean Hindu family that barenness in woman is so much feared and reproached that not only the word for barenness in Kannada, *banje* is forbidden in expression but also the term for the root of a certain plant *banje* is also avoided in usage. Both these words are tabooed in expressions of newly married wife and her husband.

The very knowledge of conception is a blessing to her, and she feels greatly relieved; she has proved her utility among the members of the family.

The important expected role of the wife now starts. Within herself as well as for the members of her husband's family, she now awaits to play her role of mother.

During this period of stringent responsibility, a young wife is also more isolated than ever before or again. Her mother-in-law is supposed to be more of a disciplinarian than a comforter, and the other women in the household are not her allies. They remain more or less indifferent if not hostile.

The male elders in the family remain even more distant to her, they are expected to keep a respectable distance lest there develops misunderstandings about her undesirable intimacy. Her husband's younger brother can be her only companion owing to his usually falling in the same age group and having emotionally similar ideas. But even it takes time for him to develop easy relations with her. It depends much upon his own nature and courage and his parent's and other member's capacity to overcome inhibited outlook towards him.

Her own husband, for whom she may have waited for long and for whom she is now expected to have most of her thoughts apparently cannot show an active interest in her behaviour pattern in his natal family. She, in turn, is also expected not to show special interest in him though all know obviously that she must perforce pin her hopes and foster her thoughts on him alone. In the most tradition bound families, she is not expected to address him directly and never to utter his name in proper noun. In fact she often refers to him in third person; *ye* (meaning He) is highly popular in Hindi. When a child is born to them she addresses his a "father of so and so". Agehananda Bharati (1966)[38] has specially stressed this role expectation in his study of teknonymy in the Hindu family.

The position of wife is also affected by village exogamy. The wife has been brought from outside the town and has no companions of her childhood; nor any relatives of her family with whom she can share her feelings and problems. She remains rather physically isolated from them and feels rather lonely, particularly in her mother-in-law happens to be authoritative and aggressive. But even where this physical isolation does not exist and even where her own mother lives in the same village or town, or in close neighbourhood, and has daily contact with her, she has to show that she is under hegemony of her mother-in-law. The traditional precept in Indian family structure, as emphasized by Mandelbaum (1972) and also by some other sociologists is that on marriage a woman comes under the authority of the husband's family and that this authority is mainly and more directly exerted by her mother-in-law than by her husband.

The traditional conventional prevailing in the Hindu families since ages is that nothing, neither her relations with her husband nor those with her parents should impair that legitimate authority or her willing submission. The husband usually shows a bowful obeissance to his mother and does not interfere in their mutual conflicts. More often than not in many conflicts between the two he truly tries to side with his mother and justify his role of son. His expected role of husband does not come in the way of discharge of his role towards his mother.

The situation of a young wife in a Hindu family can easily be depicted in more sombre tones than is the common reality; she is relatively isolated within the family structure, but she is actually not is solitary confinement. She can well maintain somewhat easy, or what is called a "joking relationship" with some of her affinal kin in the family, husband's younger brother enjoys a privilege to joke with her. Her husband's younger sister and younger brother's wife are usually her emotional companions. This gesture may well be an expression of ambivalence about the true nature of the relation, yet it also relieves the strained taintness of her conduct. She is usually quite a young girl and has the resilience of girlhood. In rural society, a chore such as getting water from the well can be used as a refreshing relief from the presence of the elders. There are other factors too. In the new home there is the excitement of new sights, new people, and the discovery of the person and personality of her husband.

While the wife feels concerned about her own position in the new family, her expression and her adjustment according to expectations of her mother-in-law, husband and other family members, the sole anxiety of the family is to see her pregnant at the earliest possible month. So synchronising her feelings with that of her family she also feels herself relieved. The very news breaks out as a pleasing communication to everyone. Her authoritativeness also relaxes a bit, and she can now take an awakened interest in seeing that she eats well and rests easily. This carefulness may be perhaps more for the expected child than for the expectant mother. This first bourgeoning also marks the beginning of her family status.

The tradition in the Hindu families in many cultural regions of

India is that the birth of the first child should take place in her parent's family. This custom is more particularly observed in the south. In the Central India and upper India, this is not necessary; the child may be born even in the husband's family. But soon after the child birth she usually goes to live with her parents for a considerable period. Karve (1953) and Lewis (1958) have specially discussed this convention in their works. There she meets a familiar recognition of her status. She had gone as a daughter from the parent's family. She now returns as a mother. Her status becomes raised in the parental family as well as in the immediate society. She is a daughter of the house and a daughter of the village. But she is also now mother of the child. Her own child has now become a grandchild in her parent's family. She has proved her motherly worth and she has acquired a new status. The family status has to be given a due recognition in her own parent's family too. She is given affection and support and her individual personality is now more specially recognized.

The wife and the mother is now apt to use quite a different mode of conduct when she visits her old home. It is a less restrained, more outgoing conduct and in a few places she may even assume different standards of personal morality. Karve, (1953) and Majumdar (1944) have pointed out towards this aspect of her conduct.

The return of the daughter with a child of her own, the young wife's status gets some change in her natal family. In her own family also it gets considerable improvement. She is now no longer considered the lowly probationer as she was at first. If the first child happens to be a son, her position gets even a better status. She has proved herself in the most important way of all and her confidence is the more secured. She has assured the cultural norm. Her son is her redeemer and thenceforth her importance in the family tends to gradually increase. Mayer (1960) has illustrated how the change in her position is symbolized in the eating pattern. When she first arrives in the household, she eats last of all, not only after men but also after the other women. Later she eats at the sametime, but turns away from the other woman as a sign of respect and of her diffidence before them. Mayer further points out that finally, when she feels secure, she will face the other women, even those of the elder generation while eating, or may eat side by side with them is a sign of equality inside the family because as it is also a public feast. The role of wife is undergoing changes in the modern age. There are various new strains on her. She has newer areas of operations and new avenues of expressing her personality.[39]

Intra-personal Relationships between other Women of the Family

Family roles are determined by role obligations, and role obligations are ultimately dependent upon intrapersonal behaviour and relationships between different members of the family. The members who act and interact under a family set-up perform different roles, under the expectation-obligation patterns are both agnatically and affinally related to the head of the family. It thus becomes significant to observe and discuss how these different roles interact with and influence each other in their intrapersonal relationships. We have discussed some of the important intrapersonal relationships of men in the earlier part of this discussion. We are discussing now here the intrapersonal relationships between other women of the family.

The most important relationship here is that of the main woman in the family who usually combines in herself different roles simultaneously. She acts as mother, as wife, and as mother-in-law to three different sets of relationship.

I have preferred to call the role or mother, a role of sentiments. The status of mother is enjoined with motherly sentiments, and she is supposed to be the custodian of all sentiments and emotional care and caressing and she is expected to show affection for her children, have tender feelings for their discomforts and miseries and support their emotional wants. She is the best confidee of all adventures, frivolities, jokings and small secrecies within the family circle. Her sons to a limited extent and daughter to any extent can best confide in her for their private affairs and secrecies. The father is usually the authoritative head and may keep reasonable distance with his sons and daughters up. He may also be upset by smallest disturbance of the family code of behaviour. But the mother is expected to be more patient, sober and tolerant to listen to different tone-expressions and demands for adjustments. She acts in her role of sentiments not only for her own children, but she is also expected to have attention for children of her husband's younger brother's wife, and moreover often for children of other women in the family.

When she acts in her role of mother-in-law towards her son's wife, she expects to perform her role with different orientations. Her first and foremost motive here is to keep her daughter-in-law under a constant discipline so that the equilibrium of family may not be disturbed. But as the younger woman becomes more experienced and adjusted to the new family situation, she feels more self-assured, as she grows more mature, physically and psychologically. She becomes less complaisant and less automatically yielding to the directives of her mother-in-law, and it becomes not uncommon to see quarrels often tending to erupt over small issues and lending into unwanted dialogues and frictions. The only safeguard in quarrels of women among themselves is perhaps that women do not feel constrained in venting hostility against other women as men normally do in a family and their quarrels are not taken as seriously as are struggles among men. Different authors have pointed out towards these frictions of women within the family.

Opler (1958)[40] who studied the phenomenon of spirit possession under close vicinity of Banaras remarks that a young wife pushed to desperation may take to extreme measures. In Senapur village, near Benaras she may even become possessed by an evil spirit.

The common feeling persisting in the minds of elderly men in the family is that women of the family are not expected to get along well. There may be grave experience of many years behind this attitude, but there may as well be a prejudice against womenfolk. Thus a state of conflict and friction prevails in the family. But the thesis of generation – gap and conflict cannot be much emphasized in the context of intra-personal relationships among women. The relations among women of the same generation also do not feel amicable in the family. Sarma (1951) remarks on the Bengali family situation that a young wife can have very friendly relations with the girls, her husband's sisters, in her new home. She is pleased to accept her. But when they marry and leave the family, the situation as well as the relation alters. Each of them becomes more and more cut off from their father's household, and each can hardly help being envious of her brother's wife, who is, or will be, mistress of her former happy home. The wife of the brother, on her part, is not overjoyed by her husband's gifts to his sister. Even while the sisters are unmarried and on close, friendly terms with their brother's wife, they can be her severest critics, if they think that she is not behaving properly. Folk-literature in many regions characterize a man's wife and his sister as natural enemies in family. This conflict and antagonism can be better understood by conceding the psychological fact that both want to be possessive of the man, one out of her filial love, the other by her womanly love in which she is drawn by her marriage. Besides Sarma, Karve (1965), Madan (1965) and Srinivas (1942) have also remarked on this growing conflict and friction in the family in more or less similar vein.

It is commonly believed by the people in the traditional family that the women who have married into the family, the wives of the brother must live in close proximity.

Dube (1955) who studied a Hindu village in Deccan, writes that the brother's wives have rivalry, jealousy and suspicion for one another. There is always considerable back-biting and telling of tales. He adds that alliances are formed and broken periodically. The intrigues and jealousies among the womenfolk in a joint family are the despair of men. These observations on intrapersonal relationships indicate one relevant fact that the popular stereotypes omit important aspects of a woman's family roles. Though boys are indeed favoured over girls in a traditional Hindu family, yet girls seem to suffer little emotional deprivation on that account. And after a girl's marriage, the favouring among siblings is almost reversed. A young woman is expected to feel the shock of transfer from daughter to daughter-in-law, and typically enough she does fell it keenly. Her low status as a young wife is a part of the systematic separation between agnatic and affinal bonds. But though the young wife is taken to be a person of little consequence in the family, her role is one of great importance. Few family roles are subject to such close scrutiny and are so liable to such quick redressive action. The fact, however, remains that the formal subordination of women in the household does not bar an elder woman from dominating her domestic scene nor does it hamper a younger woman from competitive struggle with other women of the house. Though a young woman may have the lowliest place in her conjugal family, she nevertheless may be a main vehicle for a rise in status of her natal family. And although marriage must be normally between two who are considered "ritual equals in the traditional *jati* system, the two may be from families that are unequally endowed within the *jati.* A principal lever in the competition for family status is the prestigious marriage of a daughter.

The intra-personal relationship of women of the family, whether it is nuclear or small-joint of are thus determined by family roles of the different members.

The Change in Roles

Roles are set according to the cultural needs of society. The roles in a rural society are somewhat different from the roles in an urban society, but if there has been a continuity between the two in the form of physical mobility or what has, been called, folk-urban continuity, the latter can borrow most of its cultural traits from the former and would only be reflecting a variation according to the new situation. The role of authority was a very important role in a patriarchal large joint family of the classical type. Three of four, sometimes even more, generations lived together and vested their authority in the eldest male members of the family.

All authority was centred in him. He controlled authoritatively the members of his family group as the supreme head of the family. He supervised their activity within the family, and fixed individual responsibilities upon them, and all these members were directly responsible to him. He controlled the economics of the family and pooled all the income of different family members in a common purse of the family. He also became the supreme custodian of all property in the family which was considered "joint" and was given a joint legal sanctity. And he was the supreme authority to whom family disputes and conflicts were referred for counselling and decision. His authority was final here had his decisions became binding upon all. This authority of the head of the family was commanded usually by father's father or father's eldest brother or father according to the exact nature and extent of jointness.

The role of authority vested in and expected of the centralised authority thus became identical with father's role as frequency of father combining the supreme authority became more common in the joint family. As the large joint family started breaking into smaller joint families and individual families, the father usually became now the actual authoritative head of the family. The role of authority was directly transmitted to father's status from father or father's brother's status as the families started decentralizing. As physical mobility to towns and industrial centres became more common, many a joint family underwent this structural change. But the different spheres in which power was infested became obsolete, since different kinds of kin did not live together, their expected roles became unimportant and were gradually submerged in the small family group, the purse was also not common since there were not many earners and the head of the family, often the father, became the main earner in the family and sometime the only earner. In the last four or five decades he has in some cases also become the co-earner with his wife. To his wife he is already related by the role of husband.

The role of authority thus gradually changed on mobility and in the new environment; it lost its original potential. The raised status of women in society in recent years owing to her education and enlightened views has grown more important and the need for a rational approach towards her position and personality. This has further delimited the husband's authority over his wife. The educated housewife has earned for herself a better status in the family than her predecessor in the Hindu family could claim.

They cannot now be treated in the same manner with a force of authority in which her predecessor was treated. Often the educated wife also becomes the co-earner with her husband. She shares the burden of the family with her husband in the small-joint and individual family. And through this sharing she earns for herself her relatively more independence. The husband's role of authority towards his wife in the traditional joint Hindu family is now gradually getting transformed into a role of companionship and a role of cooperative behaviour. It is thus also more congenial to the new circumstance and is promotive of more healthy relations between husband and wife. It has lessened conflicts and tensions of the family through the traditional attitude of authority still persists in some degree in the husband's basic psychology of male ago as a persistent cultural heritage.

The economic independence of the wife has also compelled her husband to make minor adjustments and allowances. The rational need for more cordiality for better living and prosperity of family life is being felt both by the husband and the wife. This realization has directly encouraged the development of companionship approach mutually between husband and wife in the urban Hindu family.

The role of authority is thus becoming gradually disintegrated in the urban Hindu family; some of its expressive forms have become dormant and some others have undergone a kind of mutational change; still some others have assumed new forms in view of the changed needs, new situations and new pressures. In the reference of husband-wife relationship, we find that this has changed from role of authority and egoistic behaviour to a role of co-operative companionship. In the references of parent-child relationship and more particularly the father-son relationships, it has changed into a role of conciliatory guardianship and in case of grown up sons, it often becomes even a relationship of companionship oriented guardianship.

The modern education and science have made the young generation realize the need of time. These have made them more conscious about their rights and privileges. It has also disillusioned their faith in conventional values. It has made them agitative against the old order and apathetic to old social norms and values. The people of new generation born in the post-independence period do not now consider it worthwhile to surrender their will and interests to the old generation, simply because they are elder to them. They now want to weigh each issue on its own merit and want to question highly controversial values. They want to have their own individuality and an autonomy in their own sphere. They are thus refusing the authoritativeness in the family. They are more in favour of democratic ideas in the family atmosphere of freedom and individual discretion and decision.

They are willing to concede a relative authority to elders on the basis of their experience of the age and talent. But they are not in favour of the rule of physical law.

The only way to maintain a relationship with them lies in the development of friendly guidance. The modern educated fathers living in metropolises and large cities like Bombay, Calcutta and Delhi are fast adopting to this new situation and are accordingly adjusting to the related new role behaviour.

NOTES

1. M.S. Gore, "The Traditional Indian Family" in ed., M.F. Nimkoff, *Comparative Family Systems* (Boston, Houghton Mifllin Co., 1965) p. 216.
2. T.N. Madan, *Family and Kinship: A Study of the Pandits of Rural Kashmir* (New York, Asia Publishing House, 1966), p. 76.
3. Adrian C. Mayer, *Caste and Kinship in Central India,* (Berkeley, University of California Press, 1960), p. 214.
4. Kathleen Gough, 'Brahmin Kinship in a Tamil Village', *American Anthropologist,* 58, 1956, 835-838.
5. G. Morris Carstairs, *The Twice Born: A Study of a Community of High Caste Hindus.* (London, Hogarth Press, 1957), pp. 68-69.
6. S.C. Dube, *Indian Village* (Ithaca, New York, Cornel University Press, 1955), p. 143.
7. T.N. Madan, *Family and Kinship: A Study of the Pandits of Rural Kashmir* (Bombay, Asia Publishing House, 1965).
8. Henry Orienstein, *Gaon: Conflict and Cohesion in an Indian Village.* (Englewood Cliffs, N.J. Prentice Hill Inc., 1965), pp. 45, 48.
9. Alan R. Beals and Siegel, Barnard, J., *Divisiveness and Social Conflict; An Anthropological Approach* (Stanford, Stanford University Press, 1966).
10. Louis Dumont, *Une sous Caste De 1'Inde du sud* (Paris, Mouton De Co, 1957), pp. 206-207.

11. G. Morris Carstairs, *The Twice Born: A Study of A Community of High Caste Hindus* (London, The Hogarth Press, 1957), p.70.
12. Irawati Karve, *Kinship Organization in India,* (Poona, Deccan College 1965), Monograph Series No. 11, p. 131.
13. Aileen D. Ross, *The Hindu Family in its Urban Setting* (Bombay, Oxford University Press, 1961), pp. 110.
14. Adrian C. Mayer, *Caste and Kinship in Central India* (Berkeley & Loss Angeles, University of California Press, 1960) pp. 219-223.
15. Jyotirmayee Sarma, 'Formal and Informal Relations in the Hindu Joint Household of Bengal', *Man in India,* 31, 1951, p. 54.
16. William Z. Rowe, 'The Marriage Network and Structural Change in North-India Community,' *Southwestern Journal of Anthropology,* 16, p. 304.
17. Leigh Minturn, Leigh and Hitchcock John T., *The Rajputs of Khalapur,* Vol. 3, Six Cultures Series (London, John Wiley Sons, 1963).
18. Leigh Minturn and Lambert, William W., *Mothers of Six Cultures* (New York, John Wiley & Sons, 1964), p. 234.
19. G. Morris Carstairs, *The Twice Born. A Study of High Caste Hindus* (London, The Hogerth Press, 1957), p. 71.
20. Louis Dumont, 'Marriage in India'. The Present State of the Question', *Contributions to Indian Sociology,* Vol. 5, 1961, p. 84.
21. Ralph W. Nicholas, 'Factions: A Comparative Analysis' in eds, Max Gluckman and Fred Eggan, *Political Systems and the Distribution of Power* (London, Tavistock Publications, A.S.A. Monograph No. 2, 1965).
22. William McCormarck, 'Sister's Daughter's Marriage in a Mysore Village', *Man in India,* vol. 38, 1958, pp. 44-46.
23. Promilla Kapoor, *Marriage and the Working Woman in India* (Delhi, Vikas Publications, 1971).
24. Wiser, William H. and Charlotte Viall Wiser, *Behind the Mudwalls* (Berkeley Los Angeles, University of California, 1963).
25. S.C. Dube, *Indian Village* (Delhi Ithaec, New York, Cornell University Press, 1955).
26. Alan Beals, *Crime and Conflict in some South Indian Villages* (Mimeographed, 1965).
27. Adrian C. Mayer, *Caste and Kinship in Central India* (Berkeley and Los Angles, 1960), pp. 225—227.
28. Edward B. Harnerd, 'Spirit Possession and Social Structure' in ed, Bala Ratnam, *Anthropology on the March* (Madras, the Book Centre, 1963), pp. 171-173.
29. Edwin D. Driver, *Differential Fertility in Central India* (Princeton, Princeton University Press, 1963) p. 41.
30. Leigh Minturn and Hitchcock, John H., 'The Rajputs of Khalapur' in ed., B.B. Whiting, *Six Cultures, Studies of Child Rearing,* (London, John Wiley & Sons, 1963).
31. Morris E. Opler, 'Spirit Possession in Rural area of Northern India', in ed. W.A. Lessa, and Vogt, E.Z., *Reader in Comparative Religion,* (Evenston, Row Peterson, 1958), p. 561.
32. Rambai Ranade, *Himself, The Autobiography of a Hindu Lady,* translated from original Marathi Language, by Katherine van Akin Gates. (New York, Longmans, Green & Co. 1938) pp. 20-21.
33. Irawati Karve, Deccan College, 1965, Monograph Series 11, pp. 135-136.

34. Jyotirmayee Sarma, 'Formal and Informal Relations in the Hindu Joint Household of Bengal', *Man in India*, 31, 1951, pp. 57, 67.
35. Irawati Karve, *Kinship Organization in India*, Deccan Collage Monograph Series No. 11, (Poona, Deccan Collage, 1953), p. 134.
36. S.C. Dube, *Indian Village,* (Ithaca, New York Cornell University Press, 1955) p.155.
37. Tadashi, Fukutate, Ouchi Trutomu, and Nakane, Chie, *The Socio-economic Structure* (Tokyo, Institute of Asian Economic Affairs, 1964) pp. 43-44.
38. Agehananda Bharati, *The Decline of Teknonymy: Changing Pattern of Husband-wife Appellation in India,* Mimeographed, p. 12.
39. A.C. Mayer, *Caste and Kinship in Central India* (Berkeley, Los Angeles, University of California Press, 1960).
40. Morris Opler, "Spirit Possession in A Rural Area of Northern India" in eds, W.A. Lesa and Vogt, E.Z., *Reader in Comparative Religion* (Evanston, Raw, Peterson, 1958), pp. 553-566.

6

ROLE EXPECTATIONS, ROLE OBLIGATIONS AND ROLE DISCHARGE IN THE URBAN HINDU FAMILY AND CHANGE

All of us in the world fulfil some role in one time of other in our life time. These roles are often different in nature and expect from us a different form of role discharge according to a particular life situation. The roles vary not only in nature from among persons having different social status in the social or family group, but also in their expected functions in different periods of life of the same person. With this expected role discharge, there become associated some related role obligations. Role is a set of conditions calling for a particular action. Roles in the family are an integrated set of our actions discharged in response to meeting certain family expectations and obligations which are closely connected with our rights, duties and special privileges in the family. All our performances in meeting different obligations of family ultimately form a part of our family roles.

Role set comprises of three things: role obligations, role taking and role playing. The first two are the formative processes of role while the third is the process of actual or frictional role discharge. All the three things in their "integrated whole" make the total function of family effective and meaningful.

Roles are always related to a status, the two are understandable in reference to each other. There can be role without its actor having some definite social status. Role and status thus go together and are inseparable. Roles are knit together in a larger circle of their operation which is called a group or unit. Each role is created to meet certain situations or demands or social behaviour; they get associated to a particular status which is endowed with certain responsibilities, thus it calls for a complete attention to ensure an optimum discharge. The first aspect of role is formed here.

No sooner these roles are set in a social unit like family, certain expectations are raised in regard to their discharge, and the actor is expected to play some definite, often predefined role here. And the second aspect or role, the "role expectation" gets formed here. With the functional discharge of the roles in accordance with their related expectations, the actual process of role playing starts here and becomes one of the most cognizant forms of social behaviour.

'Role is a social concept implying a relationship between ego and alter, between self and at least one other person. The delineation of any role implies the existence of at least one other role in a relation to complementary responses' (Ogburn and Nimkoff: 1947).

The basic conceptual units of the role-theory according to Ogburn and Nimkoff are (i) the role, which is the unit of culture; (ii) the position (status) the unit of society and (iii) the self, the unit of personality. Reciprocal action occurs between persons in terms of roles, and there is an interaction of role and self, contemporary role theory regards human conduct as the product of the interaction of role and self.

This appears to be basically a social-psychological approach to the process of role in society. It provides a better understanding in the whole phenomenon of social life. The "theory of role" provides own integrated approach to the understanding of social behaviour and intra-personal and inter-personal relationships in the family circle.

It assumes that a certain role always remains in operation and even where it is in its latent form its function is not lost. The role playing can thus be assessed both in its present and historical perspectives.

Merton remarks in the context of family role that it is the family which is a major transmission belt for the discussion of cultural standards to the oncoming generation. "But what has until lately been overlooked is that the family largely transmits that portion of the culture accessible to the social stratum and groups in which the parents find themselves. It is, therefore, a mechanism for disciplining the child in terms of the cultural goals and mores, which are characteristic of this narrow range of groups. Nor is the socialization confined to direct training ad disciplining. The process is, at least, in part, inadvertent. Quite apart from direct administration of rewards and punishments, the child is exposed to social prototypes in the witnessed daily behaviour and casual conversations of parents. Not infrequently, children detect and incorporate cultural uniformities even when these remain implicit and have not been reduced to rule."[1]

Roles in the family are set according to the large cultural traditions which assign a definite responsibility to a particular member of the family and expect a minimum behaviour from him or her in response to these expectations. Roles are thus culturally ingrained in the minds of children who are trained accordingly to ensure their minimum fulfilment and they are linked to certain cultural goals and cultural aspirations. The family expects an optimum discharge of these assigned roles from the members and attributes rewarding and punitive actions in accordance with the norms and the degree of their satisfaction. The family as an institution in action may sometime even develop apathy or antipathy, if these expectations are not satisfied for a long time, or if a particular member remains indifferent to the discharge of his expected role.

Failure of role discharge on account of physical disability or financial hardship were condoned by joint family and adjustments were made. On the other hand such members who were unable to discharge their expected role because of these conditions were helped out of their difficulty in such circumstances. This joint family role is gradually disappearing with the break up of joint family structure and formation of individual families in towns and metropolises. In the joint family, because of its large composition, members could make allowances and adjustments within its structure. Certain other members of family either voluntarily offered themselves to discharge these roles, or were asked by the head of the family to discharge these failing roles. This situation is now getting lost in the new situation an individual family set up which has already a tight charter of the duties for its a few members.

Besides some new situations have also brought a change in the role discharge. A daughter in the traditional Hindu family was entrusted the role of caring and tendering of young children. She was expected to bathe and dress the young children. She was expected to take them out for play and stroll. Besides, she was also expected to assist the mother or sister-in-law in the kitchen and other domestic duties like embroidery and knitting and decorating the house. These roles are still expected from the daughter who is going to school or college and who subsequently takes up a job. The busy hours of her new career do not leave anytime for these expected roles; moreover, a girl's inclination and interest in these family duties also get gradually lost. She finds them drab, uninteresting and unrewarding. These roles left by the daughter are now distributed among some other members of the family. Her mother normally assumes the whole responsibility of kitchen-duties, and her younger sister or an employed main servant takes up other domestic jobs. But those which cannot be shared by either are left unattended. The role discharge in a new set up has thus two or three new possibilities of its expression; either it gets discharged by some other members having a particular status in the family and from whom it is most expected of or it is divided among different members of the family often among members of the same age group. Or a third situation may arise in the situation that the particular members may partly discharge it and leave the rest to others. Sometimes if the role is not very important, it may even be left unattended for sometime. The roles set by cultural tradition are not tolerated for their total failure, they may be allowed certain concessions and allowances but their complete "writing off" is not possible.

Often it happens that a role does not have its justification in the new set up. Looking after the old and the aged has been an important role for a housewife and daughter-in-law in traditional Hindu family. It has also been a prescribed role for son in a joint family in the native place or where two generations are living together. This role expectation and role discharge still persists in native environment where joint families are found and where two generations are living together. It does not have any functional significance in a nuclear family in an urban environment, where parents are normally not residing with the couple. It gets limited in a small joint family living in an urban area, where parents may be living with the son, but where time is so an important factor in determining most of human behaviour. It cannot be said that this role has lost its utility or that it has been lost in oblivion because of the absence of old environment and setting in of new circumstances.

What appears more probable here is that the role which was so potent in a joint family set up and atmosphere becomes dormant in the new environment.

If the atmosphere would have slightly changed, this role could be conditioned to the changed environment, but since the original cultural atmosphere is now practically absent in new environment, the role becomes latent, it can express itself again as soon as that environment becomes available again. A role in thus seldom lost. It may remain inactive or in latent form, according to the responding situation, so far as the original situation which caused its certain is not totally lost to the culture.

Norms of discipline, decorum, sobriety, truthfulness, noble behaviour, honesty, basic integrity, and good nature are now more or less questioned by the younger generation. These norms now do not get that absolute approval that they used to get some generations ago. The children in the joint family set up were taught strongly to adopt these norms and values some three or four generations ago. But this cultural atmosphere and tradition are now being lost in the individual urban family. The stresses of urban life and hard economy are pressing hard on the urban family. The members in the individual small joint family are now more occupied with hard struggle to sustain their family. A sense of insecurity surrounds them more. Surrounded by such practical factors, they develop a questioning attitude towards these norms and values. They do not now accept things as they are preached or idealized, but they wish to accept them as they actually occur; they have started cross-examining them crucially at their very roots.

A kind of conflict between the old and new generations seems to have been developing during past few decades. It has been generating more during the past one decade.

This has given rise to a state of utter restlessness and dissatisfaction among the members of two generations and the two have been finding to be living at a disparity at many levels of thinking or acting. It has alarmed the elder generation against the indiscriminate and absolute use of authority and has introduced a cautionary approach.

The educated fathers in the urban families are now very much alive to a kind of growing need to understand the younger generation in their emotional background and expressive demands of their personality. They seem to be understanding that authority, power of force have very limited effect in a modern society now, where younger generations are asserting their rights and privileges and are in a constant state or revolt against authoritarianism in the family. The only way to deal with them, as psychological knowledge also suggests, is to approach them more sympathetically and affectionately, give them maximum tolerance and free expression. With this realization, the emphasis on companionship approach is being made in the contemporary urban Hindu family, more specially in the individual or nuclear family.

The educated fathers are not realizing that this does not only make a better, congenial approach to the younger generation but it also builds up better personalities. They find it a good investment for future besides reassuring them about a peaceful and congenial atmosphere at home, which prevents those bickerings, bitings, and tensions which were the natural order of day in the traditional joint family under an oppressive atmosphere of the authoritative head. It is a kind of adjustment to the new demand and strains of the modernizing society that the father's generation is now prompted to accept.

The change in the roles of the modern Hindu family has come in several ways. One important way is through the difference marked in expected roles and the actual role-discharge, the other is by marked conflicts, arising in the discharge of the different roles; sometimes the same role in family is discharged by people of different status and situation of conflict arises very often between these different people. Sometimes there is an overlapping of roles which causes this conflict. Otherwise too, there is a strange situation of role conflict which makes various role-actors to stand in conflict with each other.

Role and Status

The concept of role and status is helpful in understanding a functional family, that is to say a family in its operational behaviour in relation to its different roles, and intra-personal and inter-personal relationships. I have, therefore, used it in an analytical sense, which may help most systematically.

Role and status are the inter-related concepts. Status is usually defined as the rank or position of an individual in a group or of a group in relation to other groups. Some sociologists use the term "position" in preference to status. Role refers to the behaviour of one who occupies a certain status. Children occupy a status usually subordinate to adults and are expected to show some degree of deference to the adult authority. Soldiers occupy a status different from that of civilians, and their role calls for risks and duties which the general populace is not expected to bear; women have a different status from men; their role calls for "feminine" behaviour, whereas men's role calls for "masculine" behaviour and each is characterised by a particular kind of behaviour. Each person may occupy a number of statuses and be expected to perform the roles appropriate to them. In a sense, "status" and "role" are two interpretations for the same phenomena. 'A status is a set of privileges and duties, a role is the acting out of duties and privileges.'[2]

Status may denote slightly different meanings in different cultures, but broadly it indicates the position acquired by birth, being a member of a particular social group, or it can be ascribed to a person with certain position to enable him to discharge certain roles. Normally, members of a family group first acquire a definite status in the family such, as son and daughters, as other siblings are born in the family, they also acquire the status of an elder brother or elder daughter to their youngsters. As they grow in age and are sent to education, they acquire the status of a student in school and college, and status of a friend to their classmates, and other introductions made in society. When sons get into service and start earning they get an ascribed status of a particular occupation in which they get in, i.e., of a teacher, lecturer, engineer, doctor or research worker in the associated office or institution, while within the family organization, he may normally be ascribed the socio-economic status of "earner".

Ralph Linton (1936) speaking about the social roles has noted that statuses are of two sorts: those ascribed to us by our society, irrespective of individual qualities or efforts, and those which we achieve through our own efforts.

Ascribed Status and Role

Roles are prescribed by society to its people in order to let them function properly. The social performances are made effective and better organized by ascribing different responsibilities to different persons. The common bases devised for ascribing status are sex and age.

The simplest way to ensure the performance in a given society is to parcel most of the routine work of the society into a series of *ascribed* roles and socialize people to accept and fill their ascribed roles. Since role training must begin at early childhood, ascribed roles, therefore, must be assigned according to some criteria which can be known in advance. Sex and age are universally used as a basis of role prescription; race, nationality, social class and religion are also used in many societies.

The concept of role implies a set of expectations, both of one's own behaviour and of the reciprocal behaviour by other people in the situation. Whether a new role is taken on a pretended basis or as a genuine result of acquiring a new status, the person is forced to analyse the attitudes and behaviour of himself and of those about him (Turner; 1956).

The change in the role according to a changed status can be explained by way of an example from the family. The married woman bears a different status from that of the single girl, for her role becomes different and in many ways she will seem a different personality. Occupational roles may also produce personality changes, so that without knowing a person's occupation we may say that he "acts like" a teacher, a farmer, a businessman, or a minister. Personality and role have a reciprocal relationship in the sense that certain personal characteristics which favour or hinder the playing of social roles, while social roles in turn develop the personal characteristics required. The extrovert, for instance, is a personality type who may find it easy to adjust to the role of salesman, while conversely, the daily routine of the salesman helps to develop an extroverted type of personality (Horton and Hunt: 1968). The family roles are assigned to both, the born status and the ascribed status.

Achieved Status and Role

As different from ascribed status and role there are achieved status and role. A social position which is secured through individual choice, effort and competition is known as *achieved status.* Just as each person occupies a number of ascribed statuses, assigned without regard to individuality, ability or preference, so he also occupies a number of achieved statuses which are secured through his ability, performance, and possibly good or ill fortune (Horton and Hunt: 1968). The difference between the two can be marked by reference to an example from the family. Being male is an "ascribed status", it is determined at birth, either one is a male or he is not. There is no choice involved here. But being a husband in his future life is an "achieved status", it does not naturally come forth by one's just being a male. It depends upon his making a deliberate choice in his youth. Where he decides to marry a particular girl of his choice with whom he then unites to form a family. He achieves a definite status of husband with which certain other roles also get subsequently associated. Similarly, when a man takes up a job out of his own choice, or because of necessity to maintain himself, and becomes professor, doctor or researcher, he assumes the role related to his profession to which one is not born as in his profession; one achieves it by one's own talent, choice, industry, perseverance or action. And with this ascribed status, one starts discharging his expected role or a series of roles in his profession. In traditional societies like the Hindu society as described in classical literature most statuses are ascribed, with one's occupation and general social standing determined at birth. Industrialized societies have a greater range of occupations, they require a greater mobility of labour and allow greater scope for the individual to change his status through his own efforts.

Ascribed and achieved statuses are basically different yet they interact with each other and may overlap. Thus it is often easier for one with the ascribed status of a male to reach to the highest position of President of India though achievement possibilities are now becoming equal for both. Ogburn and Nimkoff (1947) suggest that when functions in various social systems are publicly recognised and appreciated, they are called "roles". Each interacting individual in a social system has a role or several roles to perform.

Some sociologists and social psychologists have referred to the concept of "role taking" in their discussion of socialization and personality formation of the child. Ogburn and Nimkoff (1947) in this context say, "The child starts life as a biological organism with certain potentialities for learning in the presence of certain agents of socialization who serve as cultural models. The most prominent of these are parents, siblings, friends, and teachers. Those with whom the individual becomes identified become his reference groups, the sources of his perceptions and values. In the process of role taking, the person undertakes to learn to anticipate the responses of others who are implicated with him in social situation. He aims to acquire insight into the behaviour of others. In the process of role-taking, the person also develops a self, a concept of personal identity, an answer to the question "who am I?" The process of socialization orders behaviour, inculcates basic discipline, establishes aspirations and furnishes skills. Socialisation occurs at both the conscious and the unconscious levels.[3]

Role Taking and Role Paying

The theory of role assumes two more aspects in the process of role discharge. In the interests of clarity, a distinction needs to be made between the two, the role-taking, and the role-playing. Some sociologists prefer to employ a third concept, "playing at a role". According to this usage, *role-playing* refers to the performance of one's own roles in a given set up or situation. *Role-taking* is putting oneself in the position of another person or actor playing at role. I prefer to use specifically the concept of "role-playing" in this manner. Role-taking for my purpose of discussion would mean taking up such roles of others by an individual which are not socially or conventionally ascribed to that person, but which he adopts either out of his own will or in order to make circumstantial adjustments (Table 6.1).

Roles are taken when they are not one's own, as with the actor on the stage, or the child when he undertakes to unite with his elders. But both the actor and the child have roles of their own, which they fill when they are not "acting" and which consist of an organised set of socially expected patterns of behaviour. Role-taking may be purely for amusement or for better understanding of another's role, or in anticipation of playing that role at a later time. Role-taking may be incorporated in role-playing. This may be done either quite explicitly as in the case of the actor whom we expect to act out the roles of others, or more deviously by those who take other roles like the young college instructor who in the classroom imitates a favoured teacher of his own."[4]

Role Differentiation

One more concept that needs a little exemplification, as it will be used in this study is *role differentiation.* Among the types of role found in human society, two of the more basic ones are the *instrumental* and the *expressive roles.* The former refers to the "performance of tasks" and latter to "the manifestation of sentiment". Generally speaking, the roles of men are organised more largely than those of women around instrumental roles, and the roles of women more largely around expressive roles. This is what we mean when we say men are mainly the bread winners and women chiefly the source of affection. In traditional Hindu family, the role of head of the household has been invariably ascribed to the eldest man in the family as the society has been organised on patriarchal lines from the very beginning. And this can be called the *instrumental role.* Parallel to this the eldest woman in the house was considered to be the sole repository of all affection and sentiments. She was usually the grand mother in a joint family, and sometimes father's elder sister, a woman necessarily belonging to the elder generation than to the conjugal family group or to a parallel generation. This role was organised around the expressive role of an otherhood.

TABLE 6.1: Pattern Value of the Family — Adherence to Basic Values

Type of family/ education Groups		No. of families	No. of families where some basic values govern the moral code & behaviour of family	No. of families where there basic values are still important	No. of families where basic values are still persistent in the family: Solidarity	Discipline and decorum	Chastity among girls	Development of moral character	Remarks
1		2	3	4	5	6	7	8	9
1. Joint Family	1	5	5	5	5	5	5	5	5
	2	3	2	2	1	2	2	2	2
	3	3	3	3	2	3	2	3	3
	4	6	6	6	3	6	5	6	5
	NR		1	1					
Total		17	17	17	11	16	14	16	15
2. Small Joint	1	6	3	3	2	3	3	3	3
	2	11	10	10	9	10	9	9	9
	3	13	13	13	10	10	10	11	10
	4	19	18	18	14	17	16	16	15
	NR	—	3	3	2				
Total		49	47	47	37	40	38	39	37
3. Individual	1	15	15	15	13	13	12	12	13
	2	28	28	28	22	25	20	26	26
	3	52	49	49	37	41	41	42	43
	4	61	59	59	59	48	52	52	52
	NR	—	5	7	7				
Total		156	156	156	127	131	125	132	134

Role-differentiation for our purpose of reference in the present study would mean the basic differentiation organised on the basis of sex. Role expected from wife is naturally different from role expected from husband and role of daughter is obviously different from role of son. My reference to this concept of role differentiation will denote this differentiation on the basis of age and sex (Table 6.2).

Role Conflicts

In the functional order of the roles, different roles are exercised by different members, but sometimes a particular role is exercised by different persons in a social system. A situation of conflict is likely to emerge in such circumstances which may threaten or retard the normal functioning of the role. Besides this, the multiplicity of roles in that social system causes some conflicts between different actors of roles. These conflicts give rise to several problems of adjustment. The problem of adjustment is complicated for most of us by virtue of the fact we have not just one role to perform in our family, but have rather two or three roles at a time in reference to the intra-personal relationship in the family groups and in response to the expectations of the family. Sometimes, some roles are performed by more than one member of family, and this causes "an overlapping of roles". This situation also introduces the possibility of a role conflict. For example, every man is first a son to his parents and at some later time he also becomes a lover to his beloved, and if he marries her, he combines this role and starts playing the role of husband. Of if he marries another woman, he leaves his former role and now enters into a role obligation with this woman whom he calls his wife and discharges towards her/his role of husband and companion concurrently. He can then be a friend to his other several friends, even in his wider social circle, which may include sometimes girl friends too. These roles simultaneously operate and do not come in conflict with each other unless understanding breaks off, or some crisis arises.

Role conflict can arise in the discharge of different roles, but it is often temporary. The role conflict does not ordinarily lead to lasting maladjustments. Were it not so, society would have been in a state of chronic disorder. But often it so happens in social process as role conflicts between members of different status arise that they are either resolved over sometime or get adjusted to the new developing situation for there are many role conflicts, especially in a complex and dynamic

TABLE 6.2: Opinions Regarding Importance of Different Values: Ethical, Social and Family Values

Type of family/ Education Groups		No. of families	No. of families where joint family is considered a value-ideal	No. of families where education is regarded as a cherished value	No. of families where economic superiority is considered a cherished value.	No. of families where aspiration by an individual encouraged as a value	No. of families where initiative & individualing encouraged individual
1		2	3	4	5	6	7
Joint Family							
	1	5	5	5	3	4	3
	2	3	3	2	1	2	1
	3	3	3	3	2	2	—
	4	6	6	6	4	6	5
	NR	—	—	1	1	2	4
Total		17	17	17	11	16	13
Small Joint Family	1	6	4	5	5	4	2
	2	11	8	9	3	6	3
	3	13	10	13	4	5	3
	4	19	10	16	10	13	8
	NR	—	6	5	6	8	11
Total		49	38	48	28	36	27
Individual Family	1	15	7	13	6	12	9
	2	28	12	24	16	20	12
	3	52	23	47	24	41	15
	4	61	23	54	18	46	18
	NR	—	29	14	20	23	38
Total		156	94	152	84	142	92

TABLE 6.2 *Contd.*

No. of families where initiative is encouraged and not considered harmful	No. of families where parental generation feels that choice in regard to there careers should be given to young	Reasons for changing values in the families due to modern strains/conditions			
		Modern living	Education	Others	Not answered
8	9	10	11	12	13
3	5	3	3	1	—
1	2	—	—	—	—
2	2	—	—	—	—
2	2	2	2	1	1
5	5	4	4	—	—
3	1				
14	15	9	9	2	1
5	4	3	—	1	1
6	9	3	—	—	3
8	13	7	1	2	3
13	14	13	—	—	6
12	7	—	—	—	—
44	47	26	1	3	13
12	14	4	1	—	2
13	18	7	—	2	8
36	44	9	2	20	4
41	47	5	—	16	9
33	18	—	—	—	
135	141	25	3	38	23

society. The society, therefore, works out several methods to relinquish one of the two conflicting roles. A son in a family when he finds that there is a continuing conflict between his brothers to win over maximum affection of their mother who want to get some material gains out of her affection, may feel resigned to his role of "a devoted and dutiful son", and may just continue to discharge his role of son in this most ordinarily way. Here, there is no difference in his role of son, but here silently arises the difference in intensity of the role of son and in his normally expected role.

A judge who finds that he has been assigned a case in which he has some stake if he takes it and may disqualify himself as an honest and true judge may seek avoidance. A doctor according to the medical ethics is not expected to treat a member of his own family.

A second method for resolving role conflicts is to retain both roles but to compartmentalise and rationalise them individually. This is usually accomplished by a system of priorities, either of time to or of values. Thus one, may from 9 a.m. to 5 p.m. be highly competitive and self-seeking in his role as a senior administrative officer or business executive, and highly cooperative and altruistic the rest of the time in his role of the father towards his children and role of husband companion towards his wife and towards his children when he may act as a very considerate and affectionate father. Finally he may try to moderate the demands of each role while trying to meet both the roles.

This relates to role conflicts in discharging two or more divergent roles by the same role actor. There is another type of conflict which involves two or more aspects of the same role being discharged by an individual. This can be better illustrated by reference to Shakespeare's play *Hamlet*. Hamlet, a Prince of Denmark plays several roles in the drama but in discharging his one prominent role of son he combines two different aspects. One is his love for his mother as a son, the other is his role of duty to his deceased father, who has been murdered by his uncle, Cladius, and his mother, Gertrude under a conspiracy. Hamlet was torn between his personal duty towards his father and his love for his mother. The play is especially interesting as a literary source for studying "role behaviour". Hamlet entertains the king with a pageant in which he hopes "to prick the conscience of the king by a re-enactment of what is now called socio-drama. To protect himself, Hamlet also pretends madness. This is an illustrated example of "playing at a role" and not of actual "role-taking".

The roles in the family are always liable for small changes and minor adjustments as different persons often start playing some roles other than their own, either out of their own will or in meeting expectations of other members of the family group or by pressure of circumstances. Sometimes roles left by departure of some persons have to be taken up by other members. A girl in this family usually looks after the children and assists her mother in domestic work. On her marriage she leaves her parental family and enters her husband's family. Roles left by her in the family are taken up by her brother's wife. Similarly she in her husband's family assumes those roles which had been left by her sister-in-law (husband's sister).

Such changes always occur in every family and time-to-time adjustments are made. Besides these situational changes also cause some changes in expected roles of family, when families move to urban areas, certain new roles which were not necessary in native place arise and have to be adopted in the new order. These changes in roles are sometimes more prominent and sometimes less but they do effect the function of the family. It is through such changing roles in the urban Hindu family that the different trends of changes in the family are being marked and with which I am specially concerned in the present work. I shall, therefore, analyse these in the rest of this work. To provide the base line for assessment of changes in an urban context, this reference to the traditional role pattern in the Hindu family has been rather necessary.

Role Expectations, Role Obligations and Role Discharge in the Urban Hindu Family of Bhopal

With this theoretical background of status and role in the universal Hindu family, I wanted to determine my canvas of Urban Hindu family of Bhopal, how different principal roles of family members operate in view of their respective expected behaviour, that is to say in other words, how the roles of the head of the family, husband and wife, father and mother, son and daughter and brother and sister are discharged in the urban family. The role of head of household combines in itself authoritative status, hence it has been called here 'role of authority'. It usually combines in itself the role of earner in a joint household, often in a small joint household, and always in an individual household.

His wife usually an elderly lady has a tender and an affectionate attitude and approach towards children, hence it has been called the 'role of sentiments'. Usually father's mother or an elderly lady in the family in her absence discharges this role of sentiments in a joint and small joint household, but in an individual family this role is usually discharged concurrently by wife of the earner husband.

Role of husband has been examined from the point of view of an "earning husband" towards his wife-earner. This was in relation to the role of a head. Sometimes an earner-husband is also a co-earner husband.

The role of husband also includes here the role of father towards his children, and his basic approach towards him in relation to his wife. How far the husband in the urban family takes interest in rearing and education of his children. Whether the authority and discretion is concentrated in him about his children's career or does he share it with his wife. These two aspects have been the principal concern of my study. I have assessed whether there has been marked a change in father's basic attitude towards his children, and whether it is now being made more a role of companionship and friendly approach than one of authority as it used to be till a few decades ago and which is still marked among the less educated urban and rural families.

The role of wife has been examined both in relation to her obligations towards her husband as well as towards her children, and her role was examined in two different situations, where she was co-earner as well as a housewife, and when she was only a dependent housewife. It has also been assessed whether the educated wife is now assuming some new roles mainly towards her in her new home.

The data have been analysed in a way so that it may give some typical and cross-variable results to our enquiry in view of the hypothesis in the background. Income with type of family and earner's status were made variables in one situation. Table 6.3 presents this analysis.

Family Obligations Felt and Earners in Joint Family

Of 17 joint households, only one was found in the income range of Rs. 500 and below, 10 were found in the income range of Rs. 501 to Rs. 1000 and 6 in the income range of Rs. 100 and above.

In the first income range which had only one joint family, son was found to be the only earner. He accorded his consent to the enquiry whether members of family feel a joint responsibility for maintaining the family. He also affirmed that he felt it his obligation to maintain the

TABLE 6.3: Family Obligations Felt by Type of Family and Number of Earners

Type of family/ Income Gropups		No. of families	Number of earners in the family: Head of house-hold	Wife	Brother	Son	Daughter	Sister	Daughter	No. of families where all members feel joint responsibility for maintenance of family	No. of families where members feel it their obligations to maintain solidarity of the family	No. of families feel concerned about the prestige of the family	No. of families where bonds of brotherhood/or common blood and kinship bind then together
1		2	3	4	5	6	7	8	9	10	11	12	13
1. Joint family	1	1				1				1	1	1	1
	2	10	10	2	13	4				10	8	9	8
	3	6	6	3	9	9			2	6	3	6	5
	*NR											1	2
Total		17	16	5	22	14			2	17	12	17	14

TABLE 6.3 *Contd.*

1		2	3	4	5	6	7	8	9	10	11	12	13
2. Small	1	1	1		1					1	1	1	
Joint	2	30	27	7	5	6	2	2	—	24	18	24	22
family	3	18	18	11	4	8	—	1	2	16	13	16	16
	NR									4	5	5	6
Total		49	46	18	10	14	2	3	2	45	37	46	44
3. Indi-	1	11	10							9	2	4	3
vidual	2	70	70	13	2	4				48	27	25	41
family	3	75	75	20	5	8	1	1		56	25	29	30
	NR									22	86	79	72
Total		156	155	33	7	12	3	1		135	140	137	146
(Wife and other members' % to Head of House-hold as earner)				(21.15)	(4.49)	(7.69)	(1.92)	(0.84)					

NR: Not responded. Question numbers 11, 12, and 13 were meant for assessing Joint Family ties in the family.

solidarity of joint family. He also felt concerned about the prestige of the family and believed in strengthening the bonds of brotherhood by believing that bonds of common blood and kinship bind them together.

Ten families belonged to the income range of Rs. 501 to Rs. 1,000. These 10 families had a head of household who was an earner as well as had husband's status in the family. This group of 10 joint families had 9 wives, 13 brothers and 4 sons as co-earners. All these believed that members of the family should feel joint responsibility for the maintenance of family. Eight out of these 10 households felt it their obligation to maintain solidarity of the family. Nine felt concern about the prestige of the family and 8 believed in family bonds of brotherhood, blood and kinship.

The third income group, i.e. Rs. 1000 and above had 6 joint families. All these 6 had an earning head of household and had besides the heads, 3 wives, 9 brothers, and 9 sons, and 2 daughters-in-laws as co-earners in the family. All these 6 joint households believed that family members should feel joint responsibility for maintenance of family. Three out of 6 households felt it their obligation to maintain solidarity of the family.

All 6, however, felt concerned about the prestige of the family. Five households believed in family bonds of brotherhood, blood and kinship.

This suggests that the total 17 joint households had 16 heads of households who were earners, besides these had one son who was the only earner in the household but did not classify himself as earner. These households had 5 wives,. 22 brothers, 14 sons, 2 daughters-in-law as co-earners. All the 17 households believed that family members should feel joint responsibility in such matters. Twelve felt it their obligation to maintain a solidarity of the family, 16 felt concerned about the prestige of the family, and 14 believed in bonds of brotherhood, common blood and kinship.

This data of joint family when compared to data of small joint family and individual family may reveal some analytical findings.

Family Obligations Felt and Earners in Small Joint Family

There were 49 small joint families in our sample of urban Bhopal. Of these 49 families, only one fell in the income group of Rs. 500 and below, 30 fell in the middle income group of Rs. 501 to Rs. 1000 and 18 fell in the upper income group of Rs. 1000 and above.

The only family in the income group of Rs. 500 and below had an earning head of household who was assisted by his brother as co-earner. This family believed that all members of family should feel joint responsibility for maintenance of family. The family also believed that it should be members' obligation to maintain the solidarity of the family, and that members should feel concerned about the prestige of the family.

But this family did not support the idea that bonds of brotherhood or of common blood and kinship should bind them together.

Of the 30 small joint households group of Rs. 501 to Rs. 1,000 who fell in the middle income, 27 had heads of households as main earners, with 7 wives, 5 brothers, 6 sons, 2 daughters and 2 sisters, as co-earners or sub-earners. Twenty-four of these 30 families, felt that members should feel joint responsibility for maintenance of family, 18 felt that members should feel concern about the prestige of the family, and 22 families believed in bonds of brotherhood, common blood and kinship.

Those belonging to the upper income group of Rs. 1,000 and above were 18. All these 18 had heads of households as main earners, and 11 had wives as co-earners, 4 had brothers and 8 had sons, one had sister and 2 had daughters-in-law as co-earners and/or sub-earners.

Sixteen of these small joint families believed that members should feel joint responsibility for maintenance of family, 13 families believed that members should feel it their obligation to maintain solidarity of the family, 16 felt that members should feel concerned about the prestige of the family, 16 said that bonds of brotherhood, common blood and kinship should prevail in the family.

Thus, it is seen that among 49 small joint households which fell in income groups ranging from Rs. 500 p.m. and below to Rs. 1,000 per month and above, as many as 46 had heads of households as main earners, 18 had wives as co-earners, 9 had brothers, 14 had sons, 9 had daughters, 3 had sisters, and 2 daughters-in-law had as co-earners or sub-earners in the family. Fourty-five of the small joint families believed that all members should feel joint responsibility for maintenance of the family, 37 believed that members should feel it their obligation to maintain solidarity of the family. Fourty-seven believed that members should feel concerned about the prestige of the family, and 44 expressed that bonds of brotherhood or of common blood and kinship should bind them together.

Individual Family

The total number of individual families were found much more than even the total of joint family and small joint family. These were 156, and their distribution in the three income groups was as follows : Lower income group of Rs. 500 and below 11; Middle income group of Rs. 501 to Rs. 1000 70, and upper income group of Rs. 1,000 and above 75.

Among the 11 households of lower income group 10 had heads of households as main earners and 2 had daughters as co-earners, besides the head of household, 9 of these families believed that all members should feel joint responsibility for maintenance of family, 2 felt that members should feel it their obligation to maintain solidarity of the family, 4 felt that members should feel concerned about the prestige of the family and 3 felt that bonds of brotherhood, common blood and kinship should bind members of family together.

Of the 70 individual families who fell in the middle income group of Rs. 501 to Rs. 1,000, all had heads of households as main earners, and 13 had wives as co-earners. Besides, 2 had brothers, and 4 had sons as co-earners of sub-earners.

Fourty-eight families out of 70 individual families believed that all members should feel joint responsibility for maintenance of the family, 27 believed that members should feel it their obligation to maintain solidarity of the family, 25 felt that members should feel concerned about the prestige of the family and 41 said that bonds of brotherhood and common blood and kinship should prevail among family members.

The largest number of individual families, 75, belonged to the upper income group Rs. 1,000 and above. All these 75 individual families had their heads of households as main earners, and 20 had wives as co-earners. Besides 5 had brothers, and 8 had sons, one had daughter and one had sister as co-earners.

Of these 75 individual families, 55 believed that all members should feel joint responsibility for maintenance of family, 25 believed that members should feel it their obligation to maintain solidarity of the family, 29 believed that members should feel concerned about the prestige of the family and 30 felt that bonds of brotherhood, common blood and kinship should bind them together.

When we take an overall view of the individual family's analysis in the table, we find that among total 156 individual households, 155 had heads of households as earners, 33 had wives as co-earners and 7 had brothers, 12 had sons, 3 had daughters and one had sister as co-earners and/or sub-earners.

Of the 156 individual households, 135 families believed that all members should feel it their obligation to maintain solidarity of the family, 140 believed that members should feel it their obligation to maintain solidarity of the family, 137 believed that members should feel concerned about the prestige of the family and while 146 felt that bonds of brotherhood, common blood, and kinship should bind the family members together.

Opinions Regarding Family Obligations in Different Types of Family

Whereas statements regarding family obligations felt and discharged by members of different types of family were important for my research, opinions of these members which indicated their faith in and ties with joint family, or which otherwise suggested a trend towards individualism were also considered necessary for getting more concrete results. A set of questions was thus asked from the heads of households belonging to different economic strata and type of family, to give such answers as may be representative for the members of his family. The opinion expressed have been correlated to their economic strata and type of family. The related tables give representative picture of the interpreted opinions for each type of family (Table 6.4).

Joint Family

Among the 17 joint families, we find that there is only one family belonging to the lowest income group of Rs. 500 and below. This family expressed the opinion that joint family provides better economic security. The family also expressed the opinion that joint family provides a better training and adjustment in the family and believed that joint family provides a shelter to its members at times of crisis. This indicates that this family had full faith in the joint family and in the efficacy of this system. But this family could not give incidences when help or shelter may have been actually sought from joint family.

The next income group, Rs. 501 to Rs. 1000 had 10 families. All these expressed the opinion that joint family provides them better economic security, but only 8 felt that joint family provides them training and adjustment in the family. But again, all these 10 families

TABLE 6.4: Opinions of Family Heads Regarding Family Obligations

Types of Family/ Income Groups		No. of families	No. of families who feel that joint family provides them better economic security	No. of families who feel that joint family provides them a better training and adjustment in the family	No. of families who feel joint family provides a shelter at times of crises	Occasions on which joint families help was sought by individual				Column 6 to 5 Non-respond to col. 6 to 9
						Unemployment	Transfers	Marriages	Including religious occasions & sickness	
1		2	3	4	5	6	7	8	9	10
1. Joint	1	1	1	1	1					
	2	10	10	8	10					
	3	6	6	5	6					
Total		17	17	14	17					
2. Small Joint	1	1	1	1	1				1	
	2	30	20	1	20			3	6	8
	3	18	16	12	18		1	2	5	2
	NR									
Total		49	42	40	44		1	5	12	10
3. Individual	1	11	4	4	5			1	4	4
	2	70	33	21	43		1	17	32	13
	3	75	26	20	45	3		14	36	15
	NR	—	86	93	34					
Total		156	149	138	127	3	1	32	72	32

expressed the opinion that joint family provides a shelter at times of crises. But this group also did not cite any actual instances from life, such as unemployment, transfer, or marriage, when help from the joint family may have been imperative and was actually sought.

The upper income group of Rs. 1000 and above comprised of 6 families. All these six families expressed the opinion that joint family provides them better economic security, but only 5 of them felt that joint family provides them a better training and adjustment in the family. All six, however, again believed that joint family provides a shelter at times of crisis, though they also did not mention any occasions on which shelter or help may have been sought.

This appears quite interesting that all three economic groups of joint family who expressed the opinion in favour of efficacy of joint family did not themselves have any occasions to cite when they may have actually sought help or support of the joint family. This becomes all the more important when we compare this with two other family groups, the small joint family and the individual family, who mentioned such instances.

Small Joint Family

In our sample of 222 urban families of Bhopal, we had found 49 small joint families who belonged to three different economic classes, that below Rs. 500, that between Rs. 501 to 1000 and that of Rs. 1000 and above.

Of these 49 families, only one small joint family belonged to the first economic class whose income was found below Rs. 500. This one family believed that joint family provides them better economic security and that joint family provides members a better training and adjustment in the family. This family also expressed the opinion that joint family provides a shelter at times of crisis. But this family group did not enlist any such incidences from life where anyone of its member may have actually sought help or support from the joint family. But this family said that it shared joint family obligations during religious occasions and sickness.

The next economic class, ranging between Rs. 501 to Rs. 1000 comprised of 30 small joint families. However, only 20 of these showed a faith in joint family, saying that joint family provides them better economic security, and that joint family provides a shelter at times of crisis, but only 19 felt that joint family provides them a better training and adjustment in the family. Three of these small joint families said in actual life they sought help from joint family, during occasions of marriage, one said that it sought help during transfers and 5 said that help was taken during religious occasions while 8 said it was done during sickness. The third economic group, that is above Rs. 1000 consisted of only 18 families; 16 of these families maintained that joint family provides them better economic security and also that joint family provides a shelter at times of crisis. Only 12 of these 30 families also believed that joint family provides them a better training and adjustment in the family.

As for the actual instances from life they sought help of joint family. One head of household said that his family had sought such help during his transfer, 2 said that their family had sought help during marriage, 5 said that joint family's help was taken during religious occasions and 2 said that such help from joint family was needed during sickness.

Individual Family

In our sample we had 156 individual families. Of these 11 fell in the first and lowest income group, Rs. 500 and below. Out of these 11, only 4 felt that joint family provides a better economic security, and that joint family provides them a better training and adjustment in the family, and 5 families felt that joint family provides them a shelter at times of crisis. Only one of these, however, cited transfer as an occasion on which joint family s help was sought, 4 cited religious occasions and another 4 cited sickness as an actual instance.

The next income group consisted of 70 families, 33 of whom believed that joint family provides them a better economic security, 21 felt that joint family provides them a better training and adjustment in the family. Fourty-three felt that joint family provides a shelter at times of crisis, only 2 cited transfers and 17 cited marriages from their life-time when they had sought joint family's help; 32 cited religious occasions and 13 cited sickness as occasions for such help.

The third economic group,one whose income was found Rs. 1000 and above, consisted of 76 families. 26 of these 76 individual families in this group believed that joint family provides them better economic security 20 of these families felt that joint family provides them a better training and adjustment in the family, and 45 felt that joint family provides a shelter at times of crisis.

As for actual instances from their own life when they may have sought help of joint family, only 14 cited marriage and 15 sickness; 36, however, said that joint family's help was sought on religious occasions.

This suggests that a large number of members of small joint family and individual family who do not now live in joint family, still repose some kind of faith in the efficacy of the joint system and find its opportunity desirable.

Opinions Regarding Preference to Individual Family

Joint family continuity has been a subject of debate in Indian sociology. Desai and others in their studies of the sixth and early seventh decades had tried to prove that though joint family may change its structure as its members move to towns and urban areas and form there their own individual families, joint ties are still maintained and that the members of individual families continue to discharge their joint family obligations. This has been interpreted sometimes of suggest joint family continuity.

Keeping this in view, author had wanted to examine how far people still believe in the continuity of joint family system. Author had invited in his schedule opinions of members from different types of family on what they feel about joint family and how they consider it a better system.

Author had also wanted to know whether they prefer individual family to joint family and, if so, in what ways. Author had asked a set of questions on the efficacy of individual family. Author had also asked a set of questions on the factors responsible for breaking off of joint family system. Author had analysed the answers by correlating these to type of family and education groups. The following table represents these (Table 6.5).

The analysis reveals that out of 17 joint families, 5 families whose heads belonged to the undergraduate level of education, believed that individual family is the only feasible type. They also believed that individual family is preferable to joint or small joint family. Among factors responsible for breaking off of joint family we had given them a number of options: modern conditions of living, modern ideas, financial crisis, opinions and habits-differentiation, migration due to employment, need for and emphasis upon more individual freedom, and several other than these factors.

TABLE 6.5: Opinions of Family Heads Expressing Preference to Individual Family

Type of family/ education groups.		No. of families	Individual family is the only feasible type (yes)	Individual family is preferable to joint/ small joint (yes)	Reactions Responsible for Breaking up of Joint Family: Modern conditions of living	Modern ideas	Financial grounds	Opinions and habits differ	Migration due to employment	Individual provides more individual Freedom	Other factor	N.R.
1		2	3	4	5	6	7	8	9	10	11	12
1. Joint	1.	5	3	3			2	1			5	
	2.	3	2	3				1				2
	3.	3	1	1			1	1			2	1
	4.	6	3	2			4	2			1	1
	NR											
Total		17	9	11			7	5			8	4
2. Small Joint	1.	6	1	4			1	3			2	4
	2.	11	5	6		2	3	6	3			5
	3.	13	5	9		2	3	3	5			5
	4.	19	7	11			4	4	3		6	6
Total		49	18	34		4	11	16	11		8	20
3. Individual	1.	15	14	12	1	—	6	6	4	—	—	2
	2.	28	20	24	2	1	15	8	3	3	—	3
	3.	52	34	34	2	1	28	8	8	3	2	6
	4.	61	40	45	4	1	17	6	20	3	4	9
Total		156	120	124	9	3	66	28	35	9	6	20

TABLE 6.5 *Contd.*

		Ways in which individual family is better				
		Offers opportunity to plan family affairs	Freedom to plan children's future	Tension etc. are avoides	Others	N.R.
1		13	14	15	16	17
1. Joint	1.	1	1			3
	2.	1	1			2
	3.		1			2
	4.					5
	NR					
Total		2	3			12
2. Small	1.			1		3
	2.	2	1	3	1	3
	3.	2	—	1	2	6
	4.	4	3	—	1	8
	NR	—	—	—	—	—
Total		8	4	5	4	20
3. Indi-vidu-al	1.	2	5	—	4	5
	2.	5	13	5	1	7
	3.	22	17	4	2	15
	4.	14	14	8	6	13
	NR					
Total		156 43	120 49	17	13	40

Of these 5 joint families, 2 believed that financial crisis in the joint family owing to a number of members living upon one or two earners is the main factor for breaking off the joint family system. Another one family believed that members of joint family differ in their opinions and habits. All these 5 families, however, considered other factors also responsible for breaking off of joint family system.

Author had also offered our respondents a number of options to suggest ways in which, individual family was considered a better family system. These were: individual family offers opportunity to plan family affairs; it offers freedom to plan children' future; tensions, frictions, conflicts and strains are usually avoided in individual family, and some other ways which the respondent may like to indicate.

Only one of the families in this group of 5 suggested opportunity to plan family's affairs and freedom to plan children's future as a positive point in favour of individual family. Three families did not respond this query.

Those joint families whose heads were educated up to graduate level were three. Of these 2 families expressed that joint family is only feasible type in these days, however, all 3 families agreed on the point that individual family is preferable to joint or small joint family. Only one of these said that differences of opinions and habits among members of family are the main factors for breaking off of joint family; other 2 did not answer this aspect of enquiry. Only one considered that individual family is better because it offers opportunity to plan family affairs; other 22 families did not answer on this point too.

The third education group comprised of 3 families whose heads were found to be post-graduates. Out of these 3 families, one head believed that individual family is the only feasible type and also that individual family is preferable to joint or small joint family.

One head of family believed that financial crisis and difference of opinions and habits cause break up of joint family. Two believed that "other factors" cause it; one head only believed that individual family is a better type, as it leads to freedom to play children's future, 2 did not respond this aspect.

The last education group was of professionals who were six. Out of these six, 3 believed that individual family is the only feasible type, and 4 believed that individual family is preferable to the joint or small joint type. Four families, again, suggested that financial crisis in the joint family is the main factor for breaking up of this system, 2 families suggested differences in opinions and heads of members as probable factors, one suggested other factors. As for the query on the ways in which individual family is better than joint family, 5 did not respond it.

Small joint families which were 49 in our sample also expressed different opinions on feasibility of individual family.

Out of 49 families, 6 were such whose families were educated up to undergraduate level. One of these believed that individual family is the only feasible type. Four believed that individual family is preferable to joint family or small joint family. 1 family had attributed responsibility to family crisis in breaking up of joint family, 3 said that it has been caused by difference in family member's outlook and habits, and 2 said that other factors are responsible for it, one family head said that individual family is better in the sense that tensions are avoided there which are usually frequent in a joint family; 3 did not respond here.

Eleven small joint families heads were found to be educated up to graduate level.

Five of these believed that individual family is the only feasible type, while 6 believed that individual family is preferable to joint and small joint family.

Two of these 11 heads considered modern ideas, 3 considered financial crisis, whereas 6 considered difference of opinions and habits, 3 considered migration due to employment as a factor responsible for breaking up of joint family.

Two of these 11 heads considered modern ideas, 3 considered financial crisis, 6 considered difference of opinions and habit and 3 considered migration due to employment as a factor responsible for breaking up of joint family.

Two of these believed that individual family is better in the way as it offers opportunity to plan family affairs, one believed that it is better because it gives freedom to plan children's future, and 3 believed that it is better as tensions, conflicts and strains common in joint family are avoided in individual family. One suggested other ways in which individual family is better.

Those having a postgraduate degree were 13, in all, 5 of these said that individual family is the only feasible type. Nine said individual family is preferable to joint family or small joint family.

Two heads believed modern ideas and 3 financial crisis responsible for breaking up of joint family, 3 suggested difference of opinions and habits, and 5 considered migration due to employment as the main factor responsible for breaking up of joint family system.

Two of these said that individual family is better as it differs opportunity to plan children's future. One said that it is better because tensions, conflicts and strains are avoided here; one suggested other ways.

The small joint families whose heads were professionally educated were 19 in all. Seven of these said that individual family is the only feasible type, while 11 said that individual family is preferable to joint or small joint family. As for factors responsible for breaking up of joint family, 4 considered financial crisis, 4 difference of opinions and habits, 3 migration due to employment, and 6 other factors responsible for breaking up of joint family.

Of these 19 professionals, 4 said that individual family is better in the way that it offers opportunity to plan family affairs, 3 said that it is so, because it gives freedom to plan children's future and one said that it is better in other ways.

This analysis suggests that a large number of heads of families though themselves living in a small joint family system believe more in the desirability and feasibility of individual family and this consensus of opinion is held in a major sense by all levels of educational groups.

Individual families were found to be 156 in our sample of 222 drawn from urban Bhopal. Out of these 156, 15 belonged to the first education group, that is whose heads were educated up to undergraduate level, 14 of these and though that individual family is the only feasible type, 12 had thought that individual family is preferable to joint and small joint family, of these 1 considered modern conditions of living as the factor responsible for breaking up of joint family, 6 considered that financial condition is responsible for it, another 6 considered that difference of opinions and habits, and 4 considered migration as the main factor for breaking up of joint family. As for the question that how individual family is better than joint family, 2 believed that because it offers opportunity to plan family affairs and 5 said that it gives freedom to plan children's education. Four said that it is better in other ways.

Twenty-eight individual families were such whose heads were educated up to the graduate level. Out of these 20 felt that individual family is the only feasible type, 24, however, further said that individual family is preferable to joint or small joint family.

Out of these 2 graduates believed modern conditions of living, 1 believed modern ideas, 15 believed financial crisis and 9 believed difference in opinions and habits, 3 believed migration due to employment and 3 believed individual family's ability to provide more individual freedom to be the factors responsible for breaking up of joint family.

As for the ways in which individual family is better, 5 graduates said that because it offers opportunity to plan family affairs, and 5 said because tensions, conflicts and strains are easily avoided here, 1 said that in other (unclassified) ways it is better.

Among 52 post-graduates heads of individual family, 34 felt that individual family is the only feasible type, and also that individual family is preferable to joint family or small joint family. Only 2 of these held modern conditions of living, 1 held modern ideas and 28 held financial crisis, 8 held difference of opinions and habits, 8 held migration due to employment, 3 held individual family's ability to provide more individual freedom, and 2 held other factors responsible for breaking up of the joint family system.

Twenty two of these 52 post-graduate heads believed that individual family is better as it offers opportunity to plan family affairs, 17 believed that it is better as it gives freedom to plan children's future, and 4 believed that it is better as it avoids tensions, conflicts and strains; other 4, however, believed that it is better in other ways.

The largest education group was of professional who were as many as 61 in 156 total individual families, 40 of these professionally educated heads of individual families believing that individual family is the only feasible type of family and 45 believed that individual family is preferable to joint or small joint family.

Four of these 61 heads believed that modern conditions of living, one believed that modern ideas, 17 believed financial crisis, 6 believed difference in opinions and habits, 20 believed that migration due to employment, and 3 believed individual family's ability to provide more individual freedom are factors responsible for breaking up of joint family; other 4, however, found other reasons responsible.

Of these 61 professional heads, 14 believed that individual family is better because it offers opportunity to plan family affairs, 14 believed that because it gives freedom to plan children's future, and other 8 believed that because it avoids tensions, conflicts and strains in the family. Other 6, however, considered other ways in which this family is better.

NOTES

1. R.K. Merton, *Social Theory and Social Structure* (New Delhi, Amerind Publishing Co. Pvt. Ltd., 1968), Indian Edition, p. 212.
2. Paul B. Horton and Hunt, Chesher L. *Sociology* (New York, McGraw-Hill Book Co. 1968), p. 110.
3. William F. Ogburn and Nimkoff, Mayer F., *A Handbook of Sociology* (New Delhi, Eurasia Publishing House Pvt. Ltd., 1966).
4. ibid. p. 171.

7

ROLE BEHAVIOUR AND ROLE DYNAMICS IN THE URBAN HINDU FAMILY AND CHANGE

The author tried to assess the actual role playing in the urban Hindu family of Bhopal with a view the extent of determining the change by examining what are different principal roles in the urban family, how they are discharged, and what change is now marked in their performance.

The role of head of household, the role of father, the role of mother, the role of husband, the role of wife, the role of son and the role of daughter are the important functional roles in the family. The conventional roles in the Universal Hindu family in relation to their role expectations, role obligations have been discussed in the last chapter, here the author will examine, how these different roles are actually discharged in the contemporary urban Hindu family of Bhopal, and what kind of change and to what extent they now reflect.

The author has classified the different roles according to the nature of role implicated in and role expectations raised from them. The role of head of household has been thus called the role of authority, the role of principal motherhood, that is of emotional care discharged by an old lady like father's mother or father's sister in joint family, and in small joint family by father's mother or father's sister, has been called the role of sentiments. The role of husband and role of wife have been called the role of obligation. The discussions here will show how these different roles vary in accordance with the type of family, educational standard achieved, earning status and occupational pattern of the role player.

Role of Authority

The head of household, who is almost invariably the main earner in the family, is the repository of the role of authority. How this role of authority is discharged in different types of family, the joint, small joint and individual, and how it varies according to the educational standard and occupational pattern of the head of household is examined here. The analysis is presented separately for each type of family.

Joint Family

The joint families in our urban sample of 222 households were found to be 17. Of these 17 families, all had heads of the households who solely performed the role of authority but among these only 15 discharged the active role of earner. When I analysed the role discharge in relation to the educational standards of heads of households of the 17 joint families, I found that among 5 undergraduates, all 5 discharged the role of authority actively as all of these were also active earners in the family, though they also had other sub-earners in the families who assisted them in earning.

From among these active earners only one role player of authority commanded full power in matters of economic obligations as well as social and religious obligations.

Four of these role players of authority commanded full power in matters of economic obligations, discharge of family duties, social and religious obligations, 4 had supreme voice in social, economic and religious matters. Four, however, expressed that they took advice from their wives in the discharge of their role of authority.

Among the 3 graduate heads, 2 discharged role of authority while in case of one, it was discharged by the other earner as this virtual head of household was a retired person; all these families, however, were assisted by other members of family.

Of these, 2 exercised role of authority in discharge of economic obligations, one in discharge of economic, social and religious obligations, as well as in discharge of family duties, 3 expressed that their voice was held supreme in social, economic and religious matters and another 3 said that they took active advice from their wives in discharge of their roles of authority.

Among 3 post-graduate heads, all these contained role of authority which was discharged actively though they also had other coearners or subearners in the family. Of these 3 post-graduate heads, 2 exercised authority in matters of discharge of family duties, 1 exercised authority in matters of economic, social and religious obligations, one exercised authority in matters of economic obligation and discharge of family duties as well as social and religious obligations. All these 3 postgraduate heads expressed that their voice was held supreme in social, economic and religious matters, and they also said that they took advice from their wives.

Among 6 professional heads, 5 exercised authority as active earners and in one family, the head of household was a retired person, who was considered the virtual head of family because of his senior age and family status, but he did not exercise an active role of earner and thus did not hold the role of authority. All these 6 professional heads were assisted by other earners in the family.

Of these 6 professional heads in one family the role player of authority commanded full power in discharge of family duties, one in social and religious obligations, one in economic obligations as well as social and religious obligations, and 3 in matters of economic as well as social and religious obligations and family duties. All 6 expressed that their authority's voice was held supreme in social, economic and religious matters, but only 3 expressed that they took advice from their wives in the discharge of their authority. Two did not respond on this point.

Joint Family : Occupation as a Factor

When we make the analysis of the discharge of role of authority with occupation as a variable, we find that those who belonged to the category one of occupation, i.e. of "service" were 10 and in all of these authority was concentrated. All these 10 were active earners by themselves and all these 10 were also assisted by other coearners or subearners in the family. one of these 10 commanded full power in matters of social and religious obligations, one in economic obligations and discharge of family duties, 2 in economic as well as social and religious obligations, and 6 in economic obligations, discharge of family duties as well as social and religious obligations. Nine of these 10 expressed that their voice was held supreme in social, economic and religious matters. Seven expressed that they took advice from their wives in discharge of their role of authority.

Category 2 of occupation, i.e., those whose heads were engaged in some kind of professional duty had only one family, the head of which exercised role of authority was an active earner in the family, and had also other earners in the family. The role of authority was exercised in mattes of economic, social and religious obligations and in discharge of normal family duties. This role player of authority expressed that his voice was considered supreme in social, economic and religious matters, and he also accepted that he took advice from his wife in the exercise of his role.

Category 3 of business class had also only one family, the head of which exercised authority was the main active earner in the family, he had also other co-earner in family and he exercised his role of authority in matters of economic obligations, discharge of family duties as well as social and religious obligations.

Category 4 of other occupations had 5 families. Three of these 5 families had active earners in whom the authority was concentrated, though all the 5 families had coearners or subearners who assisted the main earner of the family.

One of the 5 heads exercised full power in matters of discharge of family duties, one commanded full power in economic obligations and discharge of family duties, 3 in matters of economic and social and religious obligations as well as discharge of family duties. All 5 expressed that their authorities' voice was held supreme in social, economic and religious matters, 4 of these also accepted that they took advice from their wives in the discharge of their role of authority. Two were retired persons, hence they have not been classified among active earners, they, therefore, did not exercise the role of authority in the family.

Small Joint Family

When we compare the role of authority in the small joint family with that in the joint family, we find the following results.

Of 49 small joint families, 9 fell in the undergraduate group of educational standards; among 7 of these 9 undergraduate persons exercising the role of authority were active earners and among 8 heads of family exercising the roles of authority were assisted by other earners in the family.

One of these 9 holding the status of authority in the family commanded full power in matters of discharge of family duties and social and religious obligations. While 7 commanded it in all three spheres, discharge of economic, family, social and religious obligations, 8 of these 9 felt that their authorities' voice was held supreme in social, economic and religious matters, but only 8 of these accepted that they took advice from their wives in exercising their role of authority.

Of the 13 graduates, 12 who exercised role of authority in their families were active earners, while 10 were assisted by other earners in the family. In one family the head exercising role of authority commanded full power in matters of economic and social and religious spheres, 3 commanded it in family and social and religious spheres, and 9 in all three, economic, family and social spheres, 9 of these 13 graduates felt that their voice was held supreme in social, economic and religious matters, while all 13 agreed that they took their wives' advice in the discharge of role of authority.

Among 9 postgraduate heads all nine exercised role of authority in their families while 6 had other earners in the family to assist them. In 1 family the person holding role of authority commanded full power in social and religious spheres, 3 commanded it in economic and family spheres, and another 3 in economic, family and social and religious spheres. In 4 families, authorities' voice was considered supreme in social, economic and religious matters, while in 9 families, the role of authority holders took advice from their wives in exercising their authority.

Among 16 families of professional heads, 13 heads exercising the role of authority were active earners in the family while in 11 families there were other coearners or subearners to assist them.

One of these holders of authority commanded full power in matters of economic obligations, 2 in discharge of family duties, 3 commanded it in economic and family spheres, one in economic and social and religious spheres, another one in family and social and religious spheres and 8 in all three economic, family and social and religious spheres. Twelve of these holders of authority considered that their voice was held supreme in social, economic and religious matters, and these 12 also took their wives' advice in the discharge of their role of authority.

Two heads of families did not respond this aspect of enquiry. Six heads of households discharging the role of head of household were retired persons.

Education works as an important variable in influencing one's role. It equips one to understand one's obligations and duties and gives him a rational outlook to understand others behaviour. I have examined this aspect here. I will show in the following papers, how the occupational role of the discharger influences or determines this other role.

Among 49 small joint families, 36 belonged to category one of occupation i.e. of "Services" class, all these 36 service class, heads of households were active earners, and 24 of these were assisted by other earners in the family, one of these heads who exercised active authority in family had full power in discharging family obligations, one had full power in discharging social and religious obligations, 6 had such power in discharging economic and family obligations, 2 had it in discharging economic and social and religious obligations and 1 had it in discharging family and social and religious obligations while 22 had full power in discharging economic family as well as social and religious obligations. Twenty-five of these respositories of role believed that their voice was held supreme in social, economic and religious matters while as many as 36 took advice from their wives in discharging their role of authority in their families.

There were no families whose heads belonged to some kind of profession, therefore, there was no response from this class.

Among 2 heads of households who belonged to category 3 of occupation, i.e. whose heads were engaged in some business both were found to be active earners of the family and thus exercised full authority though both of these were also assisted by other earners in the family. One of these commanded full powers in matters of family and social and religious obligations, and another one in matters of economic, family as well as social and religious obligations, one of these 2 role dischargers of authority had their supreme voice in social, economic and religious matters, But both took advice from their wives in the discharge of their authority in the family.

Nine belonged to category 4 of whose heads were engaged in other occupations, i.e. 3 of these 9 were active earners in the family who exercised full power in matters of economic, family and social and religious obligations. 6 of the heads of households belonging to this occupation group were retired persons. These were recognised as heads of households in the true conventional manner of the Hindu joint family, but they did not in practice exercise that much active authority in the family which was habitual with active earners.

All these 9 heads of households were assisted by other earners of sub-earners, 1 of these 9 commanded full power in mattes of economic obligations, another one commanded full power in matters of family duties while 3 commanded full power in sphere of family duties as well as social and religious matters. Seven of these 9 repositories of authority said that their voice was held supreme in social, economic and religious matters and all of these 7 took advice from their wives in the discharge of their role of authority in the family.

Two respondents did not answer this aspect of enquiry.

When an overall view of the occupation-wise role discharge of authority is taken, it is found that among 49 small joint households, 43 were active earners in the family who exercised full authority in the family, 37 of these had also other coearners and subearners in the family to assist them. 4 of these exercised full authority in economic matters, 2 in discharge of family duties, one in social and religious matters, 6 in economic and family duties, 2 in economic and social and religious obligations, 5 in discharge of family duties and social and religious obligations and 26 commanded full power in all three spheres of family obligations.

In 35 of 49 heads of households in the small joint families, voice of authority was held supreme in social, economic and religious mattes while 44 took advice of their wives in discharge of his role of authority in the family.

Individual Family

Role of authority as operative in the individual family shows some variation from that found in the joint and small joint families. It was found that among 156 individual families in the urban area of Bhopal, 15 belonged to an education group of households whose heads were educated up to the undergraduate level. Of these, 14 were such whose heads playing the role of authority were active earners, and in 5 families, they were assisted by other earners as well. In the remaining 1 individual family the role player of authority commanded full power in the sphere of economic obligations, 1 in the sphere of social and religious obligations and 12 in all the three sphere of economic, family, social and religious obligations.

Eleven of these players of authority had supreme voice in social, economic and religious matters, though 13 agreed that they had to take their wives' advice in the discharge of their role of authority.

Of the 28 individual families whose heads were graduates in arts, science or commerce, as many as 27 were active earners in the family and thus discharged the effective role of authority in the family; in 13 individual families, the main earners were assisted by other earners in the family. In one individual family, the role player of authority commanded full power in the sphere of economic obligations, one in the sphere of family obligations, 2 in the spheres of economic obligations and family obligations, one in the spheres of economic, social and religious obligations, 2 in the spheres of family, social, and religious obligations and 18 in all the three spheres of economic, family and socio-religious obligations. 21 of these active role players of authority supposed themselves to be having a supreme voice in the social, economic and religious matters and 26 agreed that they took advice from their wives in the discharge of their role of authority.

The third education group of postgraduate heads was related to 52 individual families. Of these 52 heads exercising the role of authority, 51 were active earners in the family and 16 were assisted by other earners. Four post-graduate role players of authority commanded full power in the sphere of economic obligations, 5 in the two spheres of economic obligations and family obligations, one in the spheres of family obligations and socio-religious obligations and 38 in all the three spheres of economic obligations, family obligations and social and religious obligations, 39 role players of authority in individual families considered their voice to be supreme while 46 conceded that they had to take their wives' advice in the discharge of their role of authority in their families.

The education group of professional heads was related to 57 individual families. In all these 57 individual families, the heads who discharged the role of authority in the family were active earners. In 15 families there were other earners to assist the main earners. Six of these role players of authority had full power in the sphere of family obligations. One in the sphere of socio-religious obligations, 4 in the spheres of economic and family obligations, 1 in the spheres of family obligations and socio-religious obligations and 38 in all the three economic, family and socio-religious obligations, 47 role players of authority in individual families supposed their voice to be supreme in economic and socio-religious matters while 53 conceded that they had taken advice of their wives in the discharge of their role of authority.

Four in the total 156 individual families were non-respondents who did not indicate any person playing role of authority in their families. The reasons for this non-response were not given.

When an occupation-wise approach to the role of authority is made, somwhat different results are found.

Those heads of households who belonged to the service class, which include government, semi-government, autonomous organisations and private enterprise's services, were as many as 147 in the total 156 individual families. All these 147 service class heads of individual households were active earners and accordingly exercised active role of authority in their families; in 46 individual families belonging to the service class, there were other earners in the families. Twelve of these service class role players of authority commanded full power in the sphere of economic obligations, 2 in the sphere of social and religious obligations, 11 in the two spheres of economic obligations and family obligations, one in the sphere of economic obligations and socio-religious obligations, 4 in the two spheres of family obligations and socio-religious obligations and as many as 103 in all the three spheres of economic, family and socio-religious obligations. One hundred and fourteen of these active role-players of authority belonging to the service class considered their voice to be supreme in economic and socio-religious matters, 135 of these role players conceded that they had taken their wives' active advice in discharging their role of authority in the family.

The individual families whose heads were occupied in professions were only two. In both these families, the heads were active earners and thus exercised full authority in the family. One of the role players commanded full power in the sphere of family obligations and another one in all three spheres of economic, family and socio-religious obligations.

Both these professional class role players of authority supposed their voice to be supreme in economic and socio-religious matters and they also conceded that they had to take their wives' advice in the discharge of their role.

There were no individual families whose heads were engaged in business, hence no analysis on this class of occupation could be made.

Those classified under "other occupations" were 3 heads of individual families. All these three heads of families so recognized conventionally discharged the role of authority in their families even though they were non-earners in the family. The main source of earning was provided by other members of the family who were actual earners. But they were not given the privileged status of authority merely because of it, and seniority of age was given due consideration. The status of head of family as well as status of authority were wested only in the eldest paternal head. This suggests that traditions and conventions still continue to be important in the urban individual family and are not disturbed by modern factors of economic supremacy. This observation challenges those hasty, generalised conclusions which suggest that old values traditions and convention are lost in the individual family.

Two of these role players of authority exercised full power in all three spheres of economic obligations, family obligations and socio-religious obligations. Two of these role players of authority also considered their voice to be supreme in economic and socio-religious matters. Only one of these 3 non-earner role players of authority belonging to other occupations conceded that he took active advice from his wife in the discharge of his role.

If we make an overall analysis of the whole issue, we find that among 156 individual families there wee active earner heads in 153 individual families and they exercised full role of authority in their families. In 53 individual families there were other earners available, but earning alone did not provide them the privileged status of role of authority. Nineteen of these 153 role players of authority commanded full power in the sphere of economic obligations, one in the sphere of family obligations, 2 in the sphere of socio-religious obligations. 1 in the spheres of economic and family obligations, 11 in the sphere of economic and socio-religious obligations, 4 in the sphere of family obligations and socio-religious obligations and 186 in all the three spheres of economic, family and socio-religious obligations.

124 of these active role players of authority in the individual families believed their voice to be supreme in social, economic and religious matters, and 144 of these conceded that they had taken their wives' advice in the discharge of their role of authority in the family.

The analysis of individual family reveals that role of authority continues to be more or less conventionally discharged on the basis of the family status, and is not much affected by education or occupation.The Hindu family tradition is still important in the individual family, and has not yet allowed a shift of this role of authority from the head of household to other earning members of family because of the achieved economic status. There may be individual variation in the discharge of this role, the basic approach towards this role remains the same, the mode of its operative behaviour also remains unchanged.

Role of Sentiments

The role of sentiments is supposed to be played by the mother of the family, who is expected to give utmost emotional care and caressing to children. This role is normally played by grandmother or mother in the second generation or by the eldest woman kin, father's widow-sister or sometimes mother's sister having come to live with them. It is usually played by the eldest woman kin, if she is also the additional kin living with them. It is almost invariably played by the wife of the head of household who is also mother of the children specially in the individual family.

The author wanted to know how this role of sentiments is still recognized as an important role in the urban family of Bhopal and by whom it is discharged in the family and in what manner. I had, therefore, included a set of questions on actual role playing in the urban Hindu family in the schedule. The replies of the respondents are analysed below, which trace relationship of children who are given sentimental lookafter and care by the related role player of sentiments in the family.

From our sample of 222 urban Hindu households of Bhopal, 17 respondents from the joint Hindu families, 49 respondents from the small joint Hindu families and 156 respondents from the individual Hindu families responded to our enquiry on this aspect of family function.

Among seventeen joint Hindu families in 13 joint families the "mother", and in joint families 3 grandmother of the children in the second generation played the role of sentiments in the family. In one joint family, some other kin discharged this role. In all these 17 joint Hindu families, the role players of motherhood and sentiments looked after homely comforts of children and 16 role players were entrusted with kitchen duties. In 4 cases the motherly role of sentiments was discharged by some other elderly woman on behalf of the real mother. This suggests that in all the urban joint families, the role of sentiments was well discharged.

Among fourty-nine small joint families, in 32 families the "mother" of the family and in 8 families the "grandmother" of the children in the second generation actually planned the role of sentiments. In one case the role was played by some "other" women kin and in 8 families, the respondents did not indicate any role playing of sentiments.

In 41 small joint families, mother playing the role of sentiments for the children looked after their homely comforts and in 40 small joint families, these role players were also entrusted with kitchen duties as well. In 9 small joint families, the role of motherhood and sentimental care was played by some other kin on behalf of the real mother.

This suggest that small joint families also recognised this role of sentiments as an important role and gave it an effective discharge.

Among 156 individual urban Hindu families in 132 small joint families the mother of children and in 4 small joint families, the grandmother of the children in the second generation played the role of sentiments for the children of the families. In 129 individual families this role playing was affected through looking after homely comforts and in 119 individuals families, it was affected through the discharge of kitchen duties as well. In 4 individual families, this role of sentiments was discharged by some other elderly woman of the family on behalf of the real mother. Twenty respondents in individual families, however, did not indicate this role playing of sentiments in their answers. The reasons were also not given. It is not known whether this was due to their unawareness of this role implication, its non-discharge due to non-availability of role player, or their unwillingness or indifference to answer this query.

An overall analysis of this role playing of sentiments in the urban Hindu family of Bhopal reveals that in a total sample of 222 households, the role of sentiments was played by real mothers in 177 families, by grandmothers in 15 families and by other kin in 2 families.

In 187 families the role players of sentiments looked after homely comforts of children and in 175 families, these role players were also entrusted with kitchen duties. In 17 families, the role of sentiments was played by other than actual mothers and some other woman kin discharged it on behalf of the real mother.

In 28 cases, the respondents did not indicate any role playing of sentiments in their families. The reasons for not recording this role were also not given.

This analysis thus indicates that the role playing of sentiments is well recognized in all three types of families, and it is given an effective expression. This suggests that an important traditional function of the Hindu family, that of ensuring a deep emotional care and sentimental uprearing of children is still maintained by the urban Hindu family and urbanization has not affected it to any extent. It is not disturbed here as may be found in highly industrial societies.

Family Roles of Obligation

Role expectations, role obligations and role discharge vary from member to member and their related status in the family. Sometimes one status holder discharges more than one role in the family and sometimes one role is shared by more than one member or status holder.

Role of family obligations is one such role. It is discharged by several members of family holding different statuses. Primarily, role of obligations is discharged by the husband and the wife. It is then discharged by the son and the daughter, brother and the sister and by the daughter-in-law, ordinarily in a joint family of two generations.

In a small joint family it is discharged by the husband and the wife by the son and the daughter, and often by the additional kin living with them. In an individual family role of obligation is discharged only by the husband, and wife and their children, if they are matured.

The nature of family obligation varies according to the status of the family member and role expectations raised from that member.

The analytical appraisal of each of these role of obligations in their different perspective would make a thesis by itself. I have taken here for analytical discussion the most principal role of obligation, the role of husband and wife. Both husband and wife discharge a role of obligation towards each other in certain respects and generally a role of obligation towards the whole family of living, that is, the conjugal family or what Ross calls the "Companionship family". I have tried to examine the two fold role of obligation in different types of family, the joint, the small joint and the individual, and to find out whether any variations occur in different types of family. Several sets of questions were asked from the respondents to know the nature and extent of their family obligations discharged in different spheres, role of obligation of husband towards his wife, and similarly, role of obligation of wife towards her husband, role of obligation of husband discharged towards his children as father, and role obligation of wife towards her children discharged as mother. The main purposes was to know how far each of them takes an active interest in their children's upbringing, and career, whether the husband shares this responsibility in an urban family, or he has left it to the charge of his wife and whether this delegation of authority or responsibility occurs with the educated earning status of the wife.

Role of Husband

The primary role expectation of husband towards his conjugal family is to marry to emotionally satisfy his wife to look after his individual and family interests, to raise children from his wife, to upbring them with the help of his wife, to meet their emotional demands and expectations from him as husband and father, to educate the children properly and to the best of his efforts to give them a secured future.

A few sets of questions were asked in this parlance and analysed in three different contexts of family, the joint, the small joint and the individual and further correlated these to the educational status and occupation of the husband. Table 7.1 analysis these responses in joint family.

Role of Husband in Joint Family and his Attitude as Father towards Children

The joint families, which were 17 in all had four different educational standard-holder husbands. Those who were educated up to the intermediate level were 5, those educated up to the graduate level were 3, those educated up to the post-graduate level were 3 and those educated technically or professionally were six.

Of the 5 educated up to undergraduate level, all were active earners in the family, 4 fathers who were also family heads said that they looked after their children properly. Two of these 5 felt full responsibility in bringing up their children, 4 had special ambitions about the future of educational career of their children. 3 of these, however, admitted that they had no time at their disposal to devote to the teaching of their children, while 4 of these had a basic attitude to the teaching of their children in their spare time; none of these 5 expressed that they avoided teaching their children even when they had time. Four fathers expressed that they behaved soothingly towards their children when they returned home in evening, 1 did not respond this enquiry.

As for the signing of school reports of children as guardians, 2 fathers said that they had delegated this responsibility to their wives, while 1 said that both of them discharged it equally. In 3 cases, this responsibility was exclusively discharged by the mother of the children (husband's wife), who was found to be educated in all cases.

It thus appears that education has achieved a value in achieving this goal of shared responsibility (Table 7.1).

Among 3 graduates in the joint family, 2 were active earners, while one was a retired person and was thus not an active earner. All these 3 graduate-husbands however, fulfilled their roles properly towards their wives and children. All three said that they looked after their children properly, and that they fully realised their responsibility as parents in

TABLE 7.1: Role of Husband: Role of Father in Family and his Attitude as Father Towards Children

Type of Family/ Education Group		No. of families	Attitude to children			Where father encourages a friendly intimate relationship	Approach to children	
			Strict obedience	Affectional approach	Relaxation in their behaviour		Spare the rod and spoil the child	Coax them frequently
1		2	3	4	5	6	7	8
1. Joint Family Education	1	5	1	4	—	4	—	—
	2	3	1	1	1	3	—	2
	3	3	1	2	—	3	2	1
	4	6	3	2	1	4	1	4
	NR	—	—	—	—	1	2	—
Total		17	6	9	2	15	5	7
2. Small Joint	1	6	4	1	—	1	1	3
	2	11	4	5	—	7	2	5
	3	13	2	9	1	11	4	6
	4	19	1	11	1	12	—	4
	NR	—	10	—	—	9	—	—
Total		49	21	26	2	40	7	18
3. Individual Family	1	15	3	8	2	10	5	6
	2	28	4	18	2	19	7	8
	3	52	7	35	5	43	8	10
	4	61	6	37	7	47	5	10
	NR	—	20	—	—	17	23	—
Total		156	40	98	16	136	48	34

TABLE 7.1 (*Contd.*)

Type of Family		Father's irritation over			Where father believes that affectional intimacy & emotional care provides children a stronger foundation for their personality	Basic atitude of father			Where father equally behaves with his son and daughter	If no in col. 16 preferential treatment	
		Pit falls	Trivial matters	Mischievious Acts		Basically active interest	Indifference	Avoidance		Son	Daughter
1		9	10	11	12	13	14	15	16	17	18
1. Joint Family Education	1	—	—	1	3	4	—	—	3	1	—
	2	—	—	—	2	2	—	—	3	—	—
	3	—	—	—	3	2	—	1	2	—	—
	4	—	1	2	5	6	—	—	5	—	—
	NR	4	—	—	4	2	—	—	3	—	—
Total		4	1	3	17	16	—	1	16	1	—
2. Small Joint	1	3	—	2	3	3	—	—	4	—	1
	2	3	2	3	10	9	—	—	8	—	1
	3	1	1	6	9	12	—	—	9	1	—
	4	3	2	5	11	13	1	—	12	—	—
	NR	12	—	—	10	9	—	—	13	—	—
Total		23	5	16	43	46	1	—	46	1	2
3. Individual Family	1	3	2	5	12	12	1	1	12	—	1
	2	2	3	8	20	19	1	1	20	1	1
	3	13	1	17	44	42	—	1	40	—	—
	4	5	2	18	37	40	3	3	37	—	2
	NR	30	—	—	34	35	—	—	40	—	—
Total		53	8	48	147	143	5	6	149	1	4

bringing up their children. All of these three agreed that they were anxious about a prospective future of their children and have had special ambitions in regard to these. But they admitted that they had no time to teach their children, though they had an attitude to teach them in spare time. It appears that though the basic attitude to teach one's children is possessed by fathers in this group, it is not usually realised or affected because the urban life allows little time from the busy routine. None of the graduate fathers admitted that they avoided teaching their children even when they had time.

On the point, how these fathers behaved towards their children when they returned home from office in the evening, 2 of these 3 graduates said that they behaved soothingly, while 1 said that he was quite indifferent. This indifference on his part may be a part of his nature or it may be with an intention to avoid tension in his family in the evening.

As for the guardian's responsibility discharged, in 2 cases it was discharged by mother of children, that is, by wife of husband concerned, and in 1 case brother, father and mother discharged it. This means that the wife was considered competent enough to discharge this responsibility. In 2 cases this responsibility was wholly entrusted to the wife. While 1 further analysed this, 1 found that in all three families of graduate husbands, wives were also educated. It appears thus probable that achievement of education equips the wife to discharge her role properly in her family.

Among post-graduates who were also 3 among 17 joint families, all these were active earners, 2 of them, however, only believed that they looked after their children properly, though all 3 realised their responsibility in bringing up their children properly, and all of them said that they had special ambitions about the future career of their children. But they openly admitted that they had no time to teach their children themselves, though at the same time also maintained that they held a basic attitude to teach their children in spare time. 1 of these 3 also confessed that he avoided teaching his children even when he had time.

As for their behaviour towards their children in the evening, all 3 said that they behaved towards their children soothingly when they returned home in the evening from their office.

As for discharging parental responsibility towards children's formal education in one family, mother of children signed children's reports, while in another family father signed it. In 2 cases, this responsibility was exclusively entrusted to mothers of children. In all 3 cases these wives who discharged this parental role were educated.

Among 6 professionally educated husbands, 5 were active earners, while one was a retired person. All these 6 looked after children properly, fully realised their responsibility in bringing up well their children, and they also had special ambitions about the future career of their children. Five of these six husbands said that they had no time to teach their children though all 6 held an attitude to teach their children in spare time.

As for their behaviour towards their children after a busy routine of the day, all 6 said that they behaved soothingly. And as for the guardian's responsibility discharged, in 4 cases mother of children signed children's report cards, and in 2 cases both shared this responsibility. Five, however, said that they have virtually entrusted this responsibility tc their wives.

The analysis above indicates that the role of obligation is discharged with a sense of commitment and grave responsibility felt by husbands in the educated families. The probability appears that and higher the level of education in the family, the more responsibly is felt towards the discharging this role.

It is also found that wives in all these families were educated, and they were thus endowed with a sense responsibility in the sphere of their own role obligation. Educated wives are expected to participate effectively and more or less share equally with their husbands this role of obligation. They are also entrusted parental responsibility with more confidence. It appears that education shows significant influence on raising the status of a family member, in general, and on the discharge of role of obligations as the wife and the mother, in particular.

Influence of Occupation on Role Behaviour

We have seen how education affects the role discharge of the husband in relation to his expected obligation towards his wife and children. We may now examine, whether occupational status or type of occupation held by the husband also influences his role behaviour.

Among 17 joint families, husbands in 10 families were service class persons, one was a professional-holder, one was engaged in business and 5 were engaged in some other (unclassified) occupation.

Among 10 husbands whose occupation was service, all were active earners in their families. Nine of these 10 service holders looked after their children properly, though all 10 realised their full responsibility in bringing up their children, and all 10 held special ambitions about future career of their children, 9 of these, however, said that they had no time to teach their children, though all 10 said that they had basic attitude to teach their children in their spare time. Two of these, however, said that they also avoided teaching their children even when they had time. Two of the 10 service class husbands seem to have made contradictory statements in regard to the two questions asked corollary.

Eight of these 10 husbands said that they had basically delegated to their wives the parental responsibility of signing children's reports and looking after the educational interest, as their wives were educated, and they felt confident about their discharging this role effectively, 3 said that both father and mother of children signed children's school reports, while 6 said that only the mother signed it. Nine wives among 10 service class families were educated. It, again, appears probable here that the education of wife enables her to achieve her status in the family. It also helps her to get more responsibilities in the family. It widens her sphere of activity and role obligations.

The only profession-holder husband was an active earner. He said that he looked after his children properly, and also fully realised his responsibility in bringing up his children. He also had special ambitions about his children's future career. He admitted that he had no time to teach his children though he had basic attitude to do so. He behaved soothingly to his children in the evening when he returned from his day's job. He had entrusted the responsibility of children's education to his wife and the school reports of his children were signed by the mother of children who was educated.

The third category of occupation belongs to business class. There was only one case in which husband belonged to this category, and he was himself an active earner. He looked after his children properly and he felt his full responsibility in bringing up his children. He also had a special ambition about his children. He had, however, no time to teach his children though he had a basic attitude to teach them in his spare time.

He behaved soothingly towards his children in the evening when he returned home from his busy day's occupation. He did not answer other parts of the questions about sharing of guardian's role in the family. The reason was also not given.

Among 5 husbands engaged in other unclassified occupation, 3 were earners, and 2 were retired persons, hence they were not active earners. 4 of these husbands in this class said that they looked after their children properly, 3 said that they fully realised their responsibility in bringing up their children, 4 said that they had special ambitions about the future career of their children, 4 of these also said that they had no time to teach their children though they certainly nourished a basic attitude for it. Three of these said that they behaved soothingly towards their children when they returned home in the evening while 1 said that he behaved quite indifferently. Two of these said that they had entrusted responsibility of signing guardians' reports to their wives. Three of these said that the mother of children signed children's report cards, and one said that father did it.

The occupation-wise analysis of the role of family obligations of the husband does not indicate much influence of any one particular type of occupation class on family members in increasing the capability to discharge role obligations more effectively, nor on the increase of the area of role obligations.

Role of Obligation of Husband and Father in Small Joint Family

When we examine the role of obligation of husband in small joint family, we do not find much variation. Among 49 small joint families, there were active earner husbands in 47 families; in 1 there was a retired person and in one a widower, who did not answer this part of question.

Of these 49 husbands, 6 fell in the undergraduate group, 11 in graduate group, 13 in post-graduate group and 19 in the professionally and advancedly educated group.

Of the 6 undergraduate husbands, 5 were earner-husbands and all these looked after their children properly while all 6 said that they fully realised their responsibility in bringing up their children, 4 cherished special ambitions about the future career of their children, and only one said that he had no time to teach his children, though these all 4 said that they possessed basic attitude to teach their children. Only one said that the had no time to teach their children, and he also confessed that he avoided teaching children in spare time. This may be because of his nature, disinclination to teaching, or his feeling too tiresome in the evening to be able to teach; the reason was not, however, assigned. All 5 earner-husbands, however, believed that they approached their children soothingly when they returned home in the evening after a busy day's job. Again the one husband who had said that he avoided teaching his children also confessed that he behaved towards his children with irritation when he returned home in the evening.

As to discharging parental responsibility in regard to children's education, one said that mother signed children's school reports, one said that both, father and mother of children shared this responsibility, while 1 said that he had entrusted this responsibility to his wife. Four of the six husband's wives were educated. It appears that whereas 4 wives were educated, only 2 of them could be fully entrusted with this responsibility by their husbands.

Of 11 graduate husbands in small joint families, 9 were active earners, 10 of these eleven believed that they looked after their children properly, 8 said that they realised their responsibility in bringing up children; these 8 also cherished special ambitions about their children's future career, 7 said that they had no time for teaching their children when they returned home though they held basic attitude to teach their children. Three admitted that they avoided teaching their children, though this was not properly explained.

As for their behaviour towards children in the evening, 8 graduates said that they behaved soothingly towards their children; none of this group could admit behaving irritatively or indifferently. Six of these 11 graduate husbands said that children's reports were signed by mother, one said that it was signed by father, while 3 said that it was signed by both. Wives of 8 husbands were educated. It is marked here that among 8 wives educated in the graduate group of small joint families, only 6 could be entrusted with signing children's reports. Among 13 postgraduate husbands 12 were active earners. 10 of these believed that they looked after their children properly, while 11 said that they realised their full responsibility in bringing up their children. As many as 12 cherished special ambitions about their children's future career. But 10 of these said that they had no time to spare for teaching their children though all 12 held basic attitude to teach their children. Only one of these 13 post-graduates said that he avoided teaching his children.

Of 13 postgraduates 10 behaved with their children in a soothing manner, when they returned from their day's job, one admitted his irritative behaviour, while 2 admitted their indifference.

As for the parental responsibility shared in signing children's formal reports, 9 said that reports were signed by mother of children and 2 said that it was signed by father and said that it is signed by both mother and father, as may be convenient.

It is interesting to find that of 13 post-graduate husbands, only 6 had delegated this responsibility to their wives, even though in 11 of the 13 cases, wives were educated. It thus appears that higher education of husbands did not alone ensure a delegation of powers to their wives; privileges or assured responsibility in their families and their family environment, their own circumstances and their own outlook where some other factors which also influenced their family behaviour in terms of discharging role obligations.

Among 19 professionally educated husbands, 14 were active earners, 12 of these 19 believed that they looked after their children properly, while all said that they realised their full responsibility in bringing up their children. Again 12 said that they cherished special ambitions about the future career of their children, but these 12 also said that they had no time to teach their children, though as many as 13 believed that they had a basic attitude to teach their children in their spare time. Two however, admitted that they avoided teaching their children.

As for their behaviour towards their children in evening on returning home, 11 said that they behaved soothingly towards their children. One said that he behaved irritatively, and 1 said that he behaved indifferently.

As for the responsibility of signing school reports and sharing of parental responsibility over it, 8 said that the mother of children signed these reports, while 3 said that both the mother and the father signed these. Five of these 19 professionally or advancedly educated group of husbands said that they have entrusted this job to their wives, while as many as 11 of the 19 professionally educated husband's wives were educated. It appears probable here also that education of wife alone is not able to secure for her an additional role of responsibility. Family environment and outlook of husband play a large part in making it a reality.

Certain aspects of enquiry here were not answered in full by respondents; these have been included in the NR or "No Response" category (Table 7.1).

When we review the same situation occupationwise, we get somewhat different results, though not much significant to deduce any positive conclusions thereupon.

Occupationally examined, the 49 small joint families had 41 service class, 3 business class and 5 other class occupation holder-husbands. There were none belonging to the profession class.

Of 41 service class husbands, 35 were active earners. Thirty-three believed that they looked after their children properly, 32 said that they only realised their responsibility in bringing up their children. 33, again, said that they cherished special ambitions about their children's future career, 25 said that they had no time to teach children, while 33 said that they held basic attitude to teaching them. Six of the husbands of this service class said that they avoided teaching their children even when they had spare time.

As for their behaviour towards children, 29 said that they behaved soothingly to their children in evening when they returned home from office. Three of the husbands, however, admitted that they behaved irritatively and another said that they 3 behaved quite indifferently. As for responsibility entrusted and discharged in regard to children's school reports, in 20 cases it was signed by mother, in 3 cases by father, in 5 cases by father and mother both. Fourteen of 41 husbands had delegated this responsibility to their wives. This number is, however, hardly half of the educated wives in this group. These were 30. It is somewhat peculiar that of the 30 educated wives, only 14 could be entrusted with this responsibility. The next group is of business class husbands who were only three. Of these 3, only 2 were active earners, and both of these looked after their children properly, realised their full responsibility in bringing them up, though they did not have time to teach their children, and only 1 of these cherished special ambitions about their children's future education. This one husband also said that he had basic attitude to teach his children, and one said that he avoided teaching his children over when he had spare time.

Two of the 3 husbands said that they behaved soothingly towards their children.

One of these husbands entrusted the responsibility of singing children's reports to his wife and in 1 case, it was actually signed by mother, only 1 wife was educated among 3 small joint families of 5 "other occupation-holder" husbands, 3 were active earners and 2 looked after their children's education as well as realised their full responsibility in bringing them up. Two of these 5 husbands said that they had no time to teach their children, though only 2 admitted to be holding basic attitude of teaching in spare time.

All 3 husbands said that they behaved soothingly towards their children, All 3 husbands also said that children's reports were actually signed by mothers of children. All three husband's wives were educated and seemed to have got this responsibility from their husbands because of their educational status.

It appears probable that educational status of wife is well recognized among business class husbands (Table 7.1).

Role of Obligation of Husband and Father in Individual Family

Role of obligation expected from and discharged by the husband in the individual family shows some variation from what it was found in the joint and the small joint family. This has been our primary concern when we analysed our data on the basis of type of family and educational standard of the husband and educational status achieved by his wife in the family.

Among 156 individual families in our urban sample of Bhopal, in 15 families husbands were educated up to the undergraduate level, up to the graduate level and 52 educated up to the post-graduate level. In 61 families husbands were professionally or advancedly educated. Out of 15 undergraduate husbands, 14 were active earners, and 13 of these believed that they looked after their children properly as well as they realised their full responsibility in bringing up their children. But only 12 said that they cherished special ambitions about their children's future career.

Ten said that they did not have any time to devote to teach their children at home though 12 said that they had basic attitude to teach their children in spare time. Only 2 of the fathers admitted that they avoided teaching their children even when they had time.

Fourteen of the 15 fathers said that they behaved with their children soothingly.

As for the responsibility of signing children's school reports, 10 said that they had entrusted this responsibility to their wives, one said that he himself signed it, and another one said that he and his wife both shared this responsibility. Six of husbands said that they had entrusted this responsibility to their wives. It appears worth while mentioning here that as many as 10 wives were found to be educated in this groups though only 6 of these were entrusted responsibility.

Out of 28 graduate husbands, only 25 were active earners, and these 25 looked after their children properly, only 23 of these, however, realised their full responsibility in bringing up their children, and they also cherished special ambitions about their children's future career. Seventeen of the fathers said that they had no time to teach their children while as many as 21 said that they had basic attitude to teach their children had they got time for it. Seven of the graduate fathers, however, admitted that they avoided teaching their children even if they had time. This antipathy to teaching one's own children by 7 fathers among 28 graduates may be due to their own temperament, or lack of interest in children's education or family environment, it can also be due to their exerting jobs in office which may be allowing little time for them at home.

Twenty-one of the husbands believed that they behaved soothingly towards their children on returning home in evening from their day's job, while 3 said that they behaved quite indifferently to their children.

As for the responsibility of signing children's report cards, 20 said that these were signed by mothers and 3 said that fathers signed it.

Ten of the husbands said that they had fully entrusted this responsibility to their wives. This delegation of responsibility to wives seems to have been the privilege of only fifty per cent of the educated wives, who were 20 in this group of families. The other fifty per cent wives could not secure this role for themselves inspite of their education. It appears probable that family atmosphere is more important in conceding a privilege to an educated wife. Out of 52 post-graduates husbands, 46 were active earners. 41 of these looked after their children properly, while 45 realised their full responsibility in bringing up their children, 46 fathers held special ambitions about their children's future career, 34 said that they had no time to spare for teaching their children while 41 said that though they did not have time, they held basic attitude to teach their children in spare time. Seven of the fathers admitted that they avoided teaching their children even if they had time.

Forty-two fathers said that they behaved soothingly to their children in evening, 2 admitted their irritative behaviour and another 2 their indifferent behaviour to children.

Out of 52 post-graduate husbands, 30 said that the responsibility of signing children's school reports was discharged by mothers of children, 7 said that it was discharged by fathers while 5 said that both shared it. Twenty husband said that they had fully delegated this responsibility to their wives. But this number of wives is too less compared to the number of wives educated in this group of families.

Sixty-one husbands in the 156 individual families were professionally or advancedly educated. Of these 54 were active earners, and 47 of these looked after their children properly, while 48 realised their full responsibility in bringing up their children. Fifty-one cherished special ambitions about their children's future career, 27 fathers said that they had no time to teach their children while as many as 41 had basic attitude to teaching children in spare time, 4 of the husbands, however, admitted that they avoided teaching their children even if they had spare time for it.

Fourty-six of the husband said that they behaved soothingly to their children, 2 said that they behaved irritatively and 1 indifferently.

As for the responsibility of signing the school reports discharged, in 34 cases it was discharged by mothers of children, in 6 cases by fathers and in 6 cases by both. 15 husbands said that they have delegated this authority to their wives. This delegation of authority to educated wives by their husbands is far less compared to total number of educated wives, 44 in this group.

Fourteen of the earners in these four groups of education or among the total number of families did not respond the entire part of this schedule, hence have been listed separately and against columns applicable, in the table (Table 7.1).

When role of obligation exercised by husband in the individual family is seen with occupation as a variable, it shows some variations than those which were noticed when education was made a variable.

Occupationally arranged these individual families belong to only three occupation groups : 151 to service class, 2 to professional class and 3 to other occupations, the total number of 156 individual families included 2 widowers and 1 retired person.

Of 151 service class husbands, 137 were active earners, 123 looked after their children properly and 126 realised their full responsibility in bringing up their children. One hundred twenty-nine of the fathers held special ambition about their children's future career.

Eighty-five of them conceded that they had no time to spare for teaching their children while as many as 118 said that they would have taught their children had they only got time, that is to say they had basic attitude to teaching. Eighteen of the fathers, however, admitted that they avoided teaching their children even though they got time.

As for their behaviour as father to children in the evening, 120 of these believed that they behaved soothingly, 4 behaved irritatively and 6 behaved quite indifferently.

And as regards parental responsibility discharged in singing children's report cards, as many as 93 said that these were signed by the mother of the children and 15 said that the father signed them, while 12 said both signed them, 50 of 151 husbands had fully entrusted the responsibility of singing these cards to their wives. This number seems quite less when we find that 114 of the wives in this group were educated. This indirectly suggests that educational status of wife alone is not able to achieve an additional and confident role for herself. Family environment and some other factors seem to play their part here.

Two of the fathers belonging to the professional class were both earners and both looked after their children well, realised their full responsibility, had special ambitions about their children's future career, but said that they had no time to spare for teaching their children, though both of them also admitted that they avoided teaching their children even if they had time, these 2 fathers said that they behaved soothingly to their children, and that the reports of the children were signed by fathers. But only one of them entrusted the responsibility to his wife, though wives of both were educated. This seems a case of personal choice and inclination as well as basic attitude towards as a value.

Of the 3 husbands belonging to other occupations none were active earners. These were retired persons and thus they did not enlist themselves so. only 1 of these three properly looked after his children, and realised his full responsibility in bringing up his children, only he held special ambitions about children's future career, but had no time to teach them though his basic attitude was very much for it.

It is this father alone who said that he behaved soothingly towards his children when he returned home from office. he said that his wife, who was educated signed children's reports.

A few questions on this aspect were not answered in full, these are listed separately against NR ("not responded") category in Table 7.1.

Role of Father in the Joint Family

Role of father is an important key role in the family. The status of father is always the status of the head of household, though in small joint family and joint family it may be often the status of the head of household. Sometimes it may be the next important status in the family. Thus often the father of the family combines in him the role of the head of the household, or what I have called the role of authority in the family, and he discharges this role expressively in his family. Here, it needs a special mention that specifically the role of authority is an important discharge role of father in the individual and the small joint families. Only in the joint family, some other elder member of the family, father's father, or father's elder brother may be sometime discharging the role of head of household but not necessarily the role of this context, that the role of head of household may not be role of authority, too. Sometimes the role of authority may in principle be tested in the head of household (the eldest member), but in effect it may be discharged by the earner. It is here that a situation of overlapping of roles arises.

In the present section, I am discussing the role of father, as the protector of children, the governor of discipline and the custodian of the family interests and responsibilities. The role of father is being examined here in these spheres with education as a variable.

We have shown earlier that among 17 joint families of two or more generations in our sample of urban families, there have been four educational groups; those educated up to the undergraduate level 5; those educated up to the graduate level 3; those educated up to the post graduate level 3; and those with the professional or advanced education 6.

As the Governor of Discipline and Decorum in Family

As the governor of discipline and decorum in the family, the father discharges an important role in the family. His stress on cultivating personal qualities is expected to develop character of children, and raise the status of family in the social esteem. I have, therefore, tried to examine this part of his role through a set of questions. The answers that were received reveal some significant findings and are analysed below.

As a positive approach, the father tries to instil in the minds of the children ambitions and aspirations for future development.

Out of 5 undergraduates in the family, one father believed in strict obedience, 4 believed in affectionate approach to children, 4 in father's friendly and intimate relationship as a positive approach towards enculturation of children.

As regards development of children's character with a view to let them grow into responsible youngmen and citizens, none of the undergraduate fathers believed in pursuing the children severally, or in the dictum of spare the rod and spoil the child". Only one of the husbands said that he was irrigated over their mischievous acts.

Certain questions were asked from fathers about traits which they suppose would help the child to found a basic personality. Three of the five fathers in this group said that they believed that an affectionate and intimate relationship and emotional care of children provide the children a stronger foundation for their future development. 4 of them said that they adopted basically an attitude of an active interest towards their children. None of them said that he had an attitude of indifference of avoidance towards his children (Fig. 7.1).

Three of the five husbands believed in the equal status of son and daughter and said that they did not behave partially to sons. One of these, however, conceded that he accorded a preferential treatment to his son, out of 3 graduate fathers, 1 believed in strict obedience, 1 in affectionate approach, and 1 in relaxation in their behaviour. All 3 fathers believed in encouraging a friendly and intimate relationship, While asked about their actual behaviour to children, 2 of them said that they coaxed their children frequently. Two believed that affectionate and intimate relationship with children combined with emotional care ensures a stronger foundation for their development of personality. All 3 fathers in this group believed in an equal behaviour to their son and daughter.

Out of 3 postgraduate fathers, 1 believed in traits of strict obedience, and 2 in affectionate approach towards children. All 3 believed in encouraging a friendly and intimate relationship with children, 2 of them, however, admitted that they also believed in the old punishment theory, spare the rod and spoil the child, and 1 said that he coaxed his children frequently.

All 3 believed that affectionate and intimate relationship and emotional care provide the children a stronger foundation for their personality. Two of them said that they took an active interest in their children, while 1 admitted his avoiding tendency towards his children. Two of the fathers stressed their equal behaviour towards their sons and daughters, while 1 did not make any comment on this.

Out of 6 professionally or advancedly educated fathers, 3 believed in strict obedience, 2 affectionate approach towards children and 1 in allowing them a relaxation in their behaviour. Four of these six fathers believed in friendly and intimate relationship with children, while 1 believed in the old punishment theory; again 4 admitted their coaxing the children frequently and 1 confessed his irritation over trivial matters, 2 said that they got irritated only on children's mischievous acts.

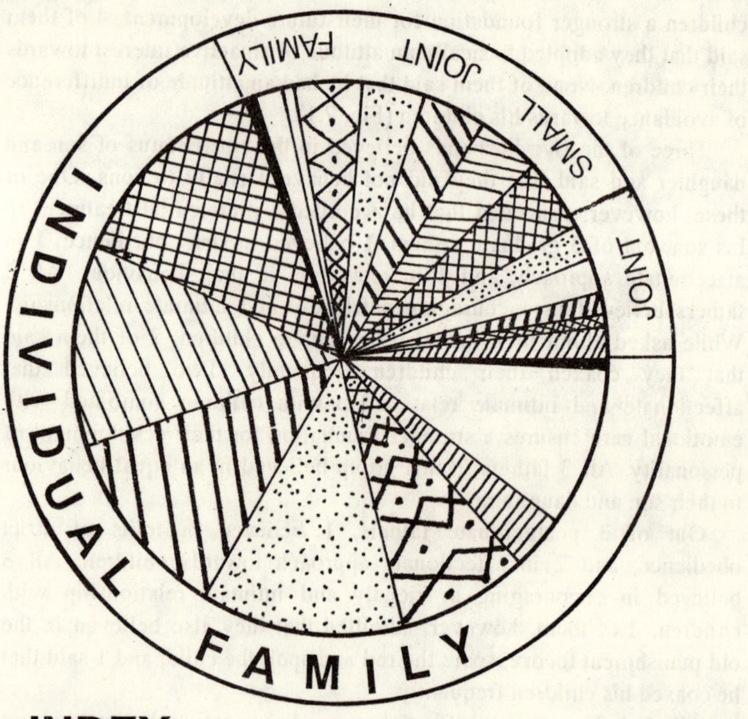

INDEX

- FATHER IS AN ACTIVE EARNER.
- FATHER LOOKING AFTER CHILDREN PROPERLY.
- FATHERS FEELING SOLE RESPONSIBILITY OF BRINGING UP CHILDREN.
- FATHERS HAVING SPECIAL AMBITIONS ABOUT CHILDREN'S FUTURE.
- FATHERS HAVING NO TIME FOR TEACHING CHILDREN.
- FATHERS WHO HAVE TIME BUT AVOID TEACHING CHILDREN.
- FATHER BEHAVES SOOTHINGLY.
- FATHER BEHAVES QUITE INDIFFERENTLY.

FIG. 7.1: Role of Father in Family and His Basic Attitude Towards Children.

Five fathers in this group believed that relationship and emotional care provide a stronger foundation for their future personality, while 6 said that they took an active interest in their children. Five of these fathers said that they behaved equally towards their sons and daughters and did not allow any discrimination. Some questions were not answered by the respondents, hence shown against "NR" category.

Small Joint Family

When the role of father in joint family is compared with the role of father in small joint family, some different findings are revealed. Out of total 49 households of the small joint family group, 6 fell in the undergraduate level, 11 in the graduate level, 13 in the postgraduate level of education, and 19 took in the professional group of education. When I analysed the importance or recognition given to different character traits, I found that affectionate approach towards children was valued more than strict obedience demanded from children in 49 small joint families when we consider them in total, but when we examine these individually, we find different results. Of 6 fathers educated up to the undergraduate level, 4 laid stress on strict obedience, and only 1 considered affectionate approach towards children more desirable. This one father also thought that a friendly and intimate relationship may be encouraged in the interests of children. Another one father, however, believed in the old dictum, "spare the rod and spoil the child". Three of the fathers said that they had to coax their children frequently.

As for occasions on which father got irritated, 3 admitted that they got irritated over petty pitfalls of children, while 2 got irritated only on children's mischievous acts. Three fathers believed that affectionate intimacy and emotional care provide children a stronger foundation for children's personality while 3 said that they took active interest in their children. Four said that they behaved equally with their children, while 1 said that he favoured his daughter more than his sons.

Among 11 graduate fathers, 4 said that they demanded strict obedience from their fathers, while 5 said that their approach towards children was more affectionate than demanding. 7 favoured a friendly and intimate relationship with children, while 2 believed in the dictum of spare the child and spoil the child", and 5 admitted coaxing their children frequently. Three said that they got irritated over their children's small pitfalls, 2 over trivial matters and 3 over their mischievous acts. Ten graduate fathers believed that affectionate intimacy and emotional care provide children with a stronger foundation for personality, while 9 said that they took active interest in their children. Eight of 11 fathers informed that they behaved equally with their sons and daughters and did not give any preferential treatment to one or the other, while 1 accepted that he gave a preferential treatment to his daughter. Another two did not say anything on this.

Among 13 postgraduate fathers, only 2 laid stress on strict obedience from children, while as many as 9 believed more in affectionate approach towards children, and 1 in allowing relaxation in their behaviour. Eleven of these 13 fathers believed in encouraging a friendly and intimate relationship with children. Only 4 believed in spare the rod and spoil the child, and 6 admitted that they had to coax their children frequently.

Among 19 fathers professionally or advancedly educated, only one demanded strict obedience, from his children, and 1 allowed relaxation in their behaviour, while 11 adopted an affectionate approach.

Twelve of these 19 fathers encouraged a friendly and intimate relationship with children, though 4 admitted their coaxing the children frequently. Three of the fathers admitted their getting irritated over pitfalls, 2 over trivial matters and 6 over mischievous acts of children. Eleven believed that affectionate intimacy and emotional care provide a stronger foundation for children's personality, and 13 said that they took an active interest in their children while 1 admitted his indifference. Twelve fathers in this group said that they showed an equal treatment to their sons and daughters.

This analysis of role of father in the small joint family reveals some interesting findings. It is found that as the educational level of father gets raised gradually the rational approach of the modern days is followed more keenly and there is less emphasis on the punitive theory or on remands. The number of persons favouring an affectionate approach and encouraging a friendly and intimate relationship is more, 9 and 11 in the two higher education groups, the postgraduate group and the professional and advanced education group, respectively. Similarly 11 of the 13 postgraduates and 12 of the professionally or advancedly educated favoured encouragement of friendly and intimate relationship with children. These two groups also ensured an equality of treatment to their sons and daughters.

It is thus found that the role of father in small joint family seems to be influenced more by education, which has shown a positive impact in relationalising father's behaviour. The fathers in the small joint families appeared to be more rational in their outlook than fathers in the joint family as far approach forwards children was concerned.

Individual Family

There were 156 individual families in our urban family. Of these there were 15 in the education group of undergraduates, 28 in the graduate group, 52 in the postgraduate group, and 61 in the professional and advanced group of education.

Of 15 undergraduate fathers, 3 demanded strict obedience from their children, 8 behaved with affectionate approach and 2 allowed relaxation in their behaviour. Ten of the 15 undergraduate fathers wanted to encourage a friendly and intimate relationship with their children but were still conservative in their outlook as they at the same time also believed in the old dictum of "spare the rod and spoil the child", while 6 admitted that they had to coax their children frequently. As for the occasions on which fathers got irritated over children's acts, 3 said that thy got irrigated over their pitfalls, 2 over trivial matters and 5 over mischievous acts. As many as 12 fathers in this group believed that affectionate and intimate behaviour and emotional care by parents would provide children a stronger foundation for their growing personality. 12 also adopted an active interest towards children, while 1 was indifferent and another was avoiding his children. Again 12 fathers believed that their approach was one of equality towards son and daughter, while only one favoured his daughter over son.

Of 28 graduate fathers in this group, 4 laid stress on strict obedience, 18 on affectionate approach towards children, and 2 on relaxation in their behaviour. 19 believed in encouraging a friendly and intimate relationship with children, while 7 were believers in the spare the rod and spoil the child dictum. Eight admitted that they indulged in coaxing of children.

Two fathers said that they got irritated over their children's pitfalls, 3 over trivial matters and 8 over pitfalls. Twenty fathers believed that affectionate and intimate behaviour and emotional care would provide children a stronger foundation for their development of personality.

As for father's basic attitude towards their children, 19 had basic interest, 1 was indifferent and another 1 had an attitude of avoidance. Twenty fathers said that they ensured an equality in their behaviour towards their sons and daughters. One favoured son over daughter and another one favoured daughter over son.

Postgraduate fathers were 52. Of these 7 demanded strict obedience, while 35 favoured an affectionate approach and 5 allowed a relaxation. Fourty-three of these 52 fathers wanted to encourage a friendly and intimate relationship between and son, while 8 wanted to strictly punish children saying that the theory of spare the rod spoil the child still works well with the parents in the treatment of their children. 10 admitted their indulging in coaxing the children, 13 said that they got irritated over children's pitfalls, 1 over trivial matters, and 17 over mischievous acts.

As many as 44 believed that affectionate behaviour, intimacy and emotional care would provide children with a stronger foundation for their personality.

Fourty-two of them thought that their basic attitude towards children was one of active interest, while 1 confessed that he avoided his children. As many as 40 said that their behaviour as father towards sons and daughters was one of equality and it admitted no preference to any one sex.

The highest number among the four education groups was commanded by professionally and advancedly educated group which had 61 individuals. Of these only 6 demanded strict obedience, more than fifty per cent, i.e. 37 fathers believed in adopting an attitude of affectionate approach towards children and 7 wanted to allow relaxation in children's behaviour. As many as 47 fathers encouraged a friendly and intimate relationship between father and son, while 5 believed in the old punitive theory, another 10 said they had to coax their children frequently.

As for occasions of irritations, 5 said that they got irritated over their children's pitfalls, 2 over trivial matters, and 18 over mischievous acts. Thirty-seven believed that affectionate and intimate behaviour along with emotional care would provide a stronger foundation for their personality. Forty said that they adopted an attitude of basic interest towards their children while 3 were indifferent and another 3 avoided children. Thirty-seven also favoured an equalitarian approach towards their sons and daughters, while 2 favoured their daughters more.

Some of the questions were not answered by respondents, and have been thus included in the "NR" or "not responded" category.

This analysis of father's role in individual family reveals that as education gets increased or deep, the modern psychological approach towards children which lays more emphasis on an affectionate and intimate approach and on the need for a tolerant attitude towards children gets more favoured. There is an increasing preponderance of this favoured trait in the postgraduate and professionally or advancedly educated groups.

Comparative Analysis

Role of father as discharged in the joint, the small and the individual family reveals some differential analysis, when an overall view of all those who believed in different family traits, the old and the conservative, is taken in comparison to those who have shown an inclination towards new trends of progressive and rational traits. It is found that there appears a tendency towards adopting modern traits in all the three types of families, the joint, the small joint and the individual. There were as many as 9 families among 17 joint families, 26 among 49 small joint families who favoured adoption of affectionate approach towards children in contrast to 6 in joint families, 21 in small joint families and 40 in individual families who favoured strict obedience from children.

The tendency towards favouring a companionship approach was also marked in another set of responses where the respondents favoured a friendly and intimate relationship with children in place of the old authoritarian approach. Fifteen among 17 joint families, 40 among 49 small joint families and 136 among 156 individual families were in favour of this, only a very small number, 5 in the joint, 7 in the small joint, and 48 in the individual families still believed in the old dictum: "spare the rod and spoil the child", and wanted to keep their authoritative hold over children.

Similarly a very large percentage of fathers in all the three types of family preferred an equalitarian behaviour towards sons and daughters. Sixteen among 17 joint families, 46 among 49 small joint families, and 149 among 156 individual families favoured an equal treatment to sons and daughters and were opposed to show any preferential treatment to one or the other sex.

This tendency is also in consistence with modern democratic ideas which stress equality. They also suggest a direct influence of education and enlightenment. It appears conclusive from this analysis that old ideas of feudal authoritarianism are breaking off gradually before the new democratic forces which have started moving in the family institution. As a core unit of society, the family is showing these influences. The impact felt in the family is suggestive of social change in the Hindu society.

Participation of Husband in Family Life

Role of husband in the family institution of his living takes different dimensions. While his role as father is very important in bringing up children and letting them grow into sound personalities, as the able citizens of society, his own role of husband in relation to his wife is equally, perhaps more, important. Here he has to meet optimum expectations of his wife, particularly if he has married her by choice. As husband, it becomes his first obligation to support her emotionally and physically and assure her a security in home and in their family life. His discharge of this expected role towards his wife comes within the purview of husband's role of obligation towards his wife. I have referred to and discussed this in earlier section of this chapter. Here I am concerned with the husband's role in a different context, viz., through his participation in family life. Considering this participation, I have tried to examine here whether higher education of the husband and educational status of wife have any direct correlation and whether these variables cast an influence on the active participation of husband and on his discharging of obligatory roles (Table 7.2 and Fig. 7.2).

Joint Family

In the group of 17 joint families, there were found 5 husbands in the educated group of undergraduates, 4 of these shared decision with their wives in matters of the family budget and expenditures. These 4 husbands did so because their wives were educated and they thought them competent enough to be consulted. Three of these also considered their wives' advice necessary and useful, and they gave their wives this privilege because they considered their wives able enough to hold an equal place in the family. But there could not be worked out a correlation between wife's attainment of equal place and decision-sharing capacity and her own status as an earner as none of these wives of the undergraduate husbands were co-earners.

TABLE 7.2: Participation of Husband in Family Life

Type of Family/ Education Group		No. of Families	Where husband and shares decision in matters of family budget and expdt. with his wife	No. of husbands who answered that their wives are educated and can share the decision	No. of husbands who consider wives' advice necessary and useful	No. of husbands who said that their wives holds or should equal place with him	Nos. where such an equal share to wife is given because she is co-earner
1		2	3	4	5	6	7
1. Joint Family	1	5	4	4	3	3	—
	2	3	3	3	3	3	2
	3	3	3	3	3	3	2
	4	6	6	5	6	5	1
	NR	—	1	1	1	1	1
Total		17	17	16	16	15	6
2. Small Joint Family	1	6	3	4	4	3	1
	2	11	8	8	7	8	4
	3	13	12	10	12	10	3
	4	19	11	9	11	10	—
	NR	—	9	10	9	9	9
Total		49	43	41	43	40	17
3. Individual Family	1	15	13	9	13	12	2
	2	28	21	18	20	17	1
	3	52	43	41	42	37	8
	4	61	41	40	43	40	3
	NR	—	24	27	25	22	26
Total		156	142	135	143	128	41

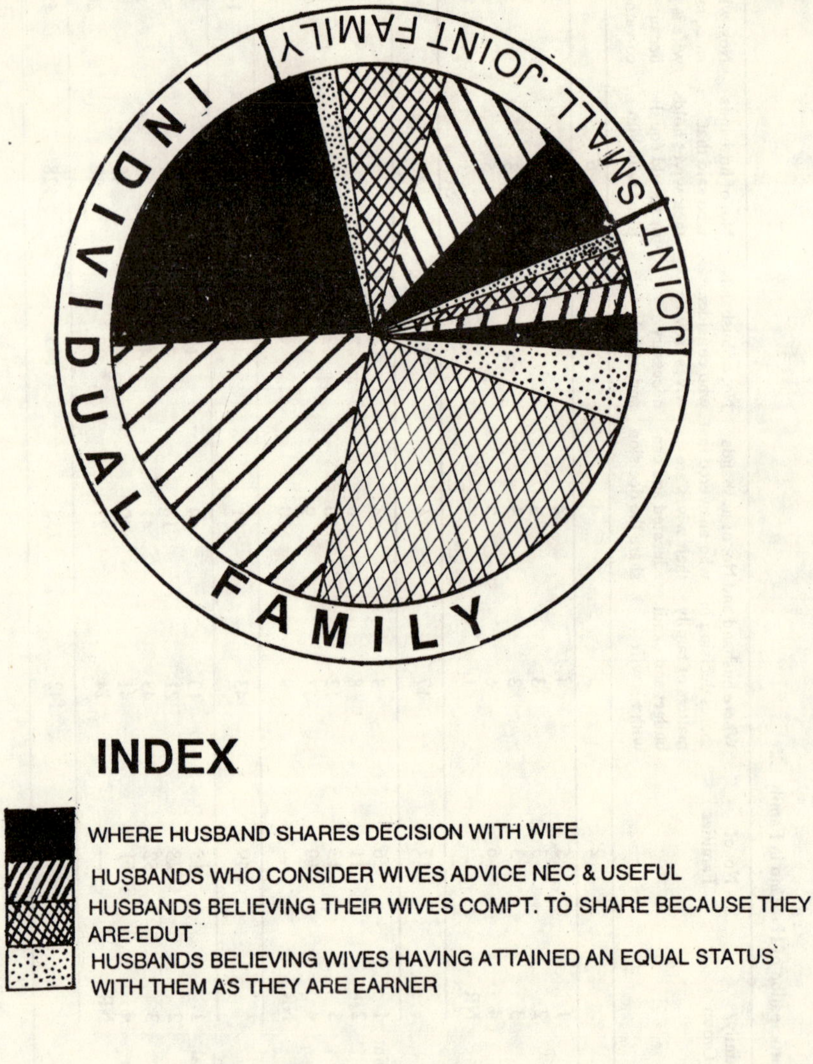

FIG. 7.2: Participation of Husband in Family Life.

Of 3 graduate husbands in the joint family, all shared decision with their wives in matters of the family budget and monthly expenditures, and they were husbands who believed that their wives are educated and could share the decision with them competently, and they were also husbands who considered their wives' advice necessary and useful in such matters. These three husbands believed that their wives held an equal place with them in their families though in 2 cases only the wives were also co-earners.

There appears here a direct correlation with equal status of wife and her capability to secure a responsible role in the family because of education. Besides there also seems a probable correlation with her earning capacity.

It may be that in this small group of 3 graduate husbands in joint family the earner's status is also an additional variable enjoined to her respectable equal status in the family.

Among the 3 postgraduates, again, all three husband's wives were educated and the husbands shared with them decision in the family budget and expenditures and they considered them eligible because the wives were educated and could competently share such decisions.

All 3 husbands considered their wives' advice necessary and useful. These husbands were convinced that their wives should hold equal place with them in the family. Here too, 2 of the 3 husbands' wives were co-earners. A direct correlation with their earning status can also be envisaged here in addition to the correlation of educational status.

In 6 joint families in which husbands were professionally or advancedly educated, all 6 shared decisions with their wives in matters of family budget and expenditure but only 5 of these husbands said that their wives were educated and could thus share the decisions. All 6, however, again considered wives' advice in this context necessary and useful.

Five of these believed that their wives hold or should hold equal with them. But only one husband clearly mentioned that equal place by his wife is commanded in his family because of her being a co-earner.

If an overall view is taken it is found that out of 17 husbands in joint families, 16 shared decisions with their wives and 15 husbands shared these decisions because their wives were educated, and these fifteen husbands also considered such advice from wives necessary and useful. Out of 17 husbands, 14 husbands believed that their wives held an equal status with them in the family. Only 5 of these 17 husbands were of the opinion that this equal share by their wives in the family has been possible because they are also co-earners with them. It thus appears that fulfilment of economic obligation probably contributes more to the securing of higher or equal status to the educated wife. This fact of equal status secured by the wife becomes all the more important in a joint family, where elder members of the second and third generation are also often found living with them.

Small Joint Family

When we compare the participation of husband in the joint family with his participation in the small joint families, we can envisage some variations, but whether his role playing in terms of his active participation reveals some important observations also needs to be considered.

In the group of 49 small joint families, 43 husbands shared decisions with their wives in matters of family budget and expenditure. When we break up this total number of husband's participation in this manner into four education groups, we find that 6 in the undergraduate group, 11 in the graduate group, 13 in the postgraduate group and 9 in the professionally and/or advancedly educated group conformed to this opinion. But of these 4 husbands believed that they could do so as their wives were educated and could share such decisions with them, though 34 agreed that they considered their wives' advice necessary and useful. Among these 34, there were 4 undergraduates, 7 graduates, 12 postgraduates, and 11 professionally or advancedly educated. Thirty-one husbands were convinced that their wives hold or should hold an equal place with them in the family. The break up of these respondents is as follows: Undergraduates 3, graduates 8, post-graduates 10, and professionally and/or advancedly educated 10, 9 husbands here and also in the former category did not answer.

Among these 46 husbands living in small joint families, only 8 husbands' wives were co-earners and their husbands believed that this equal share and status to their wives is accorded because of this fact. There were 1 undergraduate, 4 graduates, 3 post-graduates responding in this manner. Nine respondents in this category again abstained from giving any reply.

We find that there appears a close comparison between views of husbands living in the joint family with those living in small joint family, as far as their opinions about according an equal status to wife who was educated and also earner are concerned. 6 in the joint and 8 in the small joint families felt in this manner. In this group of small joint family there appears to be marked a trend of new democratic ideas of equality and recognition of the woman's status. This trend shows a gradual rise as education gets raised (Fig. 7.3).

Individual Family

When we compare individual family with that in the analysis of husband's participation in the joint family and the small joint family, we find that there is a similar trend towards democratic ideas in the higher education groups, though in all groups, the number of believers in equality and recognition for woman's status is considerably higher than the number of non-believers.

Thirteen of the 15 undergraduates, 21 of the 28 graduates, 43 of the 52 post-graduates and 41 of the 61 professionally and/or professionally educated husband's in the individual families believed that they shared decision with their wives in matters of the family budget and expenditures. Among those who felt that their wives are educated and can share the decisions, there were 9 undergraduates, 18 graduates, 41 postgraduates and 40 professionally educated and/or advancedly educated. Thirteen undergraduate husbands, 20 graduate husbands, 42 postgraduate husbands and 43 professionally and/or advancedly educated husbands considered their wives' advice necessary and useful.

Twelve undergraduates, 17 graduates, 37 postgraduates and 40 professionally or advancedly educated husbands believed that their wives hold an equal status in their families. But only 15 husbands were of the view that their wives have gained an equal status and an equal share in the decision making, because they were coearners with their husbands. A large number of respondents, 26, abstained from answering on this issue.

In comparing the analysis obtained from the three types of the urban family, the joint, the small joint and the individual, we find that there appears an agreement in the categories which express active share in the decision-making, equal status and recognition for wife's status in family in all the three types. The higher education groups reflect this more.

FIG. 7.3: Role of Wife : Wife's Participation in Family Life in Relation to her Working Women's and Housewives Status.

It is thus seen that the husband participates in his family more actively where he shares his decisions and problems in his family with wife. It is also seen that this role is being achieved by wife because of her education and also due to her own earning status. Education and employment together show a direct correlation with woman's status in family, and her getting a new and active role in her conjugal family or what Ross has called "the companionship family".

Husband-Wife Relationship; Approach of Companionship towards Wife

Education and enlightenment have helped the husband to develop an attitude of companionship towards his life-partner, whom he selects and weds to live for a long period. The attitude of his predecessor, about thirty to fifty years ago, was absolutely an attitude of authoritarianism which commanded full power over wife's life and personality and made her subjugated subordinate under her husband, which are allowed her little freedom. There has been a gradual change in his authoritative attitude of husband towards his wife. The attitude of the husband in the modern Hindu family is becoming now more an attitude of equal dealing and companionship.

My observations on the urban Hindu family had prompted me to form an hypothesis that as education and enlightenment become factors of significance, the husband's approach towards his wife becomes more of companionship and less of authoritarianism. I, therefore, put up this hypothesis to test in examining the role of husband in the different types of family, the joint, the small joint and the individual (Table 7.3).

Joint Family

Among 17 joint families, 12 husband's fully believed that husbands-wife relationship is a relationship of friendship and companionship and less a relationship of authoritative and absolute control, while 2 only party believed in this view.

When we examine this response in relation to the different educational levels of attainments, we find that out of the 5 undergraduate husbands, 3 fully believed in this view of companionship while 1 partly believed in it. Among the 3 graduates, 2 fully believed in this while 1 only party believed in it. When we

TABLE 7.3: Husband-Wife Relationship: Approach of Companionship Towards Wife — Joint Family

Type of Family/ Education Group		No. of Families	Where husband feels that husband-wife relationship is more a relationship of friend and companion and less a relationship of authority and absolute control		Is husband solely authoritative to his wife? yes	Where family matter like marriages are freely discussed with wife
			Yes	Partly agrees		
1		2	3	4	5	6
1. Joint Family	1	5	3	1	2	4
	2	3	2	1	1	3
	3	3	2	—	2	3
	4	6	5	—	4	6
	NR	—	2	—	2	1
Total		17	14	2	11	17
2. Small Joint Family	1	6	3	1	1	3
	2	11	6	2	3	8
	3	13	6	5	6	9
	4	19	8	5	7	9
	NR	—	9	—	9	14
Total		49	32	13	26	43
3. Individual Family	1	15	11	1	12	11
	2	28	17	3	10	19
	3	52	37	3	19	40
	4	61	34	9	13	41
	NR	—	28	—	25	33
Total		156	127	16	79	114

TABLE 7.3 (*Contd.*)

Type of Family/ Education Group		Correspondence for such marriages are carried out by			Where wife acts freely in carrying out such correspondence	Where husband accords agreement for sanction to marriage negotiations initiated or carried out by wife	Whose opinion is taken to be final in case of controversy over marriage proposals		
		Husband	Wife	Both			Husband	Wife	Both
1		7	8	9	10	11	12	13	14
1. Joint Family	1	4	—	—	—	2	1	—	1
	2	3	—	—	2	2	1	1	1
	3	3	—	—	2	2	1	—	—
	4	3	—	1	2	3	4	—	1
	NR	3	—	—	6	7	6	—	—
Total		16	—	1	12	16	13	1	3
2. Small Joint Family	1	3	—	—	—	2	3	—	—
	2	7	—	—	1	6	5	1	—
	3	3	3	2	6	9	5	1	3
	4	6	—	2	4	8	6	3	—
	NR	20	—	—	26	22	22	—	—
Total		39	3	4	37	47	41	5	3
3. Individual Family	1	6	3	2	4	5	4	2	—
	2	10	3	4	10	14	7	3	3
	3	16	1	2	11	19	16	—	1
	4	21	2	2	5	18	11	2	2
	NR	69	—	—	80	88	103	—	—
Total		122	9	10	110	144	141	7	6

approach the next two education groups, we find that out of the 3 postgraduates, 2 fully believed in it while among 6 professionally and advancedly educated husbands 5 fully believed in it.

When the respondents were asked: Is the husband solely authoritative to his wife, 2 undergraduates, 1 graduate, 2 postgraduates and 4 professionally and advancedly educated respondents affirmed this view. Two did not respond this question.

When I cross-examined this reply, I found that while 12 out of 17 husbands had affirmed that husband-wife relationship is more a relationship of friendship and companionship and less a relationship of authoritative control, 9 husbands of this group also affirmed the view that husband in their families is solely authoritative to his wife. There seems an apparent inconsistency in their views. It appears that these may be husbands who are living in a joint family set up but want to adopt the newer ideas of equality and companionship. They are, however, influenced by their joint family environment are unable to make their ideas a reality. The result is that they are not able to maintain a consistency in their views. It appears probable that in a joint family environment in urban Bhopal there may still be going on a struggle between the old ideas and forces and the new, and the latter may be asserting for their own place.

I wanted to examine the husband's approach of companionship in detail and from several points of views, and thus asked several other questions in corrolory which would reflect this attitude. The respondents were asked whether family matters of mutual concern, like marriage of son, daughters, brothers and sisters are freely discussed between the husband and wife. Four out of the 5 undergraduates, all 3 graduates, all 3 post-graduates, and all the 6 professionally and advanced educated husbands affirmed this opinion. Only 1 respondent from the joint family did not reply on this. This aspect was further examined by asking who usually carries out correspondence for such negotiable marriages in the family.

The findings are revealing here, 16 respondents said that the husband carried out such correspondence, while 1 of the six professionally/advancedly educated husbands said that it was carried out by both the husband and wife. It appears probable that the authority of initiative in negotiation of marriage is still kept by the husband who continues virtually to be the head of household and the authoritative head. Though in the next corollary of the questions, 2 graduates, 2 postgraduates and 2 professionally/advancedly educated, i.e., as many as 6 husbands in the joint family said that their wives act freely in carrying such correspondence, 2 undergraduates, 2 graduates, 2 post-graduates and 3 professionally/advancedly educated persons said that they usually accorded their agreement to marriage negotiations initiated or carried out by their wives. This suggests, again, a kind of inconsistency in their views. The husbands who once say that thev keep the initiative in marriage negotiations with them also silently admit later that they usually accord their approval to marriage negotiations carried out by their wives. It appears probable that as heads of their households, these husbands may be keeping the initiative for marriage negotiations with them and having once introduced such proposals, may have later on, entrusted these to their educated wives at their developed correspondence stage.

Another pin-pointed question was asked by us here: If controversies over marriage proposals occur, whose opinion was ultimately taken to be final over such controversies. Only 11 husbands among 17 joint families answered this question. One each in the undergraduate, graduate and postgraduate groups, and 4 in the professionally/advancedly educated group said that husband's opinion was final, 1 graduate suggested wife's opinion, and 1 each in the undergraduate and professionally/advancedly educated group suggested that opinions of both were considered final; it means that the matter was decided by mutual consultation.

This analysis of the joint family indicates that while there is a trend favouring development of an attitude of companionship towards wife on the part of husband, it is shrouded by a kind of conflicting views in certain cases. This conflict and inconsistency in views appears likely because of the influence of old traditions and attitude of authoritarianism on the minds of the husband still living in the joint family environment and they are expected to honour these. The younger generation appears to be more inclined towards democratic and modern ideas, but the old generation may still be pulling them back or putting a restrain on their ideas, or by exercising their elderly and parental control of the joint family organization.

These joint families in the urban set up appear to be in a transitory stage of the tradition and modernity.

Small Joint Family

We will now concern ourselves with the role of husband reflecting an attitude of companionship towards his wife in the small joint family and will try to observe if there is any variation or agreement with our findings in the joint family set up.

Among 49 small joint families, 6 husbands were found to be living in the undergraduate education group, 11 in the graduate education group, 13 in the postgraduate education group and 19 in professionally/advancedly educated group. Of the 6 undergraduates, 3 fully affirmed that their husband-wife relationship is one of friendship and companionship and less of authoritative and absolute control, while 1 partly agreed to this view. Of the 11 graduates, 6 affirmed this view in full and 2 in part; among the 13 post-graduates, 6 affirmed fully and 5 partly and among the 19 professionally/advancedly educated, 8 affirmed in full and 5 in part this contention, 9 respondents abstained from answering this aspect.

One undergraduate, 3 graduates, 6 postgraduates and 7 professionally/advancedly educated husbands said that they were solely authoritative in their approach towards their wives. 3 undergraduates, 8 graduates, 9 postgraduates, and 9 professionally/advancedly educated husbands (in all 29) said that they discussed freely with their wives' different family matters like marriage negotiations and budget. But as far as to carrying out the long formality of correspondence towards settlement of marriage was concerned, they also expressed that the central authority seemed to be kept with the husbands. Three undergraduates, 7 graduates, 3 postgraduates and 6 professionally/advancedly educated persons said that correspondence for marriage was carried but by husband. Only 3 post-graduates contented that it was carried out by wife,. and 2 in the same group contended that it was carried out by both, 2 professionally/advancedly educated also said that it was carried out by both.

In the next corollary of categorical statements, 1 graduate, 6 postgraduates and 4 professionally/advancedly educated suggested that their wives were acting freely in carrying out such correspondence. However, 2 undergraduates, 6 graduates, 9 postgraduates and 8 professionally/advancedly educated husbands said that they accorded their agreement to the marriage negotiations carried out by their wives. 22 respondents abstained from answering this aspect.

As to the final aspect of the enquiry on the husband-wife relationship, 3 undergraduates, 5 graduates, 5 post-graduates, 6 professionally/advancedly educated ones said that husband's opinion was taken to be final in case of controversy over marriage proposals, while 1 graduate, 1 postgraduate and 3 professionally/advancedly educated husbands suggested only wife and 3 postgraduates suggested both, the husband and wife.

This analysis of small joint family indicates that among 49 small joint families, as many as 23 husbands conformed to their maintaining companionship approach towards their wives, while 17 contended that as husbands they were solely authoritative to their wives. This in a way indicates that while there is all the more inclination towards adopting a rational approach of companionship towards wife, the old ideas of authoritarianism seem to cast their influence here too, as in the joint family, though their extent and degree of such influence is less marked here. Small joint family is a middle group between the joint family and the individual family. It is bound to have influences of both the environments, our sample of 49 small joint families of urban Bhopal corroborates this.

Individual Family

Interpersonal relationship shows variations in different types of family set up as well in cultural environment. We have thus examined separately the husband-wife relationship with special reference to husband's companionship approach towards wife in the joint, small joint and individual families, to see whether there are any behavioural changes in different groups and between each of the groups.

There were as many as 156 individual families found in our urban samples of Bhopal. When we break up these families into different education groups, according to levels of educational attainments, we find 15 in the undergraduate group, 28 in the graduate group, 52 in the postgraduate group and 61 in the professional/advanced education group. There are more families in the two higher education groups. Out of the 15 undergraduates 11 husbands, out of 28 graduates 17 husbands, out of 52 postgraduates 37 husbands and out of 61 professionally/advancedly educated 34 husband fully conformed to the view that their husband-wife relationship was more of companionship and less of authoritarianism of husband, 1 undergraduate, 3 graduates, 3 postgraduates and 9 professionals/advancedly educated husbands only party agreed to this view.

Twelve among the undergraduate group, 10 among the graduate group, 19 among the postgraduate group, and 13 among the professionally/advancedly educated group considered themselves as husbands holding solely an authoritative control on their wives. Eleven of under-graduates, 19 of graduates, 40 of postgraduates and 41 of professionally/advancedly educated husbands shared their family problems like marriage negotiations with their wives. However, 6 among undergraduates, 10 among graduates, 16 among post graduates and 21 among professionally/advancedly educated ones laid privilege of marriage negotiations exclusively with husband; only 3 undergraduates, 3 graduates, 1 post-graduate and 2 professionally educated husbands suggested that correspondence for marriage was carried out by wives, while 2 undergraduates, 3 graduates, 1 post-graduate and professionally/advancedly educated respondents suggested that both carried it out.

Four among the undergraduates, 10 among the graduates, 11 among the postgraduates, and 5 among the professionally/advancedly educated husbands said that their wives acted freely in carrying out such correspondence, 5 undergraduates, 14 graduates, 19 post graduates, and 18 professionally/advancedly educated husbands said that they accorded their approval to marriage negotiations initiated and correspondence carried out for them by their wives.

As to whose opinion was considered final when there was a controversy over some marriage proposal, 4 undergraduates suggested the husband and 2 suggested the wife, 7 graduates suggested the husband and 3 suggested the wife, while 3 suggested both. 16 postgraduates suggested the husband and 1 suggested both. 11 professionally/advancedly educated respondents suggested the husband while 2 suggested the wife.

When we take an overall view of the individual families' analysis, we find that in the 156 individual families, 99 husbands maintained fully an approach of companionship towards their wives while another 16 partly maintained it. Some 56 husbands found their wives acting freely in carrying out marriage correspondence. But as to the entrusting of the final verdict over the controversy, 7 husbands conceded it to their wives, while 38 husbands kept it to themselves.

This analysis indicates that there appears a marked trend towards accepting new ideas like companionship and equal status, conceding of privileges to woman more in the individual family than in the joint or small joint family. It appears probable that the atmosphere makes the difference.

And this trend becomes marked more in the higher educated groups in the individual family, who are naturally more vulnerable to changes. It may be because environment in individual family is more open and congenial to the democratic tendencies.

Role of wife in the Hindu family is an integral part of her several expected roles in the family and of a natural culmination of her girlhood in which she might have been initiated and expected to play a future role from the beginning of her young age.

As a girl she has often for long expected to play the role of wife on her wedding, and consequently with this expected role, to play all aligned roles of wife. The most primary among there are the role of housewife and the role of motherhood. And the mother has always to play this essential role of enculturing her boys and girls to perform certain roles on attaining maturity in accordance with the cultural tradition and expectations. And the adult man and woman have to struggle hard to adopt themselves in these roles and try to discharge them most effectively in the context of their own family group.

Marriage as an institution helps them to adapt to these role obligations.

Role of Wife in Urban Hindu Family

I wanted to see through this study how different natural, culturally expected and other ascribed roles of a wedded woman are performed in the urban Hindu family in the context of urbanization and change. With this objective in view, a considerable part of my schedule was related to the Role of Wife in different perspectives.

Wife's Participation in Family Life in Relation to Her Housewife's and Working Woman's Status

First of all I wanted to see how the wife participates in the family life in her husband's family, particularly in relation to her working woman's and housewife's statuses. There is often a variation in one's personality and capacity to perform an expected role in family in the background of cultural tradition and prescription. One may perform one kind of culturally prescribed roles. If one comes from the same culture and region and if one comes from some other culture and region. Wife's participation in husband's family was thus examined in the light of her belonging to the same town, or other town and/or outside the province as well.

Joint Family

Wife's role as participator in the family life of her husband was examined in three different types of family, the joint, the small joint, and the individual in relation to her occupational status.

There were 6 wives in the joint families who were engaged in service of some kind, and 11 wives who were only house-wives. Taking into consideration the most modern implication of the term "woman's occupational status," housewife's status is also included in the occupational category by modern sociologists.

Of the 6 economic earners, 3 belonged to the town itself, and the rest of 3 there from outside the town but within the same province. All these 6 were full time workers in their jobs. Four of these service holders-wives considered it their primary obligation to share their husband's burden on economic maintenance and had therefore taken an employment while other 2 joined service to pay off their husbands' liabilities, 1 said that she had taken up employment for achieving economic freedom and economic security for herself, 3 of these six women contended that they had taken up employment with a view to provide better future career to their children as their husband's monthly income was not sufficient to meet the requirements. This aspiration for better future of children and sense of security for future appears to be the natural outcome of education and enlightened outlook. Naturally all these 6 women who were employed were educated women (Table 7.4).

Of the 11 housewives, 1 belonged to the same town, 8 were from outside the town and 2 were from outside the province. Since these were housewives they felt an obligation for husband, provider of children's secured future etc.

Small Joint Family

When we compare our findings on the joint family with those in the small joint families, we find some variations. Among the 49 small joint families, 14 wives were occupation holders of service, of these 3 belonged to the town, 6 belonged to another town, and 5 belonged to another province.

All these 14 wives were engaged in full time employment. As for reasons which promoted them to take up employment, only 1 said that she had taken it for passing her time, 2 said that they had taken it for self-satisfaction, another 1 said that she had taken it for achieving her

TABLE 7.4: Wife's Participation in Family Life in Relation to Her Working Woman and Housewife's Statuses

Type of Family and occupational status of wife		Nos. who replied the questions	Native place			Whether full time worker	Where wife feels an obligation to share her husband's burden
			Belongs to the town	Belong to outside town	Belong to outside province		
1		2	3	4	5	6	7
1. Joint Family	1	6	3	3	—	6	4
	4	11	1	8	2	—	—
	NR	—	—	—	—	—	—
Total		17	4	11	2	6	4
2. Small Joint Family	1	14	3	6	5	14	14
	2	1	—	—	1	—	—
	4	27	5	14	8	—	—
	NR	7	—	—	—	—	—
Total		49	8	20	14	14	14
3. Individual Family	1	38	8	10	20	38	24
	2	2	—	—	2	—	—
	4	109	14	266	68	—	—
	NR	7	—	—	—	—	—
Total		156	22	36	91	38	26

TABLE 7.4: (*Contd.*)

Type of Family and occupational status of wife		Reasons for her accepting employment						
		For passing time	For her own self-satisfaction	For achieving economic freedom & economic security for herself	For saving extra money for future	For paying off her husband's liabilities	For providing better edn. and future career to her children as her husband's income is not sufficient	No response
1		8	9	10	11	12	13	14
1. Joint Family	1	—	—	1	—	2	3	—
	4	—	—	—	—	—	—	—
	NR	—	—	—	—	—	—	—
Total		—	—	1	—	2	3	—
2. Small Joint Family	1	1	2	1	3	2	5	—
	2	—	—	—	—	—	1	—
	4	—	—	—	—	—	—	—
	NR	—	—	—	—	—	—	—
Total		1	2	1	3	2	6	—
3. Individual Family	1	—	5	5	4	3	20	1
	2	—	2	—	—	—	—	—
	4	—	—	—	—	—	—	—
	NR	—	—	—	—	—	—	—
Total		—	7	5	4	3	20	1

Codes for occupation: Service — 1
Part-time/casual worker — 2
Business — 3
Housewives — 4

7 Schedules were not filled in case of small joint families

There were two widows and 5 wives did not report.

Note: There were no families where wives were under occupation group 2 & 3 in case of joint families and group 3 in cases of small-joint and individual families.

economic freedom and economic security, 3 said that through her employment she wanted to save for future, 2 said that she had taken it for paying off her husband's liabilities, and 5 said that she had taken it for providing better educational facilities and ensuring their future career to their children as their husband's income was not sufficient to ensure it.

One wife in one small joint family was holding a part-time employment. She belonged to outside the province. She said that she had taken up her part-time employment to augment her husband's resources for providing better educational opportunities and future career of her children.

A large number of wives, 27 in the 49 small joint families were only housewives, and were not occupied anywhere except in their house jobs. Five of these housewives belonged to the same town, 14 came from outside the town, and 8 came from outside the province.

Seven wives in the small joint families did not respond this aspect of enquiry.

Individual Family

The number of individual families composed of husband, wife and their unmarried children were the largest (156) in our sample of urban households. Out of these 156 families, wives from 149 individual families only answered the enquiry on wife's participation, among the 7 not answering, two were widows, hence their discharge of role of wife in relation to obligations towards husband was considered out of question. Besides 5 wives did not answer.

Among these 149 individual families, 38 wives come from the same town, 10 came outside the town and 20 from outside the province. These 38 wives were occupied in full time employment and 2 in part-time employment, and 109 were only housewives.

Of the 38 economic earners, 24 said that they had taken up the employment in order to share their husband's burden, 5 said that they had taken it for their own self-satisfaction. 5 said that they had taken it up for achieving economic freedom and economic security for themselves, 4, however, said that they had taken up the employment for saving extra money for future, 3 said that for paying off their husband's liabilities. Twenty of these 38 wives contended that they had taken up their employment for providing better educational and future career to their children as their husband's income was not sufficient to meet the expenses. One wife in this group did not respond this aspect of enquiry.

Two wives were only partly employed and both of these came from outside the province. These two wives said that they had taken up their part-time job as they felt it their obligation to share husband's economic burden. Both of these, however, also further contended that they had taken it for their own self-satisfaction.

One hundred nine of the wives were only housewives and did not hold any outside employment. Of these 14 belonged to the town, 26 belonged to outside the town, and 69 outside the province. I thus found that those who were from within the town in the total group of joint families were 22 while 36 in all belonged to outside the town and 91 were from outside the province.

All these housewives (109) did not respond to any other categories as these were not concerned with them. It is clearly evident that participation of housewives in their husband's family was limited to their discharging the role of housewife. Even this obligatory role of housewife is quite comprehensive. It includes performing household jobs like kitchen and other domestic works, making a budget and monthly provisions as well as looking after children. It is, thus in, one way, an insignificant role. On the contrary, it implies a concentrated discharge. It is also obligatory on the part of housewife to play the role devotedly. A wife's occupation outside her home often deprives her considerably from several of these roles, or to be active in several role situations which are then supplemented or performed by other members of family, or sometimes by paid servants. This is more so in individual families. The urban Hindu wife's participation is thus normally active in her family life where she is an earner. But it is no less active in the limited domestic sphere even when she is merely a housewife.

Role of wife in her family of living assumes a special meaning when she achieves the educated and earner's status. Her occupation of job outside her household naturally puts a strain on her personality. In the meantime, the members of her family continue to expect from her the discharge of her role of household in the same manner and degree and are not prepared to condone any of her failing roles. Even where husbands are adequately educated, and have accepted the necessity for wife's occupation to sustain family living or have promoted them to accept the job are not easily able to adjust to the new condition. Since her occupation often keeps her out for longer hours of day, her domestic jobs are likely to suffer some loss or lack of proper attention. Some of the working women do not leave their housewives' role and make some adjustments between their working women's demands and housewive's responsibilities. But in other cases several problems arise in the new situation and sometimes new strains are caused due to wife's employment. Promilla Kapur has made a detailed study of these adjustments, non-adjustments and maladjustments in her *Marriage and Working Woman in India* (1971). I am not concerned with such details here, but a reference to this seems essential in assessing the role of wife in her educated wife's and earner wife's capacity and as mere housewife, and see how far adjustments are made here or problems and strains arise.

Role of Educated and Earner Wife and Her Participation in Family Life

The author concerned more with knowing how the educated and earner wife discharges her role in an urban Hindu family and how she manages her housewife's responsibilities. I tried to assess this in the three distinct types of families, the joint, the small joint, and the individual, and in analysing this I have correlated this role with the occupation.

Joint Family

Of the 17 joint families, The author found that there were educated earner wives in 6 families. Out of these six, 4 were full time workers in their jobs. All these 4 were in service class, and said that they had entrusted their kitchen's responsibility to other family members of the joint household though they also said that they had engaged servants in the family.This suggests that they may have engaged servants for some of the domestic jobs, like cleaning of utensils and washing of clothes etc., but the more responsible role of kitchen may have been only entrusted to family members. In case of these 6 earners wives, the partial role of kitchen duties was taken by some other family member in their place, as they had probably no time for this domestic job. But these 4 also said that they continued to take an active interest in their family duties even where servants were engaged.

This indicates that the educated and earning wives, in the joint family, thought their number is small, do not loose interest in their housewife's role, because of their education and employment. Their education perhaps equips them better to discharge their housewife's role. And their earner's status which keeps them away from their homes for a major part of the day also draws them more keenly to their homes when they come back to the home in the evening. And the educated, earner wife tries to compensate her missing role of housewife during day by doing more service more keenly in the evening and at night. She makes some wholesome adjustments between her occupational duties and family obligations. There thus seems to emerge no new strain or problem in the family, because of her occupational role. There were none in other categories of earning (Table 7.5).

Small Joint Family

The role of educated and earner wife in small joint family does not show much difference from what it was found in joint family. There were 14 educated earner wives among the 49 small joint families, with only 1 part-timely employed wife. Of the 14 full time job holders in regular service, 8 service holders had engaged servants for domestic jobs, but 4 of these said that kitchen job was attended by some other family members. All these 8 earners said that they took an active interest in their family duties even when servants were engaged.

Only 1 wife was engaged as part time worker and she had entrusted her kitchen job to a kin. It is thus seen that a majority of educated earner wives were engaged in services and for part of their house-wife's role left by them in their families, they had found some other adjustments. They partly got them performed with courtesy of other family members and partly by the paid servants. It is evident that there has arisen no new problem or strain in the family because of housewife's employment. A rational adjustment between different obligations of home and service seems to have been worked out.

Individual Family

Among individual families the number of educated earner wives was 38, which appears to be more than above two types of family, but if a consideration of the total number of individual family, 156, is taken, the number appears quite proportionate. Of these 38 wives, who were engaged in full time services, 24 said that they had employed servants for their domestic jobs, and 2 had entrusted kitchen duties to their kin.

TABLE 7.5: Educated Earner Wife's Participation in Urban Family

Type of Family/ Occupation group		No. of earning wives	In case of full time workers whether servant is engaged	Are kitchen work entrusted to kin	Wife takes an active interest in her family duties even where servants are engaged
1		2	3	4	5
1. Joint Family	1	6	4	4	4
	NR	—	—	—	—
Total		6	4	4	4
2. Small Joint Family	1	14	8	4	8
	2	1	—	1	—
	NR	—	—	—	—
Total		15	8	5	8
3. Individual Family	1	38	24	2	23
	2	2	—	—	—
	NR	—	1	1	1
Total		40	25	3	24

23 of the 38 earning wives, however, affirmed that they take an active interest in their family duties and obligations even where servants are employed. Only 2 were part-time employees, and these did not answer other categories related to housewife's obligations.

The comparative analysis of individual family and joint family and small joint family reveals that there is more dependence on servants in individual families than on family kin, who are not available here, and in case of joint families, there is more dependence upon family kin for the left out jobs as they are more easily available in the family group. In case of small joint family, there is a striking of balance between the two situations. But it is revealed that occupation of an educated and earner wife has not yet introduced any new conflict or strain in the family organization, whether it be joint, small joint or individual and does not interfere with her housewife's basic role.

I had wanted to examine the role of wife in different perspectives. One important perspective was her working woman's status, and I tried to examine this in relation to her housewife's job. This has been correlated with the fact whether choosing of a working woman's career is a deliberate choice of her own, which had later got her husband's approval, or it has been initially prompted by her husband. This was expected to suggest two different lines of change, one in which woman has achieved a status of autonomy or relative independence in choosing a working woman's career, and another in which she accepts her job out of her husband's choice or to meet her husband's economic choice or to meet her husband's economic and family obligations. It was thus examined through a set of different questions which are examined below.

Acceptance of Job by Wife in Relation to Deliberate Choice and Husband's Consent and Attitude

Joint Family

Our empirical data from Urban Bhopal give us some basic revealations.

Of 6 wives in joint family who had chosen an occupation of service for themselves, 2 said that they had accepted the job by their own choice, and 4 said that they had obtained husband's prior consent to their jobs. Three of these 6 working woman, however, also further said that they had accepted their jobs at the pursuasion of their husbands.

As regards to husband's basic attitude towards their jobs, 2 women said that their husbands were opposed to their jobs while another 2 said that their husband were indifferent to their jobs.

Small Joint Family

When this situation is compared to the small joint family situation, we find that of 14 working women here, 1 accounted her acceptance of job by her own choice, while 13 said that they had obtained husband's consent. All these were engaged in service. Six of these further said that they had accepted their jobs at the persuasion of their husbands. 1 said that her husband was opposed to the job, while 3 said that their husbands were indifferent towards their jobs. There were 2 part-time employees in this group of families. One of these said that she had accepted her job by her own deliberate choice, and 1 said that she had accepted it at her husband's persuasion. Thus those who said that they had accepted their job by their own deliberate choice were far less, 2 in joint family, and 1 in small joint family as compared to those, who had accepted jobs at the persuasion of their husbands, who were as many as 10 in the combined group of joint families, 3 in joint families and 7 in small joint families.

This analysis of joint and small joint family suggests indirectly that woman's career has not yet achieved a position of value.

Among 40 working women enlisted in individual family, 38 were in regular service and only 2 were part-time employees. Ten of the regular service women said that they had accepted their job by their own deliberate choice, while 26 said that their husbands had given their consent to their jobs. Four of the working women said that they had taken up their jobs at the persuasion of their husbands, and 2 said that their husbands are rather opposed to their jobs, while 5 said that their husbands behaved rather indifferently to their employment.

Of the 2 part-time service holders, both said that they had obtained their husband's consent in accepting their jobs.

Thus we find that of these 40 working women, a large number, 28, conceded to have accepted their jobs after obtaining husbands' consent, while only 12 had accepted their jobs at their own deliberate choice, and 6 had accepted it at their husband's persuasion (Table 7.6).

TABLE 7.6: Her Acceptance of Job in Relation to deliberate Choice and Husband's Consent and Attitude

Type of Family/ Occupation group		No. of earning wives	Job accepted by: Own choice	Job accepted by: Husband's consent	Job accepted at the persuasion of husband	Husband is opposed to her job	Husband is indifferent to her job
1		2	3	4	5	6	7
1. Joint Family	1	6	2	4	3	2	2
	NR	—	—	—	—	—	—
Total		6	2	4	3	2	2
2. Small Joint Family	1	14	1	13	6	1	3
	2	1	—	1	1	—	—
	NR	—	—	—	—	—	—
Total		15	1	14	7	1	3
3. Individual Family	1	38	10	26	4	2	5
	2	2	—	2	—	—	—
	NR	—	2	—	2	2	2
Total		40	12	28	6	4	7

It thus appears that in the individual family too, husband's role seem important in motivating his wife towards working woman's career as well as in helping her to adjust herself to the new demand and himself to the new situation in family life.

Among 222 families taken in our sample, there were only 61 earning wives. This suggests that while education and employment are gaining impetus among urban women, the pace made by them is not very much marked. But this certainly indicates that educated earning wife is getting more recognition and importance in her husband's family than a mere housewife.

Role of Wife as Mother to Children

Role of wife is a multiple role, it combines in itself several family roles discharged in different family situations, I have discussed her role as house-wife and role as working woman, and examined now she discharges both these roles effectively by making due adjustments as needed from time to time. A natural corrolary that follows from the above appraisal is what is her expected role as mother of children in the family and now she discharges this role in her family of living in the three different types of family.

One primarily expected role of mother universally is enculturation of child in its family atmosphere. This enculturation implies inculcation of certain family and social virtues like discipline, etiquette, honesty, truthfulness, good and amiable behaviour, obedience to parents and other elders.

It is the primary responsibility of the mother to adapt children in these cultural traits and expect from them a minimum response to her expectations. This responsibility naturally gets increased where mother is educated. Her husband and other members of family may then leave this role entirely to her.

Besides, where she is educated, she is also expected to look after children's formal education. I had, therefore, combined these two aspects of her role expectations in my enquiry and correlated the wife's role discharge towards these with her type of occupation and the type of the family. The results are analysed here.

Joint Family

There were 6 working women and 11 housewives among the 17 joint families. All 6 working women affirmed that they are looking after well on their children's education. They said that they were teaching lessons to children in their spare time. Thus it is apparent that formal education of children was expected to be looked after by the educated and working woman. This seems a newly emergent role for the educated wife as mother who is supposed to be more equipped than her predecessor, uneducated simple and ignorant housewife. This role expectation and role discharge in joint family is in way also indicative of higher status accorded to educated and to working wife in the joint family environment which was not so favourable to woman's position and status till a few decades ago. This is thus evidently a new trend of change in the joint family.

All 6 working wives also affirmed their contribution in children's informal family education. All these said that they encultured their children into codes of family behaviour and they also said that they considered this informal education as essential.

The respondents were given a list of certain family traits and asked to affirm which of the traits they laid emphasis upon for their children. Five of the working mothers said that they stressed upon good, polite and amiable behaviour, 4 upon obedience to parents and other elders, 4 upon discipline and etiquette. Five of these mothers expected to develop intelligence and talent in their children, 4 wanted personal skill, 6 expected them to develop strong will and determination and strong personality. It thus appears that family and social virtues are still considered desirable cultural character traits in the urban joint family.

Among the 11 housewives, who were not engaged in any external occupation, 8 said that they looked after their children's education, 8 said that they were teaching lessons to their children in spare time. This indicates that housewives are also expected to look after children's education. It appears probable that these 8 may have been educated mothers though they were not earners.

All these 11 housewives said that they are also teaching codes of cultural behaviour in family to their children and they also deemed considered this informal education essential.

As regards inculcation of different family and social virtues, 11 wives said that they were emphasising upon good, polite and amiable behaviour, 10 upon obedience to parents and other elders, and 8 upon discipline and etiquette.

Nine housewife mothers expected their children to develop intelligence and talent, personal skill, strong will and determination and development of strong personality.

This analysis indicates that the role expectation of looking after informal and formal education is well discharged by the working woman as well as the housewife in the joint family and that where wife is educated she is considered more competent to discharge this role. Education ascribes a definite status to the housewife.

Small Joint Family

When this role of wife as mother is examined in the small joint family it shows some variations though it does not show much different results.

Of the 14 working women engaged in service in the 49 small joint families, all looked after children's education, they all also taught them lessons in their spare time. This indicates that role of looking after formal education of children is entrusted to working wives and they are discharging it well in their families. These 14 working women also teach their children the code of behaviour in family, while 13 of them only felt that this informal education is essential.

As for the stress laid on different qualities of character, 12 emphasized good, polite and amiable behaviour, obedience to parents, discipline and etiquette, while 11 of them emphasized upon development of intelligence, personal skill, strong will and determination, and 12 upon full development of children's personality. 1 of these 14 working women, did not suggest any of these character traits.

There was only 1 part-time working woman in this type group of family. She said that she was looking after children's education as well as teaching them lessons in their spare time. One said that she was responsible for enculturation of children in the family and taught them the codes of behaviour in family and she considered this informal education in family necessary.

She believed in all desirable qualities of children enlisted viz., good, polite and amiable behaviour, obedience to parents and other elders, discipline and etiquette, and development of intelligence, talent, personal skill, strong will and determination, and strong personality.

There were 27 housewives in these 49 small joint families. 22 of these said that they looked after their children's education, and 21 said that they also taught lessons to their children in spare time. It thus appears that among 27 housewives 22 are actually entrusted with care of children's formal education as they may have been considered competent for it, because of these education.

Among 27 housewives only 24 said that they were teaching their children codes of behaviour i.e., informal education in their family. While 26 considered this informal education essential, 24 housewives laid stress upon good, polite, and amiable behaviour, 23 upon obedience to parents and elders, 22 upon discipline and etiquette, 17 upon intelligence and talent, 16 upon personal skill and 15 upon strong will and determination and development of strong personality. One housewife did not respond on this aspect.

This analysis of role of mother in the small joint family indicates that both working women and housewives are discharging their role of mother to children in an active manner. Where they are educated, the role expectation of looking after the children's formal and informal education is made more from them.

Taking an overall view of the situation in the small joint families were find that among 42 respondents, 37 wives acted as mother to children and looked after their children's education, while 35 of these also actively imparted them school lessons at home. 39 of these also encultured their children in the code of behaviour in family, and 40 considered informal education essential. As regards inculcation of desirable character traits in children, 37 stressed upon good, polite and amiable behaviour, 36 upon obedience to parents and other elders, 35 upon discipline and etiquette, 29 upon intelligence and talent, 28 upon personal skill, 27 upon strong will and determination and 28 upon development of strong personality.

Individual Family

Among 156 individual families, response was received from 149 respondents only. Seven wives did not respond. Among these 149 respondents, 38 were working women in full time service, 2 part-time service and 109 were solely housewives.

Of 38 service holders, 33 wives said that they looked after their children's education in an active manner and 34 said that they also taught their children.

This indicates that these working women were entrusted with the role of looking after children's formal education. It appears that these working women are also educated wives hence considered competent to discharge this important role.

Two part-time working women said that they looked after their children's formal education and enculturation of children and both of them affirmed all categories of cultural virtues, except inculcation of character trait of strong will and determination in which only 1 had agreed.

Among the 149 respondents there were 109 housewives who were solely engaged in their house jobs. Eighty-nine of these housewives said that they looked after their children's education while 87 said that they also taught them lessons in their spare time. Ninety-nine of these housewives said that they adapted their children to the expected codes of behaviour in the family, and 101 considered such informal education essential.

These working women were also expected to enculture children into family values. Thirty-four of these working women said that they were teaching codes of behaviour to their children while 33 considered such informal education essential. Thirty-three working women laid emphasis upon good, polite and amiable behaviour and obedience to parents and elders, while 31 stressed upon discipline and etiquette, 27 upon development of intelligence and talent, 25 upon personal skill and strong will and determination, and 26 upon development of strong personality.

As for inculcation of desirable character traits considered necessary, 93 laid emphasis upon good, polite and amiable behaviour, 95 upon obedience to parents and other elders, 87 upon discipline and etiquette and 78 upon development of intelligence and talent, 67 upon personal skill, 62 upon strong will and determination and 5 upon development of strong personality.

Taking an overall view of the situation in the individual family it is found that out of 149 respondents, 124 wives acting as mother to children looked after children's formal education, and 123 wives actually imparted teaching to their children in spare time. Eighty-nine wives in individual family were also concerned with teaching cultural codes of behaviour in family to children and 88 considered such informal education essential.

As far desirable character traits stressed upon children, 128 of the wives said that they laid stress upon good, polite and amiable behaviour, 130 upon obedience to parents and other elders, 120 upon discipline and etiquette, 107 upon development of intelligence and talent 94 upon personal skill, 88 upon strong will and determination and 103 upon development of strong personality (Table 7.7).

TABLE 7.7: Her Role as Mother in Children's Education

Type of Family/ Occupation group		No. of wives	Wife looks after children's education	Wife teaches lessons to her children in spare time	Wife teach them the code of behaviour in family	Where wife thinks that this informal education is essential
1		2	3	4	5	6
1. Joint Family	1	6	6	6	6	6
	4	11	8	8	11	11
	NR	—	—	—	—	—
Total		17	14	14	17	17
2. Small Joint Family	1	14	14	14	14	13
	2	1	1	—	1	1
	4	27	22	21	24	26
	NR	7	—	—	—	—
Total		49	37	35	39	40
3. Individual Family	1	38	33	34	34	33
	2	2	2	2	2	2
	4	109	89	87	96	101
	NR	7	5	5	7	3
Total		156	129	128	139	139

TABLE 7.7 (*Contd.*)

Type of Family/ occupation group		Where wife lays emphasis on the following characteristics of children							
		Good, polite and amiable behaviour	Obedience to parents and other elders	Discipline & etiquette	Intelligence and talent	Personal skill	Strong will & determination	Full development personality	No response
1		7	8	9	10	11	12	13	14
1. Joint Family	1	5	4	4	5	4	6	5	—
	4	11	10	8	9	9	9	9	—
	NR	—	—	—	—	—	—	—	—
Total		16	14	12	14	13	15	14	—
2. Small Joint Family	1	12	12	12	11	11	11	12	1
	2	1	1	1	1	1	1	1	—
	4	24	23	22	17	16	15	15	1
	NR	—	—	—	—	—	—	—	—
Total		37	36	35	29	28	27	28	2
3. Individual Family	1	33	33	31	27	25	25	26	—
	2	2	2	2	2	2	1	2	—
	4	93	95	87	78	67	62	75	—
	NR	8	—	—	—	—	—	—	—
Total		136	130	120	107	94	88	103	—

Note: Figures in Cols. 3 to 7 under individual family group (HR) are excluding the number given in Col. 7.

This analysis of individual family indicates that both the working women and the housewives are expected to play upon the role of looking after the children's informal and formal education. This role expectation appears to have been ascribed to them mostly because of their education and also because of their earning status. Both the education and the earning have raised the status of woman in family in all three types of family though their influence varies in different degrees. And this status appears to be marked more in the individual family than in the joint and the small joint family.

Role of Wife as Mother to Children in deciding their Education and Planning Their Future

Role of wife is usually a role of companionship to her husband these days in an urban environment and where she is educated and also co-earner with her husband. Ross has called the contemporary individual family of husband, wife and children, "a companionship family", and I agree basically with her definition. It defines very rightly the contemporary urban individual family as well as the atmosphere in which this family now lives.

As a companion to her husband the modern wife discharges a significant role in educating and training their children. Not only this, she also decides often in consultation with her husband the particular line of education for their children, such as whether they will choose arts, science or commerce, and whether depending upon their temperament and individual capacity which course and career will be more suitable to them. This is definitely a modern approach towards children's education and with the growing emphasis upon healthy child development more and more educated parents are feeling concerned to adopt this approach in bringing up their children. This approach also suggests dealing with children's problems psychologically. This consideration was almost lacking in the joint family organization of some fifty years ago. Considering this as a trend of change I had wanted to examine how far wife participates with her husband in deciding their children's education and act as an enlightened and responsible mother to her children. The results are analysed in Table 7.8.

TABLE 7.8: As Mother to Children in Deciding and Designing Children's Education in View of their Future Career

Type of Family/ Occupation group		No. of wives	Where wife herself chooses a line of education for her children such as Arts, Commerce, Science etc.	Where husband wife mutually discuss among themselves about the future edu. of their children	Where wife feels that it is necessary to accept her in such decisions about children's future	Does husband's decision always dominates such issue		Where wife feels that concerned son's/daughter's opinion should also be taken in deciding about their educational career	Who acts formally as guardian to children		
						Yes	Equal share in decision-making		Wife	Husband	Both
1		2	3	4	5	6	7	8	9	10	11
1. Joint Family	1	6	5	6	6	2	4	4	1	3	2
	4	11	7	10	9	3	6	8	—	10	1
	NR	—	1	1	1	1	—	3	—	—	—
Total		17	13	17	16	6	10	15	1	13	3
2. Small Joint Family	1	14	3	13	10	1	13	10	1	11	2
	2	1	1	1	1	—	1	—	—	1	—
	4	27	7	24	20	12	13	12	3	17	6
	NR	7	—	—	—	—	—	—	—	—	—
Total		49	11	38	31	13	27	22	4	29	8
3. Individual Family	1	38	20	31	30	9	26	19	5	24	8
	2	2	—	2	2	—	2	1	1	1	—
	4	109	37	95	89	21	76	49	8	73	19
	NR	7	8	10	11	9	—	14	10	—	—
Total		156	65	138	132	39	104	83	24	98	27

Joint Family

Among 17 joint families, 6 working women chose a line of career for their children such as arts, science or commerce in view of their temperament and individual capability, while those 6 working women also said that they mutually discussed with their husbands about the future education of their children. All these 6 working women felt that it is necessary to consult the husbands in deciding about children's future. As regards the question, whose decision was considered final, 2 wives said that husband's decision always dominated such issues, while 4 wives said that they equally shared the decision with their husbands.

A pin-pointed question in this context was that whether the concerned son or daughter was also consulted about his or her future educational career. Four working women affirmed this view while 2 differed.

In educated families the role of guardianship to children is not exclusively left to father, it is also shared by mother. Both the husband and wife realise their responsibility towards children jointly try to share this function. In an urban family, the busy husband often does not find enough time to look after the children's problems and formalities of school, and often entrusts this role to his wife. With this view, the respondents were interrogated specifically on this issue. Out of 6 working women, only 1 said that she acts formally as guardian to her children, while 3 said that their husbands solely discharged this role and 2 said that both of them acted formally as guardians.

When we compare the responses of working women with those of housewives in rest of the joint families, we do not find much variation. Of the 11 housewives, 7 said that they chose a line of education for their children, while 10 said that they mutually discussed with their husbands about the future education of their children. Nine housewives expressed that it is necessary for the husband to co-opt his wife in taking decisions about their children's future.

As regards the issue whose decision ultimately dominates, 3 housewives said that their husbands' decision always dominates such issue, while 6 housewives said that they shared it equally with their husbands.

Eight of the housewives expressed the opinion that son's and daughter's opinions should also be taken in deciding about the future educational career of the children.

As regards the guardian's role, 10 housewives said that it is solely exercised by husband, while 1 said that both the husband and wife exercise it. None of these suggested that this responsibility has been entrusted to wife.

Small Joint Family

When we compare the analysis of joint family with that of small joint family, we find that there are three categories of respondents answering these, the working women in service, the part-time women and the housewives. Among 14 working women, only 3 said that they as mothers chose a line of education for their children, while as may as 13 said that the husband and wife mutually discussed among themselves about the future education of their children. Ten working women said that it is necessary to co-opt wife in such decisions about children's future. Thirteen working women considered their equal share in such decision making while 1 said that the husband's decision always dominates much issue irrespective of the fact whether she is consulted or not.

As may as 10 out of these 14 working women felt that they concerned son's and daughter's opinions should also be taken in deciding about their educational career. Eleven working said that husbands act formally as guardians to children in their families while 1 said that wife acts as guardian and 2 said that both act as guardians.

Of the 2 part-time working women, only 1 responded and said that she chose a line of education for her children. She also said that both the husband and wife should mutually discuss among themselves about future education of their children and that it is necessary to coopt the wife in making decisions about children's future. She also said that she shares the final decision equally with her husband and that her husband acts formally as guardian to children and she feels no objection to this.

Out of 27 housewives, 7 expressed that they chose a line of education for their children, 24 said that they mutually discussed with their husband about the future education of their children, and 20 said that it is necessary to co-opt her in such decisions about children's future. Thirteen of these said that their husbands' decision always dominated such issue, while 12 felt that they had an equal share with their husbands in decision making. Twelve housewives also expressed that the concerned son's and daughter's opinion should also be taken in deciding about their future education. Seventeen housewives said that their husbands acted formally as guardian to their children, 3 housewives said that this responsibility was entrusted to them while 6 said that both the husband and wife exercised this responsibility.

This indicates that while there is a good deal of consciousness about woman's status and wife's equal place in the family organisation and her participation in several important roles such as deciding and designing children's education. Though the main role of guardianship traditionally still rests with the husband, the educated husbands have now started delegating this role to their educated wives. In as many as 29 out of 49 small joint families and in as many as 13 out of 17 joint families, the role of guardianship was solely discharged by the husband. Tradition exercises still a strong influence on the joint and small joint Hindu family organization.

Individual Family

Among 156 individual families, 38 wives were found to be working women in regular service. Twenty of these working women said that they participated in choosing a line of career for their children, 31 said that the husband and wife mutually discussed among themselves about the future education of their children and 30 said that they considered it necessary to coopt wives whenever such decisions are taken.

Nine working women felt that the husband's decision always dominates the issue of children's education, while 26 felt that they had an equal share with husbands in decision making about their children. Nineteen working women said that the concerned son's and daughter's opinion should also be taken in deciding and designing their educational career.

As regards acting as guardian to children, 24 working women said that the husband solely acted as guardian, while only 5 said that the wife acted as guardian. Some 8 working women said that both the husband and wife exercised this role.

Among 2 part-time working women in the individual family, both said that they mutually discussed with their husbands about the future education of their children, and stressed that wives should be coopted by their husbands in taking decisions about their children's future. Both of these part-time working women felt that they had an equal share in decision-making, while only one of them felt that the concerned son's or daughter's opinion should also be taken in deciding about their educational career.

One part-time working women said that the guardian's role was acted upon by husband, and one said that she herself acted upon it.

Among 109 housewives in the individual families, 37 expressed that they chose a line of education for their children, while as many as 95 said that they discussed with their husbands about the future education of their children. Eighty-nine of these housewives expressed the opinion that it is necessary to co-opt wife in such decisions about children's future.

Twenty-one of these housewives said that husband's decision always dominated the issue of children's educational career, while as many as 76 said that they exercised an equal control in such decision making.

Forty-nine housewives considered that the concerned son's and daughter's opinion should also be taken in deciding about their own educational career.

A very large number of housewives, 73 said that husbands acted formally as guardians to children while only 8 said that wives were entrusted this role, and 19 said that both the husband and wife exercised this role of guardianship.

This analysis of individual family indicates that where a large number of wives, both working women and housewives, are participating in the educational planning of their children, and are acting in coordination with their husbands in this sphere, they are to an extent also sharing the decision-making with their husbands. While this may be a privilege of the educated wives, the formal role of guardianship still rests often with the husband, as may as 98 wives in the individual families suggested that the husbands acted formally as guardian to children, as against 34 wives who said that they were exercising this role. In 27 cases both the husband and wife shared the role of guardianship.

It thus appears that some trends of change are being marked in all the three types of family, the joint, the small joint and the individual in the areas of participation in children's education and planning, liberal attitude towards children conceding of more privileges to educated wives, and sharing of certain family roles jointly by husbands and wives and in developing an attitude of companionship towards the wife. However the formal roles expected in the tradition, like the role of guardianship to be vested in the authoritative head, still continue to be performed more or less conventionally in the household. It appears probably that one important reason behind this is that the Hindu wives even though educated do not themselves want to deprive their husbands from a long culturally ingrained traditional role.

Wife's Role of Socio-Economic Participation with Husband

The educated and the employed wife is expected to perform one more important role in her family life, and that is of socio-economic participation with her husband. Education has made her more enlightened and rational and her own earning has equipped her well to realise her responsibility towards her children and towards her husband. I have discussed in the preceding pages how the acts upon her new role of caretaking of children's education. I have also discussed how the educated wife has realised her own responsibility of assisting her husband in the sustenance of family and has thus made her to accept an employment.

Here I will now see how the educated-employed wife fulfils this role obligation by participating socio-economically with her husband in their family life.

This socio-economic participation is assured through a number of family activities. I have picked up a few of these to assess in what way, and to what extent this socio-economic participation of wife with her husband has been affected in the family, and whether a particular type of family and the fact of occupation make any variations in her discharge of the obligation.

Joint Family

Among 17 joint families there were 6 working women who were employed in a full time job. One wife among these working woman said that she was entrusted the responsibility of initially preparing the budget, while as many as 6 of housewives said that they were discharging this responsibility of budget-making even though they were not co-earners. It appears probable that the occupation of wife has not much affected this family activity in the joint family. It also appears probable that education alone equips her well to assume this responsibility (Table 7.9).

Another activity related with socio-economic participation is the control of purse. Traditionally, the husband or the head of household was the Chief Controllor of Purse of the Family. Tendencies of individualism and nuclearization of family have taken away this

TABLE 7.9: Wife's Socio-Economic Participation with Husband in Family

Type of Family/ Occupation group		No. of wives	Wife initially prepares family budget	Who controls the purse			Where wife is obliged to join her husband in any social ceremonies	Where wife feels that she is playing equal role in the family
				Husband	Wife	Both		
1		2	3	4	5	6	7	8
1. Joint Family	1	6	1	3	2	1	5	6
	4	11	6	5	3	2	9	9
	NR	—	1	1	—	—	1	1
Total		17	8	9	5	3	15	16
2. Small Joint Family	1	14	7	4	5	5	12	14
	2	1	1	1	—	—	1	1
	4	27	12	11	11	5	21	24
	NR	7	—	—	—	—	—	—
Total		49	20	16	16	10	34	29
3. Individual Family	1	38	13	16	12	9	33	36
	2	2	—	—	1	1	2	2
	4	109	51	45	34	22	91	95
	NR	7	15	9	—	—	7	9
Total		156	79	70	47	32	133	142

Note: Figures in Cols. 3, 4 & 7 under Individual Family Group (NR) are excluding figures given in Col. 2.

function from the authoritative head of the family and distributed it among individual heads of residential families. Education and earning of women have in some cases transferred this responsibility to the housewife.

Of the 6 working women, 3 said that their husbands control the purse, while 2 said that the wives and 1 said that both the husband and wife control it. As against this, 5 housewives indicated husband, 3 indicated wife and 2 indicated both.

Participation in social and religious ceremonies is a feature which indicates whether the urban educated wife finds it her obligation to joint her husband in such activities and whether this obligation is now discharged with more sense of responsibility. Nine of the 11 housewives said that they were obliged to join their husbands in social and religious ceremonies. It appears that here too, education to a great extent makes the wife more equipped to ensure this participation and the occupational status of the wife in a secondary way only accelerates it.

An appropriate question was asked from the wife about her actual, recognized status of wife in the family related to her equal playing of role. All 6 working women and 9 housewives affirmed that they are playing an equal role by participation with their husbands in their families. It seems probable that education and employment have together earned the recognition for the wife for her equal playing of role in the family with her husband.

Small Joint Family

When findings on joint family are compared to those on small joint family, it is found that there are not many variations.

Among 49 small joint family, 7 of the 14 working women in regular service, 1 in part time employment and 12 housewives said that they were primarily entrusted with preparation of family budget. Four working women, 1 part-timely employed woman and 11 housewives said that the family purse is solely controlled by their husbands, whereas 5 working wives, 1 part timely employed wife, and 11 housewives said that it is controlled by the wife. As different from these 5 working women and 5 housewives said that it is controlled by both the husband and the wife.

As regards social participation of wife with her husband in social and religious functions, 12 working women, 1 part-timely employed women, and 21 housewives expressed that they were participating with their husbands in social and religious ceremonies. And as regards their own assessment of their equal role in the family, all 14 working women, 1 of the 2 part timely employed wives and 24 of the 27 housewives said that they were playing an equal role with their husbands in their families.

This indicates that all those wives who are educated are playing an equal role with their husbands in their families, as they are supposed to be more equipped and their husbands may be feeling confident in entrusting certain responsibilities to them. Where the wives are also coearners this may further accelerate their playing of equal role with their husbands in their own families. It appears probable here that jointness or small jointness of family does not in any way retard or hinder this playing of equal role by wife in her family of living. Education has certainly raised her status in the family, and her own earning has tended to ascribe her better status. Considerations and concessions are usually made when wife is also engaged in her own occupation outside her home.

Individual Family

Individual family is expected to mean more freedom to wife and therefore findings here were expected to reveal some significant variations from those on the joint and the small joint families. There were 38 working women in regular service, 2 in part-time service, while there were as may as 109 housewives among 156 individual families though among the respondents in the individual families 7 did not respond at all on this issue.

Thirteen of these 38 working women and 51 of the 109 housewives affirmed that they were entrusted with the responsibility of initially preparing the family budget. Sixteen working women and 45 housewives said that the family purse is mainly controlled by their husbands while 12 working women, 1 part-timely employed woman and 34 housewives said that the wife controls it.

Nine working women, 1 part-time woman and 22 housewives, however, said that both the husband and wife control it.

On social and religious participation, 33 working women, 2 part timely employed women and 91 housewives believed that they were obliged to join their husbands in any social and religious ceremonies. Having answered all these aspects of family activity, as many as 36 of the 38 working women, 2 part-timely employed women and 95 of the 109 housewives felt that they were playing an equal role with their husband in their families.

This indicates that a large number of wives are actively participating with their husbands in discharging many family obligations, of which socio-religious participation also forms an important part.

This role may have been assumed by the wives themselves in certain cases, and it may have been entrusted by their husband in other cases. But in both ways it is indicative of a new change that has come in the husband-wife relationship. The husband's attitude towards his wife is now becoming more respectful and more equalitarian, and he wife's response to her husband has now become more considerate and sympathetic. It is also more realistic. She now feels her obligation to share here husband's socio-economic burden, a function which was probably not at all understood or realised by her predecessor some fifty years ago.

Husband-Wife Relationship

The most vital aspect of the functional family roles is the relationship between husband and wife which ensures a healthy environment for the development of children's personality. I had hypothetically assumed that with increasing education and enlightenment during past three or four decades there has been a promotion in mutual understanding of the husband and wife. This has certainly, affected their relationship. I had, therefore, wanted to put this hypothesis to test in my enquiry on these aspects.

Behaviour in Joint Family

Among 17 joint families, 4 of the 6 working wives with regular jobs had felt that they are living in a kind of relationship where they can freely discuss their doubts and differences in personal and family matters with their husbands in an atmosphere of confidence. Where the husband wife relationship was different from this norm, and where wife felt scared to discuss personal and family matters, different reasons were assigned. One of the 2 working women said that she could not discuss her personal and family matters with him because her husband was rude, while another one said that he was indifferent.

Among 11 housewives 7 said that they can discuss their doubts and differences in personal and family matters with their husbands freely and in atmosphere of confidence, while 4 said that they felt scared to do so as their husbands were rather rude in their behaviour.

This indicates that while a majority of wives in both the group – co-earner and housewife groups — felt confidence to discuss their problems freely with their husbands, there are still some who feel hesitant in discussing these with their husbands. It appears that an atmosphere of old conservatism still prevails in some tradition-ridden families where husbands behave rather rudely.

Small Joint Family

Among 14 working wives in 49 small joint families, 11 felt confident of discussing their doubts and personal difference freely with their husbands. Two said that they were hesitant in discussing these as their husbands were indifferent to them, while 1 said that the husband was rather suspicious towards her.

Among 2 part-time workers, only one replied that she can discuss her doubts and differences with her husbands freely. The other one did not respond of this issue.

Among 27 housewives in the small joint families as many as 20 said that they could discuss their doubts and differences with their husbands freely and in an atmosphere of confidence. Seven said that they could not discuss so freely as their husbands did not encourage this kind of behaviour, 2 said that their husbands were rude, 2 said that the husbands were impertinent, and 1 said that he was indifferent, suspicious and had held grievances against her. Seven wives did not respond on this.

Individual Family

Among 156 individual families we had found 38 working women with regular employment, 2 part-tome working women and 109 housewives, 7 had not responded to any of these categories (Table 7.10).

Of the 38 working women 31 said that they can discuss their doubts and personal differences freely with their husbands while 3 said that they could not so freely discuss these as their husbands were rude, 2 said that they could not so freely discuss these as their husbands were impertinent and 1 was indifferent. One said that her husband held

TABLE 7.10: Wife's Opinion Regarding Her Husband's Behaviour Towards Her

Type of Family/ Occupation group		No. of wives	Where wife feels that she can discuss her doubts and differences in personal & family matter with her husband freely and in atmosphere of confidence	Where wife feels to share to discuss personal & family matters with her husband because her husband is				
				Rude	Impertinent	Indifferent	Suspicious	Has grievances against her
1		2	3	4	5	6	7	8
1. Joint Family	1	6	4	1	—	1	—	—
	4	11	7	4	—	—	—	—
	NR	—	1	—	—	—	—	—
Total		17	12	5	—	1	—	—
2. Small Joint Family	1	14	11	—	—	2	1	—
	2	1	1	—	—	—	—	—
	4	27	20	2	2	1	1	1
	NR	7	—	—	—	—	—	—
Total		49	32	2	2	3	2	1
3. Individual Family	1	38	31	3	2	1	—	1
	2	2	2	—	—	—	—	—
	4	109	99	5	—	1	1	4
	NR	7	6	—	—	—	—	—
Total		156	138	8	2	1	1	5

grievances against her. Of 2 part-timely working women both had felt that they can confidently discuss their doubts and differences with their husbands.

When 109 housewives were examined on this issue it was found that 99 of them felt confident of discussing their doubts and differences with their husbands while 5 were scared of doing so as their husbands were rude, one said that her husband was impertinent, one said that husband was indifferent, 1 said that he was suspicious, and 4 said that their husbands had grievances against them and were thus distrustful of them.

This analysis of the joint, the small joint and the individual family indicates that the husband-wife relationship in most of the urban families and in all its three types of family in most cases is cordial and full of mutual understanding. This is certainly a modern trend of change, and seems to be an outcome of higher education and enlightenment which have ultimately made the husbands rational. Educated woman's employment and her association with external world have also helped her to achieve this ascribed status.

Wife's Opinion Regarding Husband-Wife Relationship

Husband-wife relationship is not only what one normally expects to be in a family but also what both the parties actually feel towards this family relationship. I have discussed in the earlier pages of this chapter, what the husband feels about this husband-wife relationship. Here my concern is with their husband-wife relationship as viewed by the wife. I had interviewed specifically on this issue and collected responses from among three different types of family and correlated these to different occupational groups of the wife, full time working woman, part-time working woman and the housewife.

Joint Family

Among 17 joint families only two types of occupations were followed by the wives, the full time working woman's, and the housewives. The wives here expressed different opinions about their own position in the family, their rights and privileges and the status accorded to them by their husbands in their families.

Of the 6 working wives all felt that their position was respectful in their own families. Ten of the 11 housewives also felt their own position in their families respectful. One housewife did not respond on this point. These 6 working women and 10 housewives felt that they can assert their position in the family where necessary. This suggests that both, the working women and the housewives, were satisfied with their own position in the family and did not express any grudge.

These working women and housewives were further interviewed on their own opinion about their husbands, that is, what is their own image about their husbands. One working woman and 2 housewives thought their husbands to be honourable men to be respected for their good and sympathetic behaviour. Three working women and 3 housewives considered their husbands to be friends and companions, while 5 housewives considered their husbands to be authoritative heads of families who supported them in their sustenance, 3 working women and 1 housewife did not respond on this aspect.

As to the wife's opinion about the accord and support given to husband's decisions, 4 working women and 9 housewives expressed that they tried to listen to their husband's opinions and decisions in a spirit of understanding and good faith.

Four working women and 10 housewives said that they can well argue with their husbands where they think it necessary. Four working women and 9 housewives further concerned that their husbands make due allowance for their arguments and try to understand them; Three did not respond on this aspect.

This analysis of wife's opinion regarding husband-wife relationship indicates that in most cases 16 out of 17 wives had found their own position respectful and in many cases, 13 out of 17 wives, could confidently express themselves to their husbands, could argue well with their husband and in turn feel that their husbands make due allowance for their arguments and try to understand them properly. This indicates that wife's position in the joint family has shown an improvement from what it was some fifty years ago. This itself indicates a trend of change in as much as even a joint family environment is now found to be encouraging.

Small Joint Family

When I had compared my findings on the wife's opinion regarding the husband-wife relationship in the joint family with those in the small joint family, I had found some variations.

Among 14 working women, all 14, among 2 part-timely employed women 1, and among 27 housewives (who answered), 22 had their position respectful in the family while 2 housewives had found it inferior, and 1 housewife had found it rather awkward in the family (Table 7.11).

As regards their own image of their husbands, 1 working woman and 5 housewives had found their husbands an honourable men to be respected for their good and sympathetic attitude, 1 working woman and 4 housewives had found them as authoritative heads who had supported them in their livelihood and 11 working women, 1 part-timely employed woman and 14 housewives considered their husbands as friends and companions. This suggests that there has been an increase in the friendly and companionship relationship of husband and wife. All three groups of occupation of wife mostly support this thesis. In all 26 respondents in the 49 small joint families, (including 7 non-respondents) indicate it. One working woman and 4 housewives did not respond on this aspect.

Thirteen out of the 14 working women, 1 out of the 2 part timely employed women and 22 housewives in the small joint families expressed that they tried to listen to their husbands' opinions and decisions in a spirit of understanding and good faith. This suggests mutual trust and confidence.

Thirteen of the working women, 1 part time worker and 23 housewives had felt that they can argue well with their husbands where they think it necessary, and 13, 1 and 22 respectively in these groups had also felt that their husbands make due allowances for their arguments and try to understand them sympathetically.

The analysis of wife's opinion regarding her own position in the family, her rights and privileges and her esteem of her husband indicates that a large number of wives, 37 out of 49 are enjoying a respectful position in their families, and all these 37 can also assert their position where necessary. As many as 26 wives find themselves living in a friendly and companionship relationship, and as many as 37, again, can express themselves freely to their husbands and in an atmosphere of good faith and also find a congenial response from their husbands.

This indicates that there has been more a trend towards congenial and mutual faith-relationship of husband and wife which has probably resulted into an expression of wife's personality in a more free atmosphere than was possible two or three decades ago.

TABLE 7.11: Wife's Opinion Regarding Husband-Wife Relationship

Type of Family/ Occupation group of wife		No. of wives	Wife feels her position in the family is				Wife feels that she can assert her position where necessary
			Respectful	Inferior	Degraded	Awkward	
1		2	3	4	5	6	7
1. Joint	1	6	6	—	—	—	6
Family	4	11	10	—	—	—	10
	NR	—	1	—	—	—	1
Total		17	17	—	—	—	17
2. Small Joint	1	14	14	—	—	—	13
Family	2	1	1	—	—	—	1
	4	27	22	2	—	1	23
	NR	7	2	—	—	—	—
Total		49	39	2	—	1	37
3. Individual	1	38	36	2	—	—	34
Family	2	2	2	—	—	—	2
	4	109	98	2	3	—	88
	NR	7	6	—	—	—	9
Total		156	142	4	3	—	133

TABLE 7.11: (*Contd.*)

Type of Family/ Occupation groups of wife		Opinion of wife regarding her husband: An honorable man to be respected for his good and sympathetic attitude	An authoritative head of family who supports her livelihood	A friend & companion	No response given	Where wife tries to listen her husband's opinions and decisions in a spirit of understanding and good faith	Where wife feels that she can argue with her husband where she thinks if necessary	Where wife feels that her husband makes due allowance to her argument and tries to understand her sympathetically
1		8	9	10	11	12	13	14
1. Joint Family	1	1	—	3	2	4	4	4
	4	2	5	3	1	9	10	3
	NR	—	—	—	—	3	3	3
Total		3	5	6	3	16	17	16
2. Small Joint Family	1	1	1	11	1	13	13	13
	2	—	—	1	—	1	1	1
	4	5	4	14	4	22	23	22
	NR	—	—	—	—	1	1	1
Total		6	5	26	5	37	38	37
3. Individual Family	1	3	9	23	3	32	33	24
	2	—	—	2	—	2	2	2
	4	33	13	54	9	966	95	87
	NR	—	—	—	—	13	13	18
Total		36	22	79	12	143	143	131

Note: Figures in Cols. 3, 7, 10 to 14 under group (NR) are excluding the figures given in Col. 2.

Individual Family

Wife's position, status, privileges and treatment by husband is usually expected to be more free and open in individual family than in joint or small joint family.

With this assumption, I had approached the individual family and the following analysis indicates how far it was found valid.

Out of 38 working women in individual families, 36 believed their position to be respectful and 2 found it inferior. Among 2 part-time workers, both wives found their position respectful and among 109 housewives, 98 found their position to be respectful and 2 found it inferior. Six did not respond here. It appears that whereas there has been an improvement in wife's position in family in late years, owing to education and her own employment in some families and in some environments there still prevails a kind of conservative outlook towards wife and here the type of family matters little which could be found responsible for keeping her wife's position esteemed inferior or degreded. It can be said that this is like a small survival of the old attitude, a kind of cultural lag in the developing society.

As regards to wife's confidence to assert her own position in the family, 34 working women, 2 part-time working women and 88 housewives said that they can assert their own position in the family, 9 did not respond on this aspect.

In their own esteem of their husbands, 3 working women, and 33 housewives considered their husbands as honourable men to be respected for their good and sympathetic behaviour towards them, 9 working women and 13 housewives considered them as authoritative heads who supported them in their livelihood. Twenty-three working women, 2 part-time working women and 54 housewives, that is, as many as 79 wives in all, out of 149 respondents in this group of families had found them as friends and companions.

When wives were interviewed on the issue as to how they mutually deal with their husbands, 32 working women in full time job, 2 in part-time job and 96 housewives said that they tried to listen to their husbands' opinions and decisions in a spirit of understanding and good faith. Thirty-three working women, 2 part time workers and 95 housewives felt that they can argue with their husbands when they think it necessary, and 24 working women, 2 part-time workers, and 87 housewives had further believed that their husbands make due allowance for their argument and try to understand them sympathetically.

This analysis of individual families indicates that most of wives in all three categories of occupation, full time working women, part time working women and housewives are living in an open atmosphere in their individual families where they have more freedom to express themselves, receive recognition from their husbands and discuss their family problems with them more freely and in a spirit of confidence. This indicates a trend of change in the modern Hindu family, as her predecessor a few decades ago was debarred from this privilege and was living in a kind of self-repressed state and in an atmosphere where woman had little recognition.

Wife's Social Participation in Urban Family

The Hindu wife is not only expected to be a good, amiable housewife, but also to be socially acceptable. Social acceptance depends largely upon how far an individual participates in social activities and this holds true with the Hindu wife living in her husband's family, she having got once adjusted to the family expectations is now expected to meet social expectations too as far as possible. The Hindu society from the very beginning has laid emphasis on community and society. The rendering of an old, scriptural *Shloka* in Sanskrit means, personal interests have to be sacrificed for the interests of family, family interest have to be the sacrificed for the interests of the community, and community interests have to sacrificed for the interests of society. While the old society drew the traditional joint family in its web in different ways and was always interested in exerting its influence and control, the modern conditions of society which are now more complex, have also cast their pressures on the individual who is ultimately remineded about the social bond.

I had, therefore, introduced some questions pertaining to the wife's participation in the urban Hindu family in the last part of the schedule. The responses that were obtained had been correlated to the type of family and the occupational group. The analysed responses express on the one hand the various media in which this participation is made, and on the other hand they indicate the extent of social participation of the wife.

Joint Family

It was expected that wife's social participation may vary in the different types of family, hence these were examined separately.

Among 6 working women 2 felt that they had a social status outside the family as they had participated in social activities of Mahila Mandals; 2 said that they had participated in activities of lady welfare clubs, and 2 in activities of cooperative societies as well as in activities of knitting, embroidery and/or tailoring centres.

Four of these 6 working women felt that social participation in these different activities raises their social status. Three of these wives further felt that their husbands feel proud of their such participation.

The wives were also interviewed on husband's attitude towards their participation. Only 1 working wife said that her husband did not show any reaction over her social participation, she said that he remained rather indifferent.

Among 11 housewives 4 said that they had achieved social status outside the family as they had participated in activities of Mahila Mandals; 3 had participated in activities of Lady's Welfare Clubs and 2 in activities of cooperative societies. Four of the housewives felt that this social participation has raised their social status. 5 of the housewives had further felt that their husbands were proud of their participation in social activities.

Only one housewife had expressed her husband's reaction over such participation. She said that he was opposed to her social participation.

This analysis indicates that as many as 9 wives among 17 joint families were participating in some social activity and as many as 11 felt that such social participation had raised their social status, and that their husbands felt proud of such participation. This suggests the extent of participation among wives in the joint family which appears quite marked as compared to the social participation which was made some fifty years ago.

Small Joint Family

Among 49 small joint families, 14 wives were working, one was a part-timely employed working woman and 27 were housewives. Responses for rest of 7 were not given.

Two of the 14 working women, and 8 of the 27 housewives believed that they achieved a social status by participating in activities of Mahila Mandals. 1 working woman and 3 housewives participated in activities of lady's welfare clubs, one working woman and 2 housewives in activities of cooperative societies while 2 working women and 5 housewives had taken part in knitting and tailoring centres (Table 7.12).

As regards status accorded to such social participation, 3 working women and 10 housewives felt that this participation had raised their social status. Three working women and 9 housewives further felt that their husbands were proud of such participation. One part-time employed woman did not suggest any kind of social participation. Two working women said that their husbands were indifferent to their social participation.

This analysis indicates that among 42 respondents in the small joint families, (7 not replying at all), 10 wives had participated in any one kind of social activity, while 13 wives felt that such participation in social activities raises their social status and 12 of them had also felt that their husbands feel proud of their social participation.

This suggests that a lesser number of wives in the small joint families are participating in social activities as compared to wives in the joint families. The extent of participation was about half in the joint family, while it is only one fourth in the small joint family. There may not be any other specific reason behind this except that individual variations of temperament and likes and dislikes do occur in every type of family and in all cultural organizations and they accelerate or retard one's social behaviour. No further correlates could be worked out.

Individual Family

When I compare findings in the small joint and the joint families with those in individual families I find some more variations in the social participation of wife.

There were 38 working women, 2 part-time working women and 109 housewives among 149 respondent individual families (7 not replying here).

Out of 38 working women, 14 said that they had achieved a social status outside the family by participating in social activities of Mahila Mandals, 8 each in activities of lady welfare clubs and knitting embroidery or tailoring centres, and 6 in activities of cooperative societies. All these 14 working women had felt that such social participation raised their social status, and 15 of them had felt that their husbands had felt proud of their social participation. Only 38 of the working women expressed that their husbands remained indifferent to their social participation.

TABLE 7.12: Wife's Social and Extra Curricular Participation

Type of Family/ Occupation group		No. of wives	Where wife feels that she has a social status outside her family by participating in activities like				Where wife feels that participation in these activities raises her social status	Where wife feels that her husband feels proud of her such participation	Husbands attitude towards wife's participation in social activities	
			Mahila Mandals	Lady's Welfare Clubs	Co-Op. Societies	Knitt. Embr. or Tailoring centres			opposes	Remains Indifferent
1		2	3	4	5	6	7	8	9	10
1. Joint Family	1	6	2	2	2	2	4	3	—	1
	4	11	4	3	2	3	4	5	1	—
	NR	—	3	—	—	—	3	3	3	—
Total		17	9	5	4	5	11	11	4	1
2. Small Joint Family	1	14	2	1	1	2	3	3	—	2
	2	1	—	—	—	—	—	—	—	—
	4	27	8	3	2	5	10	9	—	—
	NR	7	—	—	—	—	—	—	—	—
Total		49	10	4	3	7	13	12	—	2
3. Individual Family	1	38	14	8	6	8	14	15	—	3
	2	2	1	1	—	—	1	1	—	—
	4	109	46	21	8	21	48	49	—	5
	NR	7	5	—	—	—	7	6	6	—
Total		156	66	30	14	29	70	71	6	8

Note: Figures in Cols. 3, 7, 8 & 9 under Individual group (NR) are excluding the figures in Col. 2.

Out of the 2 part-time working women, one wife said that she had achieved a social status by participating in activities of Mahila Mandal and another wife by participating in Lady's Welfare Club activities, 1 of these felt that this social participation raised her social status and that her husband also felt proud of her social participation.

Among 100 housewives, 46 said that they achieved a social status outside their families by participating in activities of Mahila Mandals, 21 in activities of Lady's Welfare Clubs, 8 in activities of Cooperative Societies, and 21 in activities of knitting, embroidery or tailoring centres.

As many as 48 housewives felt that their participation in these social activities raised their social status, and 49 housewives further felt that their husbands felt proud of their participation. Only 5 said that their husbands remained indifferent to their social participation.

This analysis of individual families indicates that extent of social participation of wives here too as quite marked, as many as 66 out of 149 responuents in individual families participated in some social activity or the other and 70 felt that this social participation raised their social status, 71 wives further felt that their husbands felt proud of their social participation. It appears that individual family provides a more open and favourable atmosphere for expression of wife's personality and in earning her recognition.

Roles of obligation discharged by the husband and the wife towards each other and towards their children as father and mother, their intricate and psycho-emotional relationships, interpersonal relationships of the husband and wife, and the wife's sense of responsibility towards her husband's family and in meeting, the familial and social expectations all work under a cultural organisation which determines particular functional family roles. All these keep the family institution integrated into "as meaningful whole", strike a balance in its multifarious operations and also keep a control over them. Cultural interests may make these imperative for the unity and stability of the family organization.

8

CONCLUSIONS

The present study on family change in India leads us to the following broad conclusions on the process and trends of change:

(1) Family change in India has been working in Indian Society as a process during past few decades. This family change has been marked not only in the family structure, but also in the functional family. The change has affected the interpersonal relations of different members of family and their role behaviour. Thus the role dynamics of the family has been much affected.

(2) The former thesis of some scholars that the joint families are more common in rural society than in Urban Society, and that the urban living essentially means individual households has been much challenged by recent researches on Indian Society. The latest finding as found by Tapan Kumar Mazumdar in his doctoral research in Kanpur, *The Structure and Composition of the Urban Middle classes in city of Kanpur* (1957) reveals that about 41.2 per cent live in joint families, 8.1 per cent in, what I have in my present work have termed small joint families, and while another 15.9 per cent though living in individual households maintain some kind of functional ties with their native family. This revealation challenges the common thesis that joint family breaks down as people move from villages to urban and industrial areas. My own finding in the research corroborators Mazumdar's findings in Kanpur, some 25 years ago. While large joint families of three generations were only 17 in my sample of 222 households in the Bhopal city there were as many 49 small joint families in the sample though nuclear families were still more as many as 156. But in the meantime further enquiries revealed that they maintained most of one kind of functional tie with their joint families in the native towns or villages and could be well included among small joint families in the manner of Tapan

Kumar Mazumdar. This suggests that though structural change comes first in family, functional change does not follow immediately thereafter but actually takes much time longer and it may come in temporal sequences.

What can be safety concluded here that urbanization naturally affects the structure of joint family, which gets changed as same members of the joint household leave the native joint family to get employment in Urban and industrial areas. But after some time the nuclear family in the new urban setting faces crisis and challenge and needs some assorted kins to help them. A widow or sister is called from the native place to look after the small children who are left at home during day time because of the both husband's and wife's employment.

Thus joint family comes into temporal existence. It may remain in form and function for some time and again cease, as assorted kins may leave or the nuclear family may move to some other place on transfer or fresh employ.

This small joint family then becomes both structurally and functionally joint over a phase of time and serves as a link between the joint family and the nuclear family.

The above findings thus warrant the conclusion that the recent changes in the Indian family in the context of urbanization, industrialization and trends of modernization have tended to break-up the joint family structure in the late years. Some times the break-up has been into an individual, typically nuclear households but quite often the joint family splits-up into a small joint family.

Often, this break up of a joint household is only a structural and temporal change, as after a periodic absence to towns or industrial joint family may often return to their native home after sometime and thus form again a joint family. Though now with passage or time the members of the old joint family may now not necessarily be there and often whole one generation may be missing but the fact remains that both structurally and functionally joint family comes into existence. The members may come and go, but joint family goes forever.

(3) This kind of change, is again, a structural change, functionally the members of such families may remain joint and continued to discharge their role obligations by regular monetary remittances

to home and by periodic visits. The feeling of belonging to a common home is maintained. It however, remains time that this functional discharge is not regularly made, and for a daily round of duties, a splitted family on migration to a town or an industrial centre works out its own independent system.

(4) It seems probable that whereas a tendency of nuclearization is being marked more in the recent years in the contemporary urban Hindu family, the joint family still persists in some areas and in certain conditions, largely out of cultural traditions, as well as because of some practical factors.

(5) The pressure of urbanization has given birth to a comparatively smaller joint family structure, which can be called the small joint family. It is getting more popular and is more conveniently continued for a larger time even in highly urbanized areas. Practical considerations like the need for a helping hand have accentuated it. But it has to be noted that this small joint family is not formed by reduction of joint family into small joint but by family growth of rather nuclear family into small joint family.

(6) The pressures of urbanization and occupation of both the husband and the wife have also given rise to a new institution called *Jhoolaghar* or creche which are now performing some of the functions of family as far as looking after children is concerned. The *Jhoolaghars* in city of Bhopal can be said to be playing the new situational role of 'child care' for the nuclear family in an urban complex. It is an important observation that the children sent to such *Jhoolaghars* or creches come mostly from nuclear families and seldom from small joint or joint families. Where helping hands may be readily available. Where additional members of family are available to look after small children, while the husband and wife are busy in their jobs, as is generally found in small joint and joint families, there is hardly any need to send children to creches. The subsitutive role of child care is played by creches, where the original role players of joint or small joint family are not available to perform the basic role and where the members of nuclear family have little time to perform this role. It is interesting to note that this living under care of creches also brings out a kind of change in the personality formation of children, as those reared in personal emotional care and caress of parents or immediate kins develop a healthier and better personality than those brought up in creches even though

the children there may be well fed and be kept only for a few hours of the day. This indirectly suggests that the functional role of joint family is still realized by nuclear families living in towns and it is only when no additional kin is available to look after the children that they are sent to *Jhoolaghars*. From the other point of view also, it can be safety concluded that though the *Jhoolaghars* are now undertaking some situational role of the family in as far as looking after the children for a limited period of day is concerned but it has certainly not yet deprived the joint family of its original role of child care. When we look at the family from the point of view of functional continuity, we find that the members of nuclear family keep some brother, sister or nephew or nieces as dependents for his or her education in the town, the functional continuity is maintained while structurally a small joint family is also formed. Even a regular remittance to the native town or village for their education or for helping them in seeking employment or establishing business, ensures a functional continuity of joint family obligations. The number of these may not be large but they indicate a basic fact, that even in an urban area like Bhopal, functional continuity may be maintained in an apparent nuclear family.

(7) There is a basic change marked in the sphere of family obligations. The educated and enlightened father is now expected to adopt a tolerant and more liberal attitude towards his children in the family. His approach towards his children is now imbued with psychological and child developmental considerations. The old authoritative role of parents is now changing into a role of tolerant patronage and companionship. This change appears to be in tune with time. This change was marked in varying degrees in all three types of families, the joint, the small joint and the nuclear in my research in Bhopal city.

(8) In the sphere of husband-wife relation also there is now marked a basic change in the roles. The husband in the old joint family was an authoritative husband who treated his wife as a sub-ordinate and absolutely dependent woman. Education, enlightenment and independent employment of woman in the modern days have earned for them a more respectable place in their husband's family. The modern husband, educated and enlightened as he is, now adopts a more rational attitude in life and discharges a role of companionship to his wife. Most of husbands in all three types

of families believed that their wives have earned an equal place with them in the family. The old authoritative role of husband is now changing into a role of companionship under the stresses and strains of urbanization. The role of authority usually vested in the Head of Household is showing a gradual decline in the modern urban Hindu family.

(9) In the sphere of marriages, it was found that though rigidity about caste is maintained in all three types of family there is now a trend towards accepting love marriage though with reluctance, in the educated families. There appears a gradual change in the attitude towards marriages. But this change is mostly marked in the nuclear and small joint families.

(10) In the sphere of values, it was found that some basic values of Hindu society culturally ingrained in the family were still considered important. As many as 220 families in the sample of 222 families reposed faith in some of the cardinal family values. This suggests the conclusion that education, enlightenment, modern ideas, now ideology and new innovations are casting their influence on the urban family, but the family institution in all its three types still fosters some faith in the conventional value pattern and derives its inspiration and strength from it.

(11) In the sphere of role of wife there appears to be a basic change. As the modern Hindu wife in an urban family is now an educated and often also earning woman, she now also learns her place in her husband's family. She is now not able to give that much time to her husband as a wife in rural family could do. But she is now sharing with her husband more concretely the burden of the family. She thus also expects proper adjustment and sympathetic consideration by her husband. Her husband is also now more educated and rational man and he often concedes her an equal status in the family. Where this is not ensured, chances of frictions and conflicts arise. It was found that it is basically husband's attitude that saved or involved a wife into a situation of conflict in her discharge of two different roles, the house-wife's and the working-woman's. There does now seem to be marked any prominent change in the urban families of Bhopal because of wife's obtaining a woman's status as had been marked in metropolises like Delhi, Bombay and Calcutta. It can be safety said that this difference is more because Bhopal falls in the first stage of urbanization, and therefore all those radical changes

which come in the later stages in the process of urbanization have not yet appeared in the urban society of this city.

(12) Role and status get changed according to variation in situations and pressurised needs. Trends of modernization influence these roles and statuses to a great extent.

(13) In the sphere of socio-economic participation of the family, it is found that tendencies of individualism and nuclearization have taken away the governing role of headship from the authoritative head of family and distributed it between individual earning heads and house-wives, and sometimes between other earning members of the family too. Education alone had equipped her more to share this participation. Her occupational status actively only accelerates it more.

It can be safely concluded here that those wives who are educated are playing an equal role with their husbands in the sphere of socio-economic participation.

(14) In the sphere of wife's expression of personality, it was found that only nuclear family provides a more open and favourable atmosphere for a development of such personality.

(15) Finally it can be said towards conclusion of this research work that roles in family in their different and multifold expressive forms all work under a culturally oriented system which determines and prescribes different roles for different family members, and then accordingly expects their obligatory performance by each set. These not only fulfil definite functions in family but also keep the family integrated into "meaning-fulwhole" and strike a balance in its multifold operations. Changes in different roles are ultimately indicators of change in the family institution.

(16) Changing roles, new emerging roles and participation of different family members in their newly expected roles suggest changes a family is undergoing and changes it is accepting and admitting within. In this way, change in family become a denominator of change in society, family change and social change thus become two interlinked processes of change in society and are important for all sociological studies as well as for those of academic value.

BIBLIOGRAPHY

Agarwala, B.R., 'In a Mobile Commercial Community', *Sociological Bulletin,* Vol. VI, No. 2.

Aiyar, C.S. Ramkrishna, 'The Hindu Joint Family', *Hindu Law Journal,* Vol. III & IV, 1921-1922.

Aiyar, S.P., 'Modernization of Traditional Society,' *Conspectus* 1, 1967.

Anshen, R.N., *The Family: Its Functions and Destiny* (New York, Harper and Brothers, 1949).

Ahmad, Saghir, 'Social Stratification in Punjab Village,' *Contributions to Indian Sociology,* New Series, No. IV, December 1970.

Bailey, F.G., 'The Joint Family in India: A Framework for Discussion'. *The Economic Weekly* Vol. XII, No. 8, 1960.

Beales, A.R., 'Interplay among Factors of Change in a Mysore Village; in eds., Mc. Kim Marriot, *Village India* (Chicago, University of Chicago Press, 1955).

Beteille, Andre, 'Family and Social Change in India and other South Asian Countries', *The Economic Weekly,* Annual Number, 1964.

——, *Castes: Old and New* (Bombay, Asia Publishing House, 1969).

——, 'Ideas and Interests: Some Conceptional Problems in the Study of Social Stratification in Rural India', *International Social Sciences Journal* Vol. XXI, No. 2, 1960.

——, 'Peasant Associations and the Agrarian Class Structure', *Contributions to Indian Sociology,* No. IV, December, 1970.

Berelson, B., *Content Analysis in Communication Research* (Illinois, Free Press, 1952).

Bharati, Agehananda, *Ethical Norms and Value Modification in Modern India,* (Calcutta, The Indian Renaissance Institute, 1967), I.R.I, Monograph Series, No. 1.

Bernard, B., Social Stratification (New York Harcourt Brace & Co. 1957).

Beeker and Boskoff, *Sociology: A Guide to Problems and Literature.*

Burgess, E.W., and H.J. Locke, *The Family* (New York, American Book Co., 1953).

Burgess, E.W., 'The Family in a Changing Society' in eds., Landis, Judson T., and Mary G. Landis, *Readings in Marriage and the Family* (New York, Prentice-Hall, Inc., 1952).

Berreman, Gerald D., *Hindus of the Himalayas* (Berkeley, University of California Press, 1963).

Bhatt, R.C., Literacy Drives for Social Change, *Indian Journal of Adult Education*, Vol. XXI, No. 5, 1960.

Breese, Gerald, *Urbanization in Newly Developing Countries* (Englewood Cliffs, N.J. Prentice Hall Ino., 1966).

Chandrashekhar, S., 'The Family in India', *Marriage and Family Living,* Vol. VIV, No. 4, 1954.

Chouhan, D.S., *Trends of Urbanization in Agra* (New Delhi, Allied Publishers, 1966).

Coser, A.B., *Sociology Through Literature* (Englewood Cliffs, N.J. Prentice-Hall Inc., 1963).

Comhaire, Jean L., 'Economic Change and the Extended Family', *Annals of the American Political Review,* No. 305, May, 1956.

Damle, Y.B., *The Nature of Industrialization and Urbanization in India,* Mimeographed, (Poona, Deccan College, 1964).

—, *College Youth in India: A Study of Elite in the Making,* Mimeographed, (Poona, Deccan College, 1966).

Danda, Ajit Kumar & Dipali Ghosh, Danda, *Development and Change in a Bengal Village,* Mimeographed, (Hyderabad, National Institute of Community Development 1968).

Desai, I.P., 'The Joint Family in India: An Analysis', *Sociological Bulletin,* Vol. V, No. 2, September, 1956.

Desai, Neera, *Woman in Modern India* (Bombay, Vora & Co., 1957).

Dube, S.C., *The Indian Village* (London, Kegan Paul, 1955).

—, *India's Changing Villages: Human Factors in Community Development.* (London, Routledge & Kegan Paul, 1955).

—, 'Modernization and Its Adaptive Demands on Indian Society' in eds., M.S. Gore, I.P. Desai, and Suman Chitnis, *The Papers in the Sociology of Education in India* (New Delhi, National Council of Educational Research & Training 1967).

—, *Contemporary India and its Modernization* (Delhi, Vikas Publications, 1974).

Dumont, L., 'Introductory Note: Change Introduction and Comparison', *Contributions in Indian Sociology,* VII, 1964.

Devenandan and Thomas: *The Changing Pattern of Family in India* (Bangalore, Christian Institute for Religion and Society, 1960).

Edwin, E., 'Some Aspects of Urban Migration from a Village in North-Central India', *Eastern Anthropologist,* Vol. VIII, No. 1, 1964.

Fispiegel, John, 'New Perspectives in the Study of Family', *Address at Annual Meeting,* National Council on Family Relations, September, 2, 1953.

Ginsberg, Morris, 'Social Change', *British Journals of Sociology,* 51, 1945.

Churye, G.S., *Family and Kin in Indo European* Culture (London, Routledge & Kegan Paul).

Gore, M.S., *The Impact of Industrialization and Urbanization on the Aggarwala Family in Delhi Area.* Ph. D Thesis submitted to columbia University, 1961.

Goode, William J., *The Family* (New Delhi, Prentice-Hall of India Ltd., 1965).

Grisby, Shaw Earl, *Erin: A Socio-Economic Study of Families Living on Marginal Land.*

Hardgrave, R., *The Nadars of Tamil Nadu: The Political Culture of a Community Under Change* (Herkeley), University of California Press, 1969).

Haimendorff, C. Von Furer : *Caste and Kin in India, Nepal and Ceylon* (Bombay, Asia Publishing House, 1966).

Hill, R., 'Genetic Features of Families under Stress', *Social Case Work,* Vol. XXXIX, Nos. 2-3, February-March, 1958.

Hoselitz. Berk F., 'A Survey of the Literature on Urbanization In India', in ed. Roy Turner, *India's Urban Feature,* (Berkeley, University of California Press, 1961).

—, *International Social Science Journal* Vol. 1. XIV, No. 3, 1962. Issue devoted to Changes in the Family.

Irongride, Charles E., *The Family in Colonial New York: A Sociological Study:* Doctoral Dissertation submitted under Columbia University (Source: Doctoral Dissertations accepted by the American Universities, 1941-42 No. 9, New York 1942).

Ivan, F. Nye and Felix M., *Emerging Conceptual Framework in FAMILY Analysis* (New York, The Macmillan Co., 1966).

Ivan, F. Nye et al. eds., *Role Structure and Analysis of the Family* (Washington, National Council of Family Relations, 1976), Saga Library of Social Research, Vol. 24.

Ivan, F. Nye, *The Working Mothers* (New York, Rand McNally, 1963).

Ishwaran, K., *Tradition and Economy in Village* (London, Routledge & Kegan Paul, 1956).

Kapur, Saroj, 'Family and Kinship among the Khatris of Delhi', *Sociological Bulletin,* Vol. IIV, No. 2, September, 1956.

Kapadia, K.M., *Marriage and Family in India* (Bombay, Oxford University Press, 1955).

—, 'Changing Patterns of Hindu Marriage and Family', *Sociological Bulletin,* Vol. II, No. 2, September, 1955.

—, 'Rural Family Patterns', *Sociological Bulletin,* Vol. No. 2, September, 1955.

—, 'The Family in Transition', *Sociological Bulletin,* Vol. VIII, No. 2, September, 1959.

—, '*The Hindu Marriage and Divorce Bill* (Bombay, Popular Book Depot, 1935).

Kapparte, *The Family, Society and Individual.*

Kannan, C.T., *Intercaste and Intercommunity Marriages in India* (Bombay, Allied Publishers, 1963).

Karve, D.D., *The New Brahmins: Five Maharashtrian Families* (Berkeley, University of California Press, 1963).

Karve, Irawati, *Kinship Organization in India* (Poona, Deccan College Post Graduate Research Institute, 1953).

Kirkpatrick, Clifford, *The Family as Process Institution,* (New York, Ronald Press Co., 1965).

Kolenda, Pauline Makar, Family Structure in Village Ionikanda India, 1819, 1958, 1967, *Contributions to Indian Sociology,* New Series, No. IV, December, 1970.

—, 'Regional Differences in Indian Family Structure' in eds. Robert Grane, *Region and Regionalism in South Asian Studies: An Explanatory Study* (Duke University Programme, Camp studies on South Asia Monograph No. 85, 1967).

Kuppuswamy, B., *A Study of Opinion Regarding Marriage and Divorce* (Bombay, Asia Publishing House, 1957).

Kuppuswamy, B. et al., *Some Aspects of Social Change* (Delhi, Sterling Publishers, 1968).

—, *Social Change in India* (Delhi, Vikas Publications, 1972).

Landis, Judson T. and Mary G. Landis, eds., *Readings in Marriage and the Family* (New York, Prentice-Hall Inc., 1962).

Landis, Paul H. 'The Changing Family' in eds. Landis Judson et al., —*Readings in Marriage and Family.*

Lawrence, S. Bee., *Marriage and Family Relations: An International Disciplinary Approach* (New York, Harper & Bros. 1957).

Leslie, Gerald R., *The Family in Social Context* (1967).

Lerner, D., *Passing of Traditional Society* (Glencoe, Free Press, 1968).

Levy, Marion J., *The Family Revolution in Modern China* (Cambridge, Mass., Harvard University Press, 1949).

—, 'Changes in the family', *International Social Sciences Journal*, 14, 1962.

Lewis, Oscar, *Village Life in Northern India: Studies in a Delhi Village* (Urbana, University of Illinois Press).

Lipset. S.M. and J. Smelser Neil, *Sociology: The Progress of a Decade* (Englewood Cliffs, N.J. Prentice-Hall Inc. 1961).

Litwek, Emgene, 'Occupation, Mobility and Family Cohesion' *American Sociological Review*, 25, 1960. (b).

Lundlow, Williams L., *A Syllabus and Bibliography of Marriage and Family* (New York, Radcliffe Press, 1951).

Madan, T.N., 'The Hindu Joint Family', *Man*, Vol. XI, No. 145, June, 1962.

—, 'The Joint Family: A Terminological Clarification', *International Journal of Comparative Sociology*, III, 1962.

—, *Family and Kinship: A Study of the Pandits of Rural Kashmir* (Delhi, 1960).

Marriott, McKim, *Village India* (Chicago, University of Chicago Press, 1955).

Merchant, K.T., *Changing Views on Marriage and the Family* (Madras, B.G. Paul, 1935).

Merton, R.K., *Social Theory and Structure* (New Delhi, Amerind Publishing House, 1972) Indian Edition.

Mencher, Joan P., 'Changing Familial Roles among South Malabar Nayars', *South-Western Journal of Anthropology*, 18, 1962.

Morris, Peter, 'Social Change and the Social Class', *The Listner*, 5, November, 1959.

Moray, V.E., *The Pattern of Caste and Family in Wai Taluka*, Ph.D. Thesis (Deptt. of Sociology, University of Bombay).

Morrison, William A., 'Family Types in Badalpur: An Analysis of a Changing Institution in a Maharashtrian Village, *Sociological Bulletin*, 8, 1959.

Moore, Wilbert E., *Social Change:* (New Delhi, New Prentice-Hall of India Ltd., 1965).

Mukherjee, R.K., 'Caste Proximity and Attitude Change in the City,' in ed., R.K. Mukerjee, et. al. *Intercaste Tensions, A Survey under the auspices of the UNESCO* (Lucknow, 1956).

Mukherjee, D.P., 'The Intellectual in India', *Confluence,* 1965.

Myrdal, Alva, *Nations and Family* (Massachusetts, M.I.T., Paperbacks, 1968)

Narain, Dhirendra, 'Growing up in India', *Paper presented at Seventh International Seminar on Family Research,* September, 1962.

Nazmul Kasmi, A.K., *Changing Society in India and Pakistan* (Karachi, Oxford University Press, 1956).

Nimkoff, M.F., 'Some Problems Concerning Research on the Changing Family in India,' Sociological *Bulletin* Vol. VIII, No. 2, September 1959.

—, *Comparative Family Systems* (Boston, Houghton Mifflin Company, 1965).

—, Joint Family, an Obstacle to Industrialization, *Journal of Comparative Sociology,* Vol. I, No. 1 March, 1961.

Nimkoff, M.F. and M.S. Gore, 'The Social Bases of the Hindu Joint Family', *Journal of Sociology and Social Research,* Vol. XLIV, 1959.

Nimkoff M.F. and Middleton Rusell, 'Types of Families and Types of Economy', *American Journal of Sociology,* 66, 1960.

Ogburn, W.F., 'Changing Functions of the Family' in ed. Landis Judson t., and Mary G. Landis, *Readings in Marriage and the Family* (New York, Prentice-Hall Inc., 1962).

Oreinstein, Henry, *Gaon: Conflict and Cohesion in an Village* (Englewood Cliffs, N.J. Prentice-Hall Inc., 1965).

—, 'The Recent History of the Extended Family in India', *Social Problems,* 8, 1961.

Oreinstein, Henry and Micklin Michael. 'The Hindu Joint Family', The Norms and the Numbers', *Pacific Affairs,* 30, 1966.

Opler, Morris E., 'Themes on Dynamic Forces in Culture', *American Journal of Sociology,* 51, 1945.

Pannikar, K.M., *Hindu Society at Crossroads* (Bombay, Asia Publishing House, 1955).

Parsons, Talcott, 'Introduction to Part Two. Differentiation in Variation in Social Structures in ed. Talcott Parsons, et al., *Theories of Society* (New York, The Free Press of Glencoe, 1961).

Paydarfar, Ali A. 'Modernisation Process and Demographic Changes', *The Sociological Review,* Vol. IV, No. 2.

Prabhu, P.N., *Hindu Social Organization: A Study in Socio-Psychological and Ideological Foundations* (Bombay, Popular Book Depot, 1954).

Parsons, Talcott, 'The Social Structure of the Family' in ed. Ruth Nanda Anshen, *The Family: Its Functions and Destiny* (New York, Harper and Row, 1949).

Parsons, Talcott and Bales, *Family' Socialization and Interaction Process.*

Ramu, G.M., *Family and Caste in Urban India.*

Rao, M.S.A., *Social Change in Malabar* (Bombay, Popular Book Depot, 1957).

Randive, C.S., *Family in Urban and Rural Areas,* Unpublished Doctoral thesis (Poona, Deccan College Post Graduate & Research Institute, 1951).

Riesman, David *The Lonely Crowd* (New Haven, Yale University Press, 1950).

Rosser, Colin, 'Social Mobility in the New Caste System in ed., C. Von-Furer Haimendorff, *Caste and Kin in India, Nepal and Ceylon* (Bombay, 1966).

Rosser, Colin, and Christopher Harris, *Family and Social Change* (London Routledge & Kegan Paul, 1965).

Rosser, Aileen D., *The Hindu Family in its Urban Setting* (Bombay, OUP, 1961).

Rowe, William I., 'The New Chauhans, A Caste Mobility Movement in North India' in eds., James Silverberg, *Social Mobility in the Caste System in India* (The Hague, Mouton & Co., 1968).

Rundbland, Bengt G. *Family and Urbanization in the Family* (Tibingen, Germany, J.C.B., Mohr, Paul, Siebeck, 1956).

Sacarlet, T., *Economic Development and Social Change in South India* (Manchester, Manchester University Press, 1962).

Sait, U.B., *New Horizons for the Family Structure* (Bombay, Macmillan Co.)

Sarma, N.A., *Woman and Society* (Baroda, Padmja Publications, 1947).

Sekhar, M.C., *Social Change in India: First Decade of Planning* (Poona, Deccan College Post Graduate Research Institute, 1968).

Sengupta, Nilkashi, *Evaluation of Hindu Marriage* (Bombay, Popular Prakashan, 1965).

Sen, Lalit K. and Pradipto Roy, 'Modernization in Village India, *Awareness of Community Development in Village India* (Hyderabad, National Institute of Community Development, 1956).

Shah, A.M., 'Basic Terms and Concepts in the Study of Family in India', *Indian Economic and Social History Review,* Vol. I, No. 3, Jan-March, 1964.

—, *The Household Dimension of the Family in India* (New Delhi, Orient Longman, 1973).

Shah, B.V. *Social Change and College Students of Gujarat.* (Baroda, Maharaja Siyaji Rao, University of Baroda, 1964).

—, 'Sociology of Education', *Sociological Bulletin,* Vol. XIV, No. 2, September, 1965.

—, 'Inequality of Educational Opportunities', *The Economic Weekly,* XII, 34, August, 1960.

Shanas, Ethel and Gordon F. Streie ed., *Social Structure and the Family Generational Relations* (New Jersey, Prentice-Hall Inc., 1965).

Shils, Edward, *Intellectual Between Tradition and Modernity.* (The Hague, Mouton & Co., 1961).

Silverberg, James ed., 'Changing Familial Roles among South-Malabar Nayars', *South-Western Journal of Anthropology, 182,* 1962.

Singers, Milton J., 'The Changing Family in A Changing Society', *Social Case Work,* Vol. XI, No. 8, October, 1959.

Singer, Milton and Cohn. S. Bernard, *Structure and Change in Indian Society* (Chicago, Aldine Publishing Co., 1968).

Singh, Yogendra, 'Cultural Integration and Changing Values', *Sociological Bulletin,* Vol. XXII, No. 2, 1964.

—, 'Symposium on Rural-Urban Relations', *Sociological Bulletin,* Vol. V, No. 2, 1956.

Savani, N.V., 'The Urban Social Situation in India', *Artha Vijnana,* Vol. III, No. 23, 1961.

Stanlay, A. Freed, 'Urbanization and Cultural Change: India', Reported at the 58th Annual Meeting of the American Anthropological Association, Mexico, D.P., December, 28, 1959.

Stephens, William N., *The Family in Cross Cultural Perspectives* (New York, Holt Rhinehart and Wingston, 1963).

Stoodbeck, F.Z., 'Family Interaction, Value and Achievement' in Mcclelland *et al., Talent and Society* (1958).

Srinivas, M.S., *Marriage and Family in Mysore* (Bombay, 1942).

—, *Religion and Society among the Coorgs of South India* (Oxford, Clarendon Press, 1952).

—, *Social Change in Modern India* (Berkeley, University of California Press, 1966).

—, *Caste in Modern India and other Essays* (Bombay, Asia Publishing House, 1970).

—, 'The Industrialization and Urbanization of Rural Areas', *Sociological Bulletin,* Vol. V, No. 2, 1956.

Sussman, Marvin B., 'The Isolated Nuclear Family: Fact or Fiction' in ed., *Source Book on Marriage and the Family* (Boston, Houghton Mifflin, 1963).

Tham, Robert, *Beyond Marriage and the Nuclear Family* (New York, Cornfield Press, 1975).

Theodore, William and Bary eds, *Sources of Indian Tradition* (New York, Columbia University Press).

—, *The Journal of Family Welfare.* Special Conference Number, Vol. XIII, No. 3, 1967.

Tropp, Ashler, The Social Functions of Education Systems', *Social and Economic Studies,* Vol. XIV, No. 1, March, 1965.

—, UNESCO: Sociological Considerations in Educational Planning for Economic Development (Delhi, 1965).

Venkatacharya, K.N., 'Some Aspects of Marriage and Family', Mysore University Journal, Vol. XVI, 1956.

Vogel, Ezra and Norman W. Beel. ed., *A Modern Introduction to the Family* (Glencoe, Ill, The Free Press 1960).

Winch, Robert F. et al., *Selected Studies in the Marriage and Family* (New York, Halt, Rhinehart and Wingston, 1962).

Wolf, A.W.M., 'Family in Literature', *Child Study,* 9, 50-2, October, 1930.

Waller, W. and R. Hill, *The Family,* (New York, Dryden Press, 1951).

Young, Martin C., *The Family in the Chinese Revolution* (Cambridge Mass: Harvard University Press, 1861).

Young, Michael and Peter Willmot, *Family and Kinship in East London* (London, Routledge & Kegan Paul, 1957).

Zimmermann, Carle, C., 'The Family' in ed., Joseph S. *Roucek, Contemporary Sociology* (London, Peter Owen, 1964).

INDEX